European Banking Union

T0330479

Recent failures and rescues of large banks have resulted in colossal costs to society. In the wake of such turmoil a new banking union must enable better supervision, pre-emptive coordinated action and taxpayer protection. While these aims are meritorious they will be difficult to achieve. This book explores the potential of a new banking union in Europe.

This book brings together leading experts to analyse the challenges of banking in the European Union. While not all contributors agree, the constructive criticism provided in this book will help ensure that a new banking union will mature into a stable, yet vibrant, financial system that encourages the growth of economic activity and the efficient allocation of resources.

This book will be of use to researchers interested in banking, monetary economics and the European Union.

Juan E. Castañeda is lecturer in economics, University of Buckingham and deputy director, Institute of International Monetary Research, UK.

David G. Mayes is professor of banking and financial institutions; chairman, Europe Institute; and director, NZ Governance Centre, University of Auckland, New Zealand.

Geoffrey Wood is emeritus professor, University of Buckingham and Cass Business School, UK.

Routledge International Studies in Money and Banking

European Banking Union

Prospects and challenges

Edited by
Juan E. Castañeda,
David G. Mayes and
Geoffrey Wood

LONDON AND NEW YORK

First published 2016
by Routledge
2 Park Square, Milton Park, Abingdon, Oxon OX14 4RN

and by Routledge
711 Third Avenue, New York, NY 10017

First issued in paperback 2017

Routledge is an imprint of the Taylor & Francis Group, an informa business

British Library Cataloguing in Publication Data
A catalogue record for this book is available from the British Library

Library of Congress Cataloguing in Publication Data
European banking union : prospects and challenges / edited by
Juan E. Castañeda, David G. Mayes and Geoffrey Wood. — First Edition.
pages cm
Includes bibliographical references and index.
1. Banks and banking—European Union countries. 2. European Union countries—Economic policy. 3. Monetary policy—European Union countries. 4. Banking law—European Union countries. I. Castañeda, Juan E., editor. II. Mayes, David G., editor. III. Wood, Geoffrey, 1925- editor.
HG2980.5.A6E877 2015
332.1094—dc23
2015023397

ISBN 13: 978-1-138-49545-6 (pbk)
ISBN 13: 978-1-138-90650-1 (hbk)

Typeset in Times New Roman
by Swales & Willis Ltd, Exeter, Devon, UK

This book is dedicated to Yolande Hinson, who with good humour and friendly efficiency organised the conference which brought all the authors together. She served as senior administrator in the University of Buckingham's department of economics and international studies from 2012 until early 2015, when she died after a short illness.

Contents

Figures

Tables

Contributors

Jens-Hinrich Binder is professor of law, chair of private law and commercial law, Eberhard-Karls Universität, Tübingen.

Juan E. Castañeda is lecturer in economics at the University of Buckingham, deputy director of the Institute of International Monetary Research and honorary senior visiting fellow in the faculty of finance at the Cass Business School.

Thomas Conlon is a lecturer in banking and finance at the UCD Centre for Financial Markets, Smurfit School of Business, University College Dublin.

John Cotter is professor in finance and the chair in quantitative finance, UCD Centre for Financial Markets, Smurfit School of Business, University College Dublin and a research fellow at the UCLA Ziman Research Center for Real Estate

Philipp Erfurth is a European economist with Morgan Stanley Research.

Charles A. E. Goodhart is emeritus professor and director of financial regulation research in the financial markets group at the London School of Economics.

Thomas F. Huertas is a partner in Ernst and Young's financial services risk practice and chairs Ernst and Young's global regulatory network.

Giannoula Karamichailidou is a research fellow in the Europe Institute at the University of Auckland.

Michael Krimminger is a partner with Cleary Gottlieb Steen and Hamilton, and former general counsel and deputy to chairman for policy at the US Federal Deposit Insurance Corporation.

Rosa M. Lastra is professor in international financial and monetary law, Centre for Commercial Law Studies, Queen Mary University of London.

Johan A. Lybeck is CEO and owner, Finanskonsult AB, Stockholm.

David G. Mayes is professor of banking and financial institutions, chairman of the Europe Institute and director of the NZ Governance Centre at the University of Auckland and is a visiting professor at the University of Buckingham.

Kate Phylaktis is professor of international finance and director, emerging markets group, at Cass Business School.

Alessandro Roselli is honorary visiting fellow at the Cass Business School and senior visiting fellow at the University of Buckingham.

Geoffrey Wood is emeritus professor of economics at the Cass Business School and emeritus professor of monetary economics at the University of Buckingham.

Preface

Simply managing to get all the measures thus far involved in banking union in the EU into law is a remarkable achievement, as is the creation of the new institutions that are involved in its implementation. It is of particular satisfaction as between us we have been involved for nearly 20 years in a campaign to address the problems of supervising cross-border banks and the orderly resolution of banks without the need for bail-outs by the taxpayer and its associated moral hazard and unfairness. Until the global financial crisis it had not been possible to make any significant headway. Politicians did not regard the issues as important enough to consider for the legislative agenda, and regulators tended to be convinced that their systems would work well in practice despite their obvious limitations.

There are some honourable exceptions, with the Reserve Bank of New Zealand investigating resolution mechanisms carefully and then starting to implement a new scheme that addressed both the cross-border issue and the need to bail in rather than bail out by 2005. The Swedish authorities got as far as a draft law, but it was not presented to parliament. The Bank of Finland also pursued these issues and Peik Granlund, Liisa Halme, Aarno Liuksila and Jukka Vesala have been co-authors in this, Aarno Liuksila in particular being an energetic proponent of the reorganisation of both assets and liabilities of a failing bank, using early intervention under a lex specialis. The successive deputy governors responsible for financial stability, Esko Ollila, Matti Louekoski and Pentti Hakkarainen, helped push the programme forward. Jon Sigurðsson from the Nordic Investment Bank pointed out the impossibility of rescuing the Icelandic banking system a full five years before it failed, leading to the development of the concept of 'too big to save'.

Despite our accolade to the EU for achieving so much in a short period, this does not mean that what has been achieved is perfect, and our purpose in writing this book is to draw attention to the actual and potential difficulties in order to help the authorities and the participants in the financial system tackle them over the future. While some of the deficiencies can be simply ascribed to the problems of achieving agreement among 28 countries, others reflect what we regard as misperceptions of the problems and the ways the solutions that have been adopted are likely to play out in practice in the future.

In particular we think it is a delusion to believe that taxpayers are off the hook or that they ever could be in the event of the threat of a widespread crisis. We remain cautious that without substantial reorganisation the largest complex banking institutions could be resolved rapidly, except perhaps by the home supervisor resolving the group where it has a holding company structure as is prevalent in the US. We also feel that, despite being early supporters of bailing in, the concept has been oversold. A large bail-in will still have substantial real effects and spillovers to the economy at large. It is simply that they will be distributed differently from those in the traditional bail-out.

The individual authors in this book have contributed their analysis of the various parts of the problem, looking both forward and backward. While they do not necessarily subscribe to what each other says, we hope that the constructive criticism provided in the book will be of value in helping the new banking union mature into a stable, yet vibrant, financial system that encourages the growth of economic activity and the efficient allocation of resources. Progress is being made on two fronts: the reduction of fragility in the system and the ability to handle problems and, in particular, to permit exit without endangering the stability of the rest of the system.

It will take a lot longer than the ten-year implementation period envisaged for the EU and indeed the EEA to achieve a full banking union in the sense observed within the member states. We must hope that any major disruption to the system does not occur before then – indeed of course we hope there is no such disruption. But if there is, another such shock may well offer the opportunity to take further steps towards eliminating the problems we identify. However, in a dynamic system there can be no final solution – the next crisis is likely to be different from the last and, almost by definition, come as a surprise.

Juan E. Castañeda, David G. Mayes and Geoffrey Wood
Auckland and Buckingham

Acknowledgements

The chapters in this book all reflect the personal views of their authors and do not necessarily represent the views of the organisations they work for or the funders of their research.

The editors are grateful for the help of Giannoula Karamichailidou at all stages of this project from organising the contributions to checking through the type-script. They thank the Universities of Auckland and Buckingham for their financial support for the workshop in Buckingham, which brought the authors together. We also thank the late Yolande Hinson and her colleagues for their help in organising the workshop.

David Mayes and Giannoula Karamichailidou acknowledge financial support for this work from the EU through Work Package 1B on The Future of Financial and Monetary Integration in the EU, through the EU Centres Network in New Zealand. David Mayes thanks the ARENA Centre for European Studies at the University of Oslo and the Research Council of Norway for support under the EuroDiv project as part of the Europe in Transition programme.

We thank the following for their copyright permission:

The European Commission for permission to use Figures 3.1 and 3.3, which are drawn from European Commission (2014) *Banking Union: Restoring Financial Stability in the Eurozone*, available at: http://ec.europa.eu/finance/general-policy/docs/banking-union/banking-union-memo_en.pdf, ©European Union, 1995–2015.

Banca d'Italia for permission to use Table 3.3 and Figure 3.5, which are both drawn from Bank of Italy (2014) *Financial Stability Report*, no 2, November, available at: https://www.bancaditalia.it/pubblicazioni/rapporto-stabilita/2014-2/en-RSF2-2014.pdf?language_id=1.

OECD for permission to use Figure 10.1, which is drawn from Dirk Schoenmaker and Toon Peek (2014) *The State of the Banking Sector in Europe*, OECD economics department Working Paper 1102, 27 January, p. 19, available at: http://www.oecd.org/officialdocuments/publicdisplaydocumentpdf/?cote=ECO/WKP(2013)94&docLanguage=En.

European Banking Federation for permission to reproduce Figure 10.2, which is drawn from European Banking Federation, March 2014, available at: http://www.ebf-fbe.eu/publications/statistics/.

1   Banking union in Europe

*Juan E. Castañeda, David G. Mayes
and Geoffrey Wood*

Before the global financial crisis (GFC) there had been some discussion of the
way the regulation of banks in Europe might evolve. Some academic contributions had set out what a functional system might look like in the future. Mayes
et al. (2011), for example, laid out a simple scheme based on US experience,
where banks which wished to operate across borders should register as European
companies, subject to a single regulatory scheme, under a new regulator – not the
European Central Bank (ECB) – and should banks fail they would be resolved
by a European equivalent of the Federal Deposit Insurance Corporation (FDIC),
a European Deposit Insurance Corporation. Treatment of purely national banks
would remain a national responsibility. However, such ideas were regarded as
something for the distant future, with integration expected to take the form of
steadily closer cooperation among national authorities and increasing harmonisation of regulation led by the Committee of European Banking Supervisors
(CEBS) based in London. (Mayes *et al.* had assumed that CEBS would become
the European level single supervisor.)

All this has now changed, and in the course of five years the European Union
(EU) has implemented a major programme of legislation, which has been labelled
as 'banking union'. Although the current plans will not be fully operational until
2024, parts of it have come into force already. This speed of action has come at
a price. The so-called 'union' is not complete – most importantly only the euro
area is fully covered by the measures – and it does not have the neatness of the
comprehensive scheme one might have expected. The reason is simple: such a
comprehensive agreement could not have been negotiated among the member
states if unanimous approval were required. Any changes which required amendments to the EU treaties would have entailed that unanimity.

The EU authorities and the member states are to be congratulated on their inge-
nuity in getting round these constraints. But the result has many flaws. The questions that are addressed in this book are: Will it work well despite these flaws?
What changes can be made – within the bounds of political feasibility – that can
improve it?

However, we need to start with a broader consideration of the pressures in the
European and indeed global financial system that banking union seeks to address.
Some of these are still with us, and it is extremely difficult to write this chapter

with the uncertainty over the future over Greece hanging over us. If any of these spill over into a new crisis in European banks, then there will be no time for the new recovery and resolution arrangements to mature and for there to be any judgement about how well they could operate once the new authorities involved, particularly the Single Resolution Board, have been equipped for their task.

In this chapter, therefore, we set out a brief outline of banking union, followed by an analysis of the short-run pressures it faces. We then consider the longer-run difficulties that banking union will have to cope with before providing an assessment of how well it may be able to meet these challenges. These sections provide an introduction to the remaining chapters in the book, whose contribution we explain in a final section.

An outline of banking union

As explained in more detail in chapter 2 by Thomas Huertas, banking union is a label being applied to a group of three main actions by the EU in response to the GFC and the discussions on the way forward for banking regulation by the G20/ Financial Stability Board and the Basel Committee for Banking Supervision.

The first action is increased harmonisation and the implementation of the Basel 3 rules for capital adequacy, through the capital adequacy directive and regulation, and through the increasing work of the European Banking Authority (EBA), which was formed out of CEBS. This harmonisation is notable for its move away from simply requiring minimum standards (which member states could exceed if they wished) to trying to set *common* standards that all must follow across the whole EU. Thus, although the main point of this action is to make banks more resilient to future shocks, it goes beyond this towards creating a more homogeneous system than is actually necessary for a single market to operate.

The second action is the creation of the Single Supervisory Mechanism (SSM), based on the ECB, to try to achieve a common high standard of supervision, especially for the largest banks that run across borders. The ECB is only supervising the largest banks directly, and the smaller banks and the non-banking activities will still be subject to the national authorities. This is not a genuine SSM, as only the euro area countries have to participate. Other countries may participate if they choose, but they cannot be full members as they are not represented on the ECB's Governing Council. This division into SSM and non-SSM countries is unfortunate as the banks in the different categories of course interact. The reason for the division is not that there is something inherently different in banking terms by being a member of the euro area. It is simply that there was not the political will among the member states to create a new single supervisor that would cover the whole EU. The only way forward that did not involve a treaty change, which would have failed to achieve the necessary unanimity, was to exercise the option for the ECB to be assigned supervisory responsibility for banks under Article 127(6) (Treaty on the Functioning of the European Union). This conflates monetary policy and financial stability and potentially creates a conflict of interest for the ECB across its two roles as well as possible damage to its independence. This latter point is taken up below.

For the large majority of banks, which do not have substantial operations across borders, there is no particular need for an SSM, but for cross-border banks there are three obvious reasons. First, it could help lower the costs of banking services if banks only have to face a single regulatory regime and not a different one in every jurisdiction in which they operate. Second, it could help reassure host countries that the supervision of both branches and the operations of the parent bank are being conducted not just to a satisfactory standard but to a standard they can influence as they are part of the mechanism. Last, that reassurance can make it easier for countries to accept the pooling of resources in the resolution of large cross-border banks.

This takes us to the third action, the establishment of a regime for being able to resolve all banks, whatever their complexity, should they get into difficulty, at minimum cost to the real economy and without the need for a taxpayer-financed bail-out. This regime has been established in two parts:

1   a Bank Recovery and Resolution Directive (BRRD), which requires all member states of the EU (and indeed, all members of the European Economic Area (EEA)) to have in place a regime which allows early action by the authorities should a bank get into difficulty – so that it can, if possible, be turned round before failure – and, should a failure become inevitable, to have all the tools necessary to effect a resolution;
2   a Single Resolution Mechanism (SRM), which matches the SSM and is run by a new Single Resolution Board (SRB) in Brussels, independent of the ECB and responsible for implementing such resolutions especially of the large cross-border banks.

As part of the BRRD, the resolution authority in each country is required to have a resolution fund at its disposal, amounting to at least one per cent of banks' covered deposits, which can be used to help finance resolutions. In the case of the SRM, these funds will be progressively mutualised as they are built up over 2016–2024.

Thus, the SRM, like the SSM, is incomplete and, since many of the most important cross-border banks lie in the UK, as does Europe's most important financial market, this deficiency is substantial. Unlike the US, the EU has not created a single deposit insurance/guarantee organisation, which can act as the resolution authority. That is not such a significant concern, as, with depositor preference as part of the BRRD, it is not so likely that these funds will be drawn on in resolution.

The BRRD, however, is a major step towards enabling an immediate resolution of any bank in a manner which keeps the functions that are essential to the stability of the financial system operating without interruption. Previously, the regulatory environment in most countries meant that there could not be intervention until insolvency, and then the available insolvency procedures precluded uninterrupted operation unless the government either purchased the bank outright or recapitalised it enough to allow it to continue. In other words, they had to bail it out. With the new tools in the BRRD and the ability to 'bail-in' creditors – either write down their claim or convert their debt into equity such that the bank becomes adequately capitalised again – the hope is that bail-outs by the taxpayer will not be needed. The problem is that many of these procedures are untested, particularly with a large bank. Hence, we do not know whether they will work. Exploring this is the purpose of this book.

There are two parts of banking union that have not (yet) taken place, but might have been expected. One is a directive relating to the structure of financial institutions. This was proposed by the Commission in January 2014, but it has not as yet moved further, partly as a result of opposition from the industry, for which it would be costly, and partly because the member states have different views about what should be done. Belgium, France, Germany and the UK, for example, have implemented their own legislation already, and the idea of making banks change their structures twice in short order with the associated high compliance costs is not welcome. The problem is partly that the large banks are very complex, and it may prove impossible to make them readily resolvable, as required by the BRRD, unless their structures are simplified. However, beyond this, banking activities can be divided in two ways: first, according to risk; and second, according to the importance of the activity for maintaining financial stability. Part of the argument is over whether more risky activity should be separated so that it does not bring down the core activities should it make major losses. (It should not be forgotten, though, that the covariances among different sources of risk are at least as important as the risks evaluated individually.) The argument is also, however, over whether a banking group should be saved in its entirety by the resolution process or whether the bail-in should only relate to the parts which are vital to the smooth running of the financial system as a whole.

There are several possible answers to this, and the future of banking union will remain somewhat uncertain until this is agreed. The most important distinction is whether one should move to resolve the group as a whole (single point of entry, SPOE) or to resolve the vital parts separately in each jurisdiction, but coordinated by the lead authority (multiple point of entry, MPOE). SPOE is simpler and involves a single jurisdiction whereas MPOE involves coordination, which has not been achieved in the past. SPOE, however, may involve a larger bail-in and may be beyond the resources of small countries with large banks.

The second omission from banking union is the unification of deposit insurance/deposit guarantees. While the EU has a common minimum guarantee of €100,000 per depositor per bank, it has not gone as far as implementing a single EU-wide scheme, mainly because they are too different to harmonise easily. Given the BRRD has required the creation of resolution authorities in each member state and has instituted depositor preference, the issue of the use of insurance funds in a crisis is no longer likely to be very important. So, although this means that the EU does not look like the US where the deposit insurer, the FDIC, covers all banks and is the resolution authority, it is not in itself a problem.

In chapter 6 Rosa Lastra argues that there is a third omission, that of a lender of last resort (LOLR) at the European level. However, the LOLR function exists in each of the member states and in the euro area. The LOLR function effectively involves two actions. The first is the expansion of market liquidity when an institution gets into difficulty and the pessimism this generates threatens to spread round the rest of the financial system, turning a problem into a disaster. The second is simply to lend to the troubled institution itself, assuming it has appropriate collateral, when the market has decided that it is too great a risk to justify lending to that institution.[1] In non-euro countries the central bank performs both functions, but within the euro area the ECB performs the first and the national central banks (NCBs) perform the second, normally with the ECB's prior agreement, but in emergency they can lend first and clear it with the ECB afterwards. The ECB insists not just on solvency of the institution concerned but that any programme of public support can be credibly repaid within a few years. This chapter by Rosa Lastra identifies legal problems, which can exacerbate or even cause economic problems. It also highlights the distinction, clear in principle but inevitably blurred in practice, between common law (primarily the law of the English-speaking world) and civil (or Roman) law. The essence of the difference, baldly stated, is that under the former one can do anything that is not forbidden, while under the latter one can do anything that is allowed. This distinction appears in her discussion of recent US changes and of a restriction on the ECB. She notes that the Federal Reserve's freedom for action in a crisis has been restricted by the Dodd-Frank Act (2010); but the ECB 'is not competent' – that is to say, is not allowed – to provide liquidity assistance to individual banks. (Professor Lastra notes that it has imposed this restriction on itself by its interpretation of the ECB Statute.)

The ECB indubitably has clear authority to provide liquidity to the market as a whole; indeed, doing so involves exactly the same action as does an easing of monetary policy. The only difference is the reason and possibly also the scale. But responsibility for individual banks lies with NCBs. This is identified as a crucial gap in banking union, for, she argues:

> While prudential supervision was at the national level, it was perhaps logical to assume that the adequate expertise and information to assess the problems of banks within their jurisdictions . . . But . . . the ECB should be . . . lender of last resort for all those institutions it now supervises.

The practical importance of this was illustrated fairly recently: the problems of dealing with Northern Rock in the UK were exacerbated by supervision not being undertaken by the Bank of England.

A further and more general problem is that there is no European 'fiscal backstop'; that is to say, there is no European body that can provide capital should it be needed to maintain banking stability. There is a body which can recapitalise the ECB should it experience substantial losses. But that body comprises national governments, which by having fragile fiscal positions may have caused problems in their banking systems and retain responsibility for their NCBs should they need recapitalising. This last observation leads to a further question.

Is this union?

Before going on to show how the chapters in this volume fit into and develop the above framework, it is necessary to consider what can be meant by the term 'banking union'.

The plans that have been described as banking union by their designers embody an implicit definition. A banking system, spread over areas and countries, is a banking union if it has a common regulatory framework and a common regulator. That implicit definition is troublingly incomplete, and it has curious implications. It says, for example, that Britain did not have a banking union until 1979 – until then British banks were regulated only by the same set of company laws that regulated other firms. There was no specific banking regulation. Also, the definition is not only odd in some of its implications; it omits, or perhaps presumes as following automatically from having a single regulator, an important aspect of what should be integral to such a union.

Certainly one reason to promote a banking union (and the same reason applies to the promotion of a capital markets union) is to increase the efficiency of resource allocation. How can this be done in the present context?

Suppose that the interest rate charged for an identical loan to identical borrowers in different parts of the euro area differed. Would that comprise a capital market imperfection, which could be eliminated by a capital market union? Lance Davis (1963) would say so: he measured the approach to a national capital market in the US by the decline in differences in interest rates among regions. But as Stigler (1967) points out: 'No-one would dream of using this criterion for wheat or automobiles'. Stigler's point generalises as follows. Price differences between the same good at different points, which are less than the transport costs between them, make the movement of the goods uneconomic. The goods will not be transported, and the remaining price difference is evidence of efficiency *not* of inefficiency. Similarly, a misallocation of capital is created, not removed, if interest rates move together without the genuine removal of what was keeping them apart. Moving them together by regulation, for example, would be damaging.[2]

Now what does this imply for the meaning of banking union? Take the example of the UK. That country has had for many years now a genuine banking union. That has come about through a system of nationwide banks. Not all banks are nationwide and many fewer banks were nationwide when interest rate differences first virtually vanished across the UK, but there is a banking union created by the ability individuals have to borrow and lend where they wish and for banks to lend and borrow in any part of the UK they wish, without regulatory impediment or barriers to entry in any part of the country (at any rate for an institution which is already in the banking system). Both supply and demand can move freely across the nation.

A genuine, efficiency improving, banking union would be one which led to such a situation in the EU. Can what has been described as a banking union be expected to do that? It is hard to see how. Centralising regulation for large cross-national banks is indeed likely, as noted above, to produce lower regulatory costs than would otherwise be the case, so that is beneficial. But barriers between national banking markets are not tackled by these arrangements, except to some extent by the 'single rule-book'. Hence, these plans may well be better viewed not as a banking union but as a device for simplifying and sharing the burden of the resolution of large banks. Indeed, one could go further and describe them as a step towards fiscal union, starting with the banking sector.

Accordingly, therefore, we do not in this book analyse the proposals from the viewpoint of whether they create, or move us towards, a genuine banking union. Rather we consider solely the narrow objectives of promoting early intervention and, if necessary, orderly and (to the taxpayer) inexpensive resolution should resolution be needed.

Short-term pressures

Even the limited banking union that is being implemented will not be fully operational until 2024 when the resolution funds have reached their target level and the Single Resolution Fund (SRF) is fully mutualised. Similarly, Basel 3 is not due for completion until 2019, and extra requirements for capital beyond that will still take some time to be implemented, as will the full capacity for bailing in (minimum required eligible liabilities, MREL, in the EU terminology, and total loss absorbing capacity, TLAC, in the FSB (international) parlance). There are, therefore, issues about how the system will work before it reaches maturity, particularly if the current pressures on sovereign debt, through Greece, cause problems for the banks.

One great hope for banking union was that it would break the vicious circle between weak banks and heavily indebted sovereigns. If the only way forward for recapitalising weak banks is a taxpayer bail-out then this route is not open for a heavily indebted country or, as in the case of Cyprus and Iceland, if the size of the recapitalisation needed exceeds the capacity of the state. Under the BRRD, it should be possible to recapitalise banks primarily through bailing in, not bailing out. Hence, although public funds may be needed to provide confidence in the financial system, the demands are likely to be more manageable. The problem is that this system will work once banks have been properly recapitalised. Banks, which are weak at the start of banking union, still need funding from other sources as they would have used markets if they could.

The ECB in coordination with the EBA has undertaken an Asset Quality Review, which was intended to make sure that all banks entering the SSM were sufficiently well capitalised; if they failed that test then they would not be admitted. The review, whose results were published in October 2014, suggested that only a dozen important banks were undercapitalised, and only one of those represented a serious problem. Lybeck criticises this assessment in chapter 9, suggesting that the test is too weak. However, it is also clear that to meet Basel 3 and the TLAC requirements very significant capital raising still has to take place. So, until that recapitalisation is complete, there will still be a question mark over both bank quality and sovereign solvency.

The problem is even worse if there is indeed a sovereign default, as local banks tend to be holders of their own country's debt. Ironically, the more problematic cases such as Greece have the lowest proportion of domestic holding of their own securities. A default in such a case would have extensive external consequences. Most Italian debt, for example, is held by Italians; hence, a default would be much more concentrated on Italy itself. Nevertheless, until Europe can escape worries about undercapitalisation, its banks will be more reluctant to lend, thereby making the recovery more difficult. Economic growth is the best route out of the sovereign debt problem.

Longer-term issues[3]

There is a strong tendency in addressing the weaknesses in regulation revealed by the GFC to fight the last war and design a system that would make it easier to avoid the same crisis again. This is a mistake. Crises normally occur because of a collective failure to realise the pressures that are building up in the system. Sometimes they occur because of a major shock that is of a known type but is inherently unforecastable, such as a serious natural disaster. Those we can prepare for, but not avoid. What we can do is attempt to set out the sorts of pressures that exist in the world today and which are likely to result in financial crises. There are some obvious candidates. One is that in both the private and public sectors there has been a build-up of debt. Much of this build-up in the private sector has been the result of underutilised resources. The assets of the private sector, particularly housing, can be used to leverage both a better lifestyle and investment in productive activity, which offers a higher rate of return at a higher risk. It has, therefore, been sensible to see private debt rise as a ratio of GDP. However, at some point the debt ratio reaches an equilibrium. At that point, the growth of private debt should slow and move in line with economic activity over the longer term.

In practice, it is likely that there will be a substantial overshooting, as it is not likely to be clear ex ante when that point is reached, for a lot of the conditions depend purely on preferences: how much we value the future compared with the present; how important housing is as a consumption and investment good compared to other opportunities; how much risk we are prepared to tolerate; and so on. Moreover, such decisions are history dependent – if there is a substantial downward shock and a lot of people lose money in the short run, it will affect their attitude to risk in the longer term. We might want to consider this as an example of multiple equilibria. If all goes well and there have been no adverse shocks, debt ratios will adjust differently from if there is an unpleasant surprise. Worse still, if there is a favourable surprise, ratios may rise much further than would make sense under normal conditions. Recognition of the error (or the occurrence of the adverse shock) will generate the crisis.

Charles Goodhart's contribution to this volume recognises that such a turning point will be one-off and may happen smoothly. At some point, society will realise that the debt build-up cannot continue anymore. Hence, we are likely to suffer any such crisis once, rather than repeatedly.

A similar argument applies to ageing and to the retirement of the 'baby boom' generation after the last world war. At some point in societies, they change from seeing steady population growth to starting to contract. At the same time, the proportion of older people in society rises. Goodhart assumes that this will increase the dependency ratio, but in a modern society this is not so obvious. People can work longer in jobs that are not physically demanding. Furthermore, the same improvement in health that helps them live longer is also likely to make them want to work longer, especially if fiscal burdens mean that their pensions would otherwise be reduced.

Again, this is probably a one-off problem from a crisis point of view. There will be a change from the build-up of assets in a growing population to one where older people need to run down their assets in order to sustain their living standards in old age. That may very well result in an adjustment of asset prices. But, given the tendency of asset prices to overshoot, the adjustment may not be smooth.

More pernicious is the failure of the developed world to adjust fully to the pressures from the rise of China and other less developed countries as more efficient and cost-competitive sources of production. To some extent the rise of China, in particular, has just enabled an expansion of consumption. But in other respects it is substitution. More of the same value added will accrue in the developing markets and less in the developed ones. This implies a slowing or even reversal in growth rates in the developed world, at least temporarily. As with other imbalances, the hope is always that it will be run down steadily rather than drastically, but the ability to change gradually is asymmetric. Those in surplus can always continue with the surplus whereas those in deficit can reach the limit of what they can borrow or the exchange rate they can defend. The difficulties then are concentrated in just some countries, giving them harsh problems. This is obviously reflected in a number of countries in the euro area.

Goodhart's final unsustainable trend is the way in which monetary policy has become progressively weaker, as has labour's share in the economy, and hence demand has fallen relative to GDP and inequality has risen over the last 35 years. While he expects this trend to be reversed in the future, the key issue in current circumstances is that a structural change can be expected.

The banking system will, thus, have to cope with several sources of long-term stress. An optimistic view would be that these problems would be resolved progressively, and hence the change can be smooth. History suggests that such smooth change is not particularly common and that further financial instability along the way could be expected. Banking union has to cope with this and may not get a long smooth run in until banks are very well capitalised.

Ironically, if there is a further period of crisis, this will give an opportunity for moving banking union from its current incomplete and asymmetric position to one which has a better economic basis and is not constrained by current political concerns. A period without strain is likely to let the current system become ingrained and make change much more difficult.

However, this discussion relates to the pressures we know that banking union will have to cope with. The more difficult are those we cannot identify explicitly.

The insistence on recapitalisation, reduced leverage, improved liquidity management and restructuring among banks to reduce the threat of financial instability
and the consequences of failure on the real economy will all help reverse the
trends of recent decades. But financial systems and institutions adapt. All of the
same pressures to reap higher returns and hence run greater risks will remain in
society at large. Concentrating on banks and banking union may simply drive the
problems elsewhere – almost by definition into shadow banking as the area where
bank-like activity is undertaken by non-banks. However, insurance and pension
funds may well find themselves perhaps taking on risks they had not appreciated –
from bailing in for example.

There is a temptation, therefore, to try to push out the frontier of bank-like
regulation ever further. However, there is a second approach, which the European
Commission appears to be adopting. This is to extend the idea of banking union
more widely to capital markets and have a capital markets union of some form
in Europe. Certainly, given the very high share of bank finance in much of continental Europe, moves towards making equity and bond markets operate more
effectively and become more attractive to investors and firms would be no bad
thing as a contribution towards increased stability. It is often argued (Levine *et al.*,
2015) that stock markets act as a 'spare tyre', providing firms with an alternative
source of finance when banks have to cut back on lending. Indeed, banking union
itself will help the growth of stock markets if the worries about the increased cost
of bank finance as a result of the withdrawal of the subsidy from the availability of
taxpayer bail-outs prove to be correct. (The counter argument is that if banks have
now become less likely to fail as a result of higher capital ratios, greater liquidity,
decreased risk and better incentives to monitor, then the cost of capital should fall –
or at least not rise very much overall.)

Thus, some of the parameters of banking union may need to be revised in the
light of the future development of the financial system, particularly in relation to
restraints on structures of financial groups.

Union or division?

Despite the many positive sides to what has been enacted, the banking union
arrangements risk dividing the EU or even encouraging countries to leave, because
its structure reflects the political difficulty of agreement not the economic logic
of the structure of the banking and wider financial system in Europe. Centralising
supervision on the ECB, in which non-euro countries are not full members, puts
them at a disadvantage. Given the problems with the euro area since 2010, there
are clear incentives for countries that are not heavily integrated with the euro area
to retain their monetary independence so that they can react to shocks, whether
favourable or unfavourable.[4] With monetary independence, the worst affected
euro area countries would have had the option of devaluation and a more rapid
course to regaining competitiveness. Moreover, financial markets would not have
allowed their debt to get into such a precarious position before the GFC, as there
would have been no possibility of a bail-out by other member states.[5] Current

non-members can now see the problems and hence have a disincentive to join. Indeed, adverse selection is likely to occur where applicants are those states most likely to need assistance from the other members.

However, having a suitable structure for dealing with cross-border banks in Europe is largely irrelevant to whether the countries are members of the euro area or even of the EU itself. Indeed, the need for close cooperation is greater when the jurisdictions have different currencies. To take an example: Nordea is the most significant bank in the Nordic region, covering Denmark, Finland, Norway and Sweden. Only Finland is a member of the euro area and Norway is not even a member of the EU. Clearly, it makes sense for them to have an organised approach to both supervision and resolution, yet this cannot happen under the current banking union if only because Norway is ineligible to join. It would make sense to have a much more variable geometry where Norway could join an independent EEA-wide organisation. (Indeed, it would make sense to try to include Switzerland as well given the role of UBS and Credit Suisse across Europe.)

A neat structure for banking union would have a single regulatory structure, a single supervisory structure and a single resolution structure that applied not just across the EEA/EU but was open-ended so that other countries could join. This would be particularly helpful for aspirant EU members that have systemically important subsidiaries/branches of EU/EEA banks operating in their territories. Complete harmonisation for banks without significant operations in other countries would appear unnecessary from experience in the US, but the existence of an EU-level regime that could be adopted by cross-border banks for their operations throughout the area would make life simpler for them and less costly for their customers. Having a single resolution framework for cross-border banks without having a single supervisory framework first would be difficult to operate, because resolution imposes losses and costs across the various jurisdictions for problems that might be the consequence of supervisory errors by one of the parties. Unless there were joint responsibility for actions beforehand it is unlikely that the consequent resolution would avoid recriminations and refusals to act.

As it is, where countries face difficulties in coordination outside the SSM/SRM it makes sense for them to follow one of two routes. In the case of the UK and Sweden (excluding Nordea), the easiest way forward is to make sure they can solve problems on their own following the SPOE approach, where they are the lead authority. Where they are a host, then trying to separate out the operations and insist on a subsidiary structure where there is practical self-sufficiency makes sense for any other systemically important institution. (Systemic importance should be interpreted very broadly in this case, as difficulties with any well-known institution where it appeared they had no adequate control could lead to a financial crisis as people begin to worry about the consequences.)

There are two problems about being a junior partner in a bank whose headquarters are in the SSM/SRM. The first is that the SRB will have dominating negotiating power so domestic problems could be overridden. The second is that it is as yet unclear how well any approach recommended by the SRB might work in practice. In so far as such a resolution involves MPOE it is not clear how well authorities may be able to coordinate, whatever their prior commitments. The Netherlands went along with the wishes of Belgium and Luxembourg in the resolution of Fortis in 2008 until it became clear that a better outcome might be obtained by carving the Dutch parts out of the bank and running them separately. Such concerns will still apply in a major crisis where countries are worried about their economic survival. The pressure from the ECB on countries such as Ireland and Cyprus when they were in difficulty is not going to encourage small countries in the future.

Hence, it would make sense for the EU to move to create a genuine separate single supervisor outside the euro area framework. The EBA was the obvious location for this, and this could still be the case, particularly since the location in London may have some appeal to the UK.

There is, of course, one potential opportunity for changing the structure of banking union, if pressure to alter the EU, precipitated by the need for the UK to reassess its position with respect to the EU, turns out to be strong enough. However, the nature of any such renegotiation is likely to lead to a reduction in some dimensions of integration rather than to any increase or to an increasing polarisation between countries that wish to move further and those who wish to take a few steps back. Similarly, should Greece default and leave the euro area, this also would tend to lead to a weakening of integration, allowing a more flexible approach to macroeconomic policy, where countries are otherwise constrained by the joint nominal exchange rate and interest rate, and having a more coherent euro area would increase the sustainability of the EU. Otherwise, the outlook is somewhat pessimistic. For the maintenance of relatively untroubled times that do not test the banking union's tools will tend to solidify the existing structures, including divisions among the member states.

Without the GFC it is highly unlikely that the EU would have implemented legislation as drastic as the BRRD and countries would have continued to believe that their existing tools would be adequate to handle serious problems and crises. Whether the increasing harmonisation through CEBS would have led to anything approaching the SSM is a much more difficult speculation. However, history is as it is; at this stage one can only hope that banking union will evolve into a more credible and complete framework – without the dramatic events that are more likely to precipitate further change. At least with the BRRD all of the member states will have much better tools to effect less costly resolutions in the future, and with the improved capitalisation ensuing from the Basel 3 rules and the FSB recommendations for systemically important financial institutions (SIFIs), the risk of failure should have fallen. Making any forecast in the current unstable conditions is likely to render the conclusion wrong between the time that the text is finalised and the date of publication.

The plan: comparison and analysis

Turning now, very briefly, to the individual chapters, we start with Karamichailidou and Mayes as that focuses on an aspect of the scheme, which should be integral to any legal framework concerning banks – recovery and resolution plans. Ever since the problems of LTCM, a firm which had to be propped up because the US insolvency code as then constituted could not handle it in an orderly fashion, there has been discussion of such plans for the banking sector. (Other parts of the financial sector have been accorded a lower priority on the grounds that they are less of a threat to financial stability.[6]) Karamichailidou and Mayes are hesitant in their welcome for current plans in the banking union. In particular, they draw attention to a problem, which is especially likely to occur in the EU – the problem of failing cross-border banks. Such banks have, however, been resolved in the past, and the chapter draws on these experiences. The authors summarise the very substantial requirements for success.

> The case of Fortis, for example, illustrated that the cross-border crisis management framework needs to be developed to be compatible with the cross-border nature of the operations of those FIs [financial institutions]. Secondly, there need to be mechanisms in place to ensure the continuity of business across all the jurisdictions where a cross-border FI operates. Thirdly, there should be arrangements for information sharing to ensure that critical information is assessed and interpreted in the same way. And lastly, financial authorities need to have powers that allow them to override shareholders' rights if financial stability is threatened (Basel Committee on Banking Supervision, 2010).

These are not necessarily easy to satisfy particularly because in order for a smooth resolution to be possible, there must be not just the will to achieve the mechanisms set out above but a common view on the nature these mechanisms must take. That too is not straightforward: to quote Mayes writing in 2014: 'It is already clear that even the Nordic countries, which form one of the most integrated groups internationally, have clear differences of opinion over the tools that should be applied in a crisis . . . '.

Furthermore, thinking just about large and important banks, without reflecting on cross-border complications, also highlights some problems. Karamichailidou and Mayes write: 'The key to a successful cross-border bank resolution is clearly that ex ante the bank appears "resolvable" to the authorities'. That applies to all banks, and here 'living wills' come in. These specify how a bank works and can be wound up. They form, at the least, a kind of road map. With these, is separation of functions in the bank necessary, as is currently being prescribed in various forms in many countries? It is hard to see why, for if the bank can if necessary be resolved, then why break it up and reduce the number of not perfectly correlated income streams? Be that as it may, much remains to be done in the EU agreements, as the extensive discussion by Karamichailidou and Mayes of the experience of other countries shows very clearly. The conclusion of Karamichailidou and Mayes that there are completely unavoidable uncertainties is hard to deny: 'So despite all the planning we can expect the normal panic and the need to take extraordinary actions, some of which are likely to involve taxpayers' money'.

Do any of the other chapters lighten the tone? Conlon and Cotter follow Karamichailidou and Mayes in looking at history, but unlike Karamichailidou and Mayes they look entirely inside the EU and use data from it to run a most interesting counterfactual experiment. They rerun the last crisis under the new rules of the game. Their findings are very striking; it appears that for large, systemically important euro area banks, equity writedowns would have been sufficient to cover losses. But adequate capitalisation for most such banks would have required conversion to equity of all subordinated and some senior debt. Depositors would, however, have been safe. So far, so optimistic. They then go on to examine whether formal resolution triggers, derived from market and balance sheet data, have provided any help in distinguishing in advance between the banks which failed and the banks which survived. The evidence that they could have done so is there, but is weak. This highlights that much reliance is being placed on the subjective triggers of the SRM. These are important conclusions. How are they reached?

Accounting data relating to European banks are drawn from Bankscope for the period 2006 to 2012. This dataset covers the 12 largest euro area countries for which banks fall under the supervision of the ECB under the SSM. (The countries included are Austria, Belgium, Finland, France, Germany, Greece, Ireland, Italy, Luxembourg, Netherlands, Portugal and Spain.) Bankscope provides data on both listed and unlisted banks, resulting in a total of 701 banks.

Conlon and Cotter then apply the bail-in tool provided for in the BRRD and SRM. To arrive at a required level of bail-in for each bank, the impairment charges accounted for over the period 2008–2012 are taken as baseline losses experienced.

The analysis is presented for writedowns and equity conversions relating to bank balance sheets from 2006, and the bail-in is structured in the way mandated by the BRRD. It is this that yields the modestly encouraging result summarised above.

But careful as this work is, there must be a note of caution. For the bail-in rules were based on the experience of the preceding crisis; hence, that they worked when applied to it retrospectively is encouraging, but certainly not a guarantee that they will work in future episodes. Turning now to trying to foresee failures, how do the authors proceed? They examine a number of potential quantitative market and balance sheet triggers. Market-based triggers are forward looking, capturing the markets' perception of a bank's position. Balance sheet triggers are backward looking, revealing the reported financial position of the bank.

Conlon and Cotter state their conclusion cautiously: 'While weak evidence exists for the ability of equity market-based triggers to differentiate between failed and surviving banks, the evidence for balance sheet triggers is unintuitive . . . '.

One could very reasonably say that their chapter is no more than modestly encouraging for the banking union proposals as set out to date.

This caution is reinforced by the concerns set out by Alessandro Roselli in his observations, which follow the paper by Conlon and Cotter. Automatic bail-ins are, he observes, an apparently attractive device (particularly to bankers), as an alternative to raising new equity. They prevent use of taxpayer's money in banking crises, are cheaper than equity, which indeed might not be available at any price, and avoid dilution of bankers' control. But while this may appear to be true in good times, Roselli observes that in a crisis they might make things worse, deepening the crisis, multiplying losses and perhaps expanding haircuts to customers' deposits, while cases of idiosyncratic risk may well evolve into systemic crises.

To reduce or avoid costly public bail-outs, he argues, we either – on the liabilities side of a banking institution – have to convert creditors into equity holders, or – on the asset side –need safer activities. While in the past emphasis has been mainly on the second (for example, the Glass Steagall Act, at least as defended by its advocates), the current approach is to address the first, partly by increasing capital requirements and partly by envisaging a panoply of instruments that should bail in the bank in crisis. It is, however, unclear what the optimal level of equity should be and still more uncertain whether bail-in clauses would protect the taxpayer, or more likely have unwanted, destabilising consequences.

What to do? Roselli suggests two possibilities. One is to eliminate bank leverage, transforming the liability side into an equity investment; but this would deprive the financial system of banks' monetary function at the centre of the payment system – their core, public utility business. The desire to maintain this core function opens the way to a second approach: the 'narrow bank', which gathers deposits and invests them only in 'safe' instruments – in the extreme, balances at the central bank.

These approaches actually complement each other, and the resulting structure of the banking system would have two components: the 'narrow bank' and a series of institutions with a substantial equity component and a wide range of activities carrying different degrees of risk. This is a greater degree of radicalism than policy makers are at the moment willing to contemplate; but who knows what a future crisis may bring?

In chapter 4 Kate Phylaktis considers the banking problems of Cyprus and their implications for European banking union. She terms the episode: 'The Cyprus Debacle'. It soon emerges from her description and analysis of what happened that the word 'debacle' is too mild for what happened.

She traces the origins of these events to a combination of Cyprus's history and what it did to join the euro. The budget deficit was sharply reduced and turned into a surplus. In consequence, the debt to GDP ratio fell from 70 per cent to 48.9 per cent. But this was produced by the combination of a one-off tax amnesty, which led to a temporary burst of payments, and a capital gains tax, which, due to a 'real estate bubble', produced a substantial rise in revenue.

This one-off gain was dissipated by the extreme left government which took over at the next election. Both social spending and the number of government employees increased. The cumulative deficit from 2009 to 2013 was some 30 per cent of GDP.

In addition to this fiscal laxity, developments in the banking sector further exacerbated problems. Before joining the EU there was interest rate regulation, with credit allocated by use of collateral and on personal guarantees. The former, of course, biased lending to real estate. Furthermore, the reliance on personal guarantees led to personal lending; private sector credit as a share of GDP reached: ' . . . 298 per cent in 2011, only surpassed briefly by Iceland in 2006'. The situation was plainly just waiting for a trigger to turn it into a catastrophe.

Joining the euro led to a rapid growth of foreign inflows, which were still largely directed to real estate. Further, banks started to increase their operations outside Cyprus, notably (but not exclusively) in Greece. Hence, when in 2011 Greek debt was restructured, Cypriot banks were very severely affected. A comparison makes the point: the private sector bail-in that took place in the Greek restructuring was 23 per cent of GDP in Cyprus, 0.14 per cent of German GDP and, perhaps much more notable, 12 per cent of the GDP of Greece itself. The banks not surprisingly did not have the capital to cover this, and the sovereign could not issue long-term debt to provide support, as it had lost market access in 2011.

This was manifestly a major problem for Cyprus. The crisis occurred in March 2013. What happened next? The government of Cyprus had already applied to the 'Troika' for assistance, but then refused to sign a memorandum of understanding. One was only signed after a change of government in February 2013. A plan was first agreed on 16 March. Notably, this plan included a bail-in of *all* depositors, insured as well as uninsured, in all Cyprus banks. Even then, the Eurogroup would lend only €10 billion out of the estimated requirement of €17 billion. This, Phylaktis suggests, was a result of two things: German belief that a large part of the bank deposits were from wealthy non-EU depositors and the IMF's unwillingness to allow the creation of an unsustainable debt burden.

At this point one really has to ask what the Troika was thinking. Had they no notion of the risks they were running by not protecting insured deposits? Widespread deposit insurance had, after all, been developed in the US in the wake of the banking collapse of the 1930s with the aim of preventing such collapses in the future. In any event, they were saved from the possible consequences of their folly when the Cyprus parliament rejected the whole deal. But insured depositors had by then realised their danger. (It still seems remarkable that such fears did not also in consequence affect at least some other euro area members.)

The ultimately accepted deal involved bank closure, exchange controls and Cyprus becoming for a time an exclusively cash economy so far as using a medium of exchange went – no bank transfers of any sort could take place. (No doubt there was also a partial reversion to barter.) There were cancellations of shares in some banks and the sale of Cypriot bank branches in Greece at a knock-down price. Regardless of the health of the parent, *all* branches of *all* Cypriot banks in Greece had to be sold. The Troika insisted on the sale of Cypriot branches in Greece to cut off any channel of contagion to the rest of the euro area. Depositors in Greece avoided the bail-in, but, at the same time, Cypriot depositors were to be bailed in much more as a result.

What lessons does Phylaktis draw explicitly from this sorry episode? She considers the 'three pillars' of European banking union: the SSM, bank resolution and deposit insurance. She suggests there are considerable benefits from the first, as it frees supervisors from local political pressure. But she is concerned about interbank linkages and the link between the banking sector and national sovereignty. Dealing with supervision, had it been done earlier, might, she suggests, have prevented the crisis. An SRM might have made the crisis less deep, as resolution might have come earlier, despite domestic political resistance in the run-up to an election. A unified deposit insurance system, while not of itself breaking the link between sovereign and banking solvency, would also make insured depositors less anxious should doubts over the sovereign's solvency appear.

Her conclusion is nonetheless a gloomy one, reflecting as it does on what happened to Cyprus.

> Had there been a European Banking Union along proposed lines . . . when Cyprus joined the EU . . . recommendations (might have been made) to put the banking sector on a better footing. European Banking Union has come too late for Cyprus.

Johan Lybeck, like most authors in this volume, looks both backward and forward. He views, surely correctly, the measures undertaken in the US and in the euro area as designed both to reduce the likelihood of a shock on the scale of the first financial crisis of the twenty-first century and also to change the way in which bank failures are resolved so that they can be done at reduced, preferably zero, cost to the taxpayer. He also shares the concern of Karamichailidou and Mayes that taxpayers' funds may be needed in a crisis, but for different reasons. While they expect that to be the result of the 'normal panic', this is because: 'A study of the bank resolutions in financial crises shows that the use of taxpayer money is an inevitable feature of successful interventions'. Also, he adds that: 'A credible resolution authority, irrespective of whether financing means are prefunded or not, depends on having the Treasury (i.e. the tax payer) as a last resort'. The last is extremely plausible, at least until there have been several failures resolved without the need for taxpayer funds.

His comparison of the US and the euro area leads him to be pessimistic that the euro area has as yet achieved anything that can be called banking union, or indeed produced a plausible resolution regime. To quote: 'The US, after Dodd-Frank, presents a consistent framework of resolution where some minor things need to be changed. Europe, on the other hand, is in a total mess.' (Observe that he is somewhat more sympathetic to what has been done in the US than is Rosa Lastra in her chapter.) The US has common supervision, common resolution and deposit insurance for the whole of the country. In the euro area there is common supervision, based in the ECB, but the resolution board lacks powers of decision, adequate resources and a taxpayer backstop. The last of course would imply at least a start to fiscal union and so one should not rely on its coming quickly. His recommendations are drastic. Either repatriate all powers for dealing with crises to individual countries, or proceed to a 'true European banking union'. That, he suggests, involves following the recommendations of other chapters in this volume. A further recommendation is that there should be host country supervision of international banks in a way pioneered by the US, where foreign banks have to operate as separately capitalised US subsidiary bank holding companies and are supervised by the Federal Reserve. These are striking recommendations, rigorously thought through.

But however limited in scope these banking union proposals are, they inevitably have legal implications and requirements. It is useful therefore to turn next to a chapter which deals with legal matters. The chapter by Binder does that and deals in particular with resolution plans, which are obviously, in view of the guarded endorsement given to the scheme as a whole by Conlon and Cotter, particularly important to the workability of the scheme. He is concerned that discussion of resolution plans and of structural banking reforms have been 'rather separate'. Now a question does of course arise at this point: if we are convinced the former will work, do we need the latter? Binder suggests that we should not be completely confident in resolution plans. The reasons he advances relate primarily to the structures of the organisations which may need to be resolved. He points to: ' . . . complexity and opacity of legal structures . . . ', to ' . . . intra-group arrangements for IT support . . . ', to ' . . . conflicting legal frameworks . . . ' and to 'conflicting national powers and interests'.

Binder considers how the plans for resolution can be 'reconciled with' the plans for structural reform that are being advanced. He further argues that it makes little sense to consider resolution plans and recovery plans separately.

But his major conclusion is on the problems of requiring reorganisation so as to facilitate resolution. Existing bank structures are not as they are for fun. Many years ago George Stigler enunciated the 'survivor principle' in his discussion of the problems of the optimal size of firm literature. The same principle surely applies to the optimal structure of banks. The structure evolved for a reason, or indeed for a variety of reasons, and one of these has been totally neglected in official discussions – the structure of tax systems. Binder's conclusion that it is not wise to propose major reforms of structure without careful consideration of: ' . . . relevant trade-offs between business models, funding arrangements, organisational and legal structures on the one hand and resolvability on the other . . . ' is surely correct. If there is not careful gathering and evaluation of evidence on this, then one can be at least moderately confident that the roots of the next crisis have been sown.

Krimminger considers another possible source of difficulty in chapter 8.

> [i]nternational standard setters and national authorities have sought to create a more resilient financial system while fashioning statutory frameworks and strategies to make the resolution of so-called SIFIs possible . . . Those strategies have begun to coalesce around approaches that focus on restructuring and recapitalising the failing SIFI through the bail-in or conversion of debt into a new capital base. This chapter examines some of the differences in the approaches taken in the US, UK and European Union and the possible implications for the industry and the financial system.

He first sets out the different approaches taken by the US, the UK and the members of the EU. The contrast he shows is clear:

> As we move from the FDIC's description of its SPOE resolution strategy, it is important to note that the focus for the FDIC remains on a transfer of operations to a temporary Bridge followed by restructuring and an exit through a recapitalisation using a bail-in of debt-holders of the failed SIFI. The approach to the SPOE strategy preferred by UK and European regulators is significantly different.

In the UK there can be bail-in before insolvency: ' . . . to ensure that critical banking services continue to be provided, while imposing recapitalisation costs on shareholders and creditors rather than meeting this cost out of UK Government funds'. In the EU: ' . . . there was no harmonisation of the insolvency regimes for resolving banks or other financial institutions in the EU and the crisis underscored a lack of adequate tools both at the EU level and in the member states to deal effectively with unsound or failing banks . . . '.

The BRRD of 12 June 2014: ' . . . is designed to fill this gap by laying out a harmonised toolbox of resolution powers that will be available to national authorities in each member state'. It is, as he writes, one of the 'building blocks' of banking union. He then goes on to compare and contrast the approaches to dealing with failing banks that are proposed in the three areas. His chapter provides an abundance of detail. But he emphasises one key point, that there is much uncertainty about the role of:

> TLAC in the US, EU and UK resolution strategies . . . With regard to internal TLAC those questions include which subsidiaries will be required to issue internal TLAC, how to evaluate whether a company is a material subsidiary given the new importance this acquires, how should internal TLAC be calibrated based on the business and interconnections between the subsidiary and its affiliates as well as its parent, and many others'.

He concludes: 'We must assume that international and national regulators will be open to a transparent discussion about these issues. They are too important to resolve without bringing the best analytics together in an open dialogue'.

That sentence can, if the reader wishes, be regarded as the summary of this chapter and, indeed, of the book as a whole. For those who wish for something a little longer, that too can in fact be brief.

The proposals for banking union aim not so much at union in the sense of achieving a fully integrated banking market across the EU, nor even that across the euro area, but at breaking the link between bank failure and government financial stress and perhaps failure. They aim to do this by better supervision, better management of risk, better procedures for failure so that it can be orderly and better or at the least clearer division of responsibilities for dealing with banks. The chapters in this volume suggest that none of the measures taken fully achieves any of these goals.

Taken individually, moving towards these desirable goals clearly represents steps in the right direction and is to be applauded. The EU has been remarkably successful in pushing through major legislative changes in a short period. Introducing the tools to resolve banks without either their ceasing trading or the taxpayer footing the bill is particularly welcome. But taking some but not enough steps to make a collaborative approach fully credible could be worse than each country moving to be able to solve its own problems. It could even be divisive, particularly in its distinguishing between euro and non-euro area countries. In some respects, banking union is an attempt to get round some of the consequences of the lack of a more developed fiscal union in the EU. By mutualising and privatising some of the costs of adjustment to adverse shocks in particular countries, this will clearly help in the crisis itself. However, such partial measures usually introduce distortions in trying to compensate for what has been left undone. A consequence can be greater imbalances and more destabilising corrections. Attempting to correct deficiencies in the structure of economic and monetary union by the back door through aspects of banking union does not address the fundamental problems and could weaken the banking union in the process.

Apart from the obvious and, perhaps, politically inevitable fact that not all EU financial markets are covered, there are legal and economic aspects that are incomplete. The ECB has been forced to live with a conflict of interest by having to be supervisor of some banks. Bail-in may spread rather than end financial sector problems. There has been a push towards common rather than consistent and transparent standards, and this unnecessary centralisation has perhaps diminished appetites for politically contentious but useful measures. It is not clear that links between failing states and failing banks have been broken – indeed, where they have been, notably in Greece at the time of writing, this was achieved without any of the changes proposed.

In summary, there remain legal and economic barriers to be surmounted before there can be reasonable confidence in the overall stability of the euro area banking system, and as for banking union in the sense of an integrated banking market in Europe, little that has been done moves the EU towards that desirable situation. Much of this may of course reflect political difficulties, but how to surmount these is beyond the scope of this book.

Naturally, our hope is that the maturation of banking union over the coming years will lead to a resolution of these problems. The SSM is a new mechanism and the SRB is yet to start work. Even where frameworks have deficiencies, well-run organisations can ensure that the practice turns out well. There is thus a huge responsibility for the ECB, the SRB and the other financial regulatory authorities in the EU and their partners in trying to ensure future success. Implementing excellent mechanisms in theory is clearly a good start, but it is not until the next crisis strikes that we will discover their true quality. Whether one regards this as a glass half full or a glass half empty problem, filling the other half is clearly the priority.

Unfortunately, even if it is possible to design a recovery and resolution system that will work under most (although not necessarily all) plausible scenarios, it is not possible to opine clearly on whether the political pressures of the time will allow it to be deployed. In a crisis everyone is under strain, and policymakers worry about the best actions to take, irrespective of the fact that they have designed a system to make that choice more straightforward. The main concerns are simply confidence and contagion. If, for example, there are worries at the time that using the bail-in tool will precipitate a far worse crisis – and all those about to be bailed in will no doubt claim that this will be the case – the authorities may well hesitate. A taxpayer-financed bail-out may still look the best way to lessen the immediate impact and punt the consequences a lot further into the future. One must not, therefore, expect perfection from banking union.

We can certainly insist that we need a system that works well in normal times, but that is a relatively easy requirement. The greater difficulty is that the system should, ex ante, plausibly appear able to operate when it is under severe stress. As this book shows, many but not all the tools to achieve this are being put in place. The authors of the various chapters show a caution about whether the omissions are so serious that the system may not work. If this caution is widely shared then banking union will be at a considerable disadvantage. Those involved will manage the risks they face differently in the light of that belief. It thus remains to be seen whether or not there will be general confidence and, hence, how the banking system will behave in trying to increase stability for its own benefit.

Notes

1 It is normally argued that any such lending should be at a margin over normal market rates, otherwise the LOLR will become a lender of first resort and risk distorting the market system. It is anticipated that LOLR lending will be short-lived as once the central bank states its confidence in the institution (based on supervisory reports) then private sector lenders can flock back in; first, because the central bank will try to protect its investment and, second, because this vote of confidence will lead to market lenders offering finance once again.
2 Stigler applies the same analysis to re-appraise asserted 'imperfections' in markets such as the US market for student loans and the market for loans to allow a small firm to ride out a price war initiated by a larger rival.
3 The work of Charles Goodhart, who gave the keynote address at the conference in which the chapters of this book were discussed, provides an important input to this section, especially Goodhart and Erfurth (2014) and of course his address, which is reproduced here in modified form as chapter 10.
4 Obviously this does not apply to the Baltic States, who were already running currency boards backed by the euro. For them membership gave added certainty and hence reduced interest rates, gave them a seat at the decision-making table and made little difference to effective monetary policy. As small countries with a difficult history as members of the Soviet Union, they lacked an alternative basis for a credible monetary policy.
5 It is important to differentiate between the countries that had the most difficulties, as Spain and particularly Ireland did not have public debt ratios that were a cause for concern. Nevertheless, with independent currencies each country would have received a continuous assessment by markets of the sustainability of their fiscal position.
6 Why this may be the case is discussed in Allen and Wood (2006).

References

Allen, W. and Wood, G. E. (2006) Defining and achieving financial stability. *Journal of Financial Stability* 2(2): 152–172.

Basel Committee on Banking Supervision (2010) *Report and Recommendations of the Cross-Border Bank Resolution Group*. Available at: http://www.bis.org/publ/bcbs169.pdf (last accessed 30 October 2014).

Davis, L. E. (1963) Capital immobilities and finance capitalism: A study of economic evolution in the United States. *Explorations in Entrepreneurial History* 1(1)(Fall): 88–105.

Goodhart, C. A. E. and Erfurth, P. (2014) *Demography and Economics: Look Past the Past*. Available at: http://www.voxeu.org/article/demography-and-economics-look-past-past (last accessed 27 July 2015).

Levine, R., Lin, C. and Xie, W. (2015) *Spare Tire? Stock Markets, Banking Crises, and Economic Recoveries*. NBER Working Paper 20863. Available at: http://www.nber.org/papers/w20863 (last accessed 27 July 2015).

Mayes, D. G. (2014) *Top-Down Restructuring of Markets and Institutions: The Nordic Banking Crises*. Paper presented at the SAFE conference on Bank Reorganisation and Resolution, Bad Homburg, Germany, October 10–11. Available at: http//:safe-frankfurt.de/fileadmin/user_upload/editor_common/Events/TT_2014/David_G_Mayes_paper.pdf (last accessed 30 October 2014).

Mayes, D. G., Nieto, M. J. and Wall, L. D. (2011) *A Deposit Insurance Model for Europe*. Paper presented at the EUSA biennial meeting in Boston, MA. Available at: http://www.euce.org/eusa/2011/papers/12d_mayes.pdf (last accessed 25 March 2015).

Stigler, G. (1967) Imperfections in the capital market. *Journal of Political Economy* 75(3): 287–292.

Treaty on the Functioning of the European Union, TFEU. Available at: http://eur-lex.europa.eu/legal-content/EN/TXT/?uri=celex:12012E/TXT (last accessed 27 July 2015).

2 Banking union

The way forward

Thomas F. Huertas

Banking union has a lofty aim: to break the so-called 'doom loop' (see Figure 2.1) that makes governments dependent on banks and banks dependent on governments (European Commission (EC), 2014).[1] Successful banking union would therefore promote financial stability and put the euro on a sounder footing.

What are the prospects that banking union will in fact succeed? At this point (November 2014), they are mixed. Initially, banking union has focused on the first part of the equation, reducing the dependence of governments on banks. The single supervision mechanism (SSM) should reduce significantly the probability that banks will fail, and the single resolution mechanism (SRM) should reduce significantly, if not eliminate entirely, the likelihood that governments would have

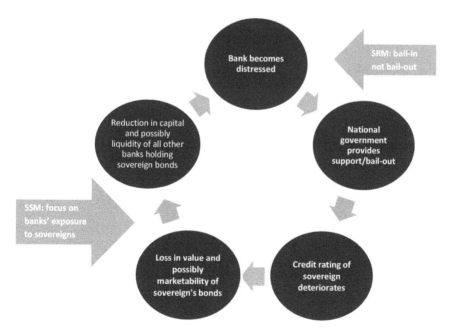

Figure 2.1 Banking union aims to break 'doom loop'.
Source: EC (2014).

to bail out the banks if they did fail. Here, the question is: will the SSM and SRM be as robust in execution as they are in design?

To date banking union has made little progress on the second part of the equation, reducing the dependence of banks on governments. Banks are still disproportionately exposed to governments in terms of credit and 'climate'. Although the SSM can (and should) address the first concern (credit concentration risk), neither the SSM nor the SRM can address the second, namely the fact that governments ultimately set the climate in which banks operate.

By far the most important element of that climate is the currency that the government adopts. It is the threat that this might change that to date has prevented agreement on what is for the man in the street arguably the most important plank of banking union, the single deposit guarantee scheme (SDGS).

For the SDGS to represent an improvement over national deposit guarantee schemes, the SDGS would have to do something that the national schemes do not: namely guarantee against sovereign risk, in particular the risk that the government of a member state would change the currency in which the depositor's account is denominated. For an SDGS to make sense, it would have to assure that a euro deposit in one member state is just as good as a euro deposit in any other member state within the banking union. This chapter suggests how this might be done.

Banking union is an exercise in variable geometry

In concept, banking union has five components: regulation, supervision, resolution, deposit guarantees and the provision of liquidity to the banking system. Banking union builds on the foundation of law and regulation applicable to all member states in the EU and develops special provisions with respect to supervision, resolution and prospectively deposit guarantees. These special provisions apply only to member states inside the banking union.

The special provisions include the SSM,[2] the SRM[3] and prospectively the SDGS.[4] Participation in banking union measures is mandatory for member states in the euro area, and open to entry via cooperation agreements for member states outside the euro area.[5]

Finally, it should be noted that neither the SSM nor the SRM affect the allocation of responsibility for providing liquidity to the banking system. Within the euro area, this remains the responsibility of the European Central Bank (ECB) (for normal facilities) and national central banks (for emergency liquidity assistance).[6]

In sum, therefore, banking union is an exercise in variable geometry, similar to the Schengen Agreement that allows a subset of member states to achieve closer integration within the broader context of the treaty applicable to all member states.

The SSM reduces the probability that banks will fail

Simply put, the SSM's mandate is to supervise banks headquartered or active in the euro area. If done well, this supervision will reinforce regulation. In its capacity as 'monitor', the supervisor assures that banks currently meet capital and liquidity requirements. In its capacity as 'minder', the supervisor induces the banks to take measures to assure that they will continue to do so in the future.[7]

Conversely, if done poorly, supervision can undermine regulation. In particular, if supervisors fail to monitor banks accurately and/or exercise forbearance, the bank can slip below minimum requirements. This would increase 'loss given failure': the losses that creditors (including the deposit guarantee scheme) would have to bear if the bank were to fail.[8]

To perform supervision well, the SSM must meet four tests:

- Does it have the right powers?
- Does it have the right profile?
- Does it have the right people?
- Does it employ the right approach?

The SSM has the right powers

The SSM clearly passes the first test. The regulation establishing the SSM passes responsibility for prudential supervision of banks headquartered in the euro area to the ECB.[9] The ECB will directly supervise the largest 130 banks and oversee the supervision of the remaining banks by the national competent authorities (NCA). The ECB will set the standards for such supervision and have the power to take any of these remaining banks into direct supervision should the bank in question become significant, or the NCA not comply with the supervisory standards set by the ECB (ECB, 2014: 39–42).

The SSM clearly meets all the core principles of effective banking supervision (Basel Committee on Banking Supervision, 2012). The SSM is responsible for the authorisation of banks, including both the decision to grant a new banking licence as well as making the determination that the bank no longer fulfils the minimum conditions for authorisation (and should therefore enter resolution).[10] As part of its assessment the SSM will evaluate the suitability of the bank's management and directors. For cross-border groups within the euro area, the ECB will function both as home *and* as host.[11]

To assess the bank's condition, the SSM may supplement the regulatory reporting submitted by the bank via on-site inspections, thematic reviews and cross-sector comparisons. The SSM will also review the bank's internal models and assess the bank's business plan.

Finally, and perhaps most importantly, the ECB has the power to put a bank into resolution, if the bank reaches the point of non-viability. This potentially gives the ECB considerable clout. Indeed, if resolution becomes feasible, its prospect should concentrate the minds of the bankers to heed the supervisor's input and instructions.

The SSM has a European profile

The SSM is not a single institution, but a construct that comprises the ECB and NCAs. As the European Council (2012) decision states:

> The SSM will be composed of the ECB and national competent authorities. The ECB will be responsible for the overall functioning of the SSM. Under the proposals, the ECB will have direct oversight of euro-zone banks, although in a differentiated way and in close cooperation with national supervisory authorities.

The SSM has a two-tier governance structure, dictated in part by the decision to create the SSM within the confines of the existing treaty, rather than establish a new institution under a separate intergovernmental agreement. At the first tier, the Supervisory Board of the SSM consists of representatives of the NCAs that are members of the SSM, the Chair of the Supervisory Board, the Vice Chair of the Supervisory Board (who shall be a member of the Executive Board of the ECB) and three additional appointees designated by the ECB.

This Board prepares decisions for ratification by the Governing Council of the ECB under a non-objection procedure (see Figure 2.2). Should the Governing Council object, the decision is referred to a mediation panel consisting of one member per participating EU member state, chosen from among the members of the Governing Council of the ECB and the Supervisory Board of the SSM. This is a very complex structure. Although it may be suited to policy decisions and may help preserve the separation between monetary policy and supervision demanded by the treaty, it may also obstruct the ability of the SSM to take decisions quickly.

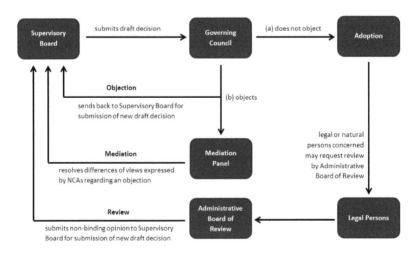

Figure 2.2 The SSM has a two-tier governance structure.

Source: ECB (2014).

This may be especially relevant in the case of a failing bank, where the opinion of the Supervisory Board (with respect to whether the bank continues to meet the minimum conditions for authorisation) may differ from those of the Governing Council (with respect to whether the national central bank should be allowed to provide emergency liquidity assistance to the failing bank).

In comparison to the governance arrangements, the management of the SSM is much more straightforward. In principle, the central SSM organisation at the ECB is responsible for organising and directing supervision of banks within the euro area. This process is now largely in place. The ECB will exercise direct supervision over approximately 130 large, cross-border banks as well as over-see the supervision of the remaining banks by the NCAs.[12] To implement direct supervision the ECB has formed a multinational team for each of the 130 banks, headed by an ECB employee who is not of the same nationality as the bank he or she supervises. The supervisory team as a whole shall consist of ECB staff and staff at the NCAs in jurisdictions in which the bank is active, with the team head empowered to give direction not only to ECB employees but also to NCA repre-sentatives seconded to the supervisory team.

Although the NCAs will conduct supervision of the remaining banks in the euro area, this will be done in accordance with policies and procedures set by the ECB. Moreover, the ECB: 'can decide to transfer to direct supervision any bank or group of banks that may be considered relevant or the origin of systemic risk' (Constâncio, 2013).

The SSM has the right people

From a standing start the ECB has recruited nearly 1000 people from around the world to staff the central functions in Frankfurt. The vast majority have prior supervisory experience at one of the NCAs. A significant minority has industry experience. On paper, this multinational team is well qualified to do the job.

The SSM has the right approach

The ECB intends to take a pro-active approach to supervision. This started with an entry examination for those institutions coming under direct ECB supervision and will con-tinue as the ECB develops and implements supervisory plans for each of those banks.

The entry examination had two parts: the Asset Quality Review (AQR) and a stress test (done in conjunction with the European Banking Authority (EBA)). The AQR was unprecedented in scope and scale, far exceeding anything that any national regu-lator had previously undertaken. Its purpose was to identify legacy problems and thus potentially avoid reputational risks for the SSM down the line (Constâncio, 2013).

The AQR was very much bottom up, with extensive examinations of actual loan files to determine whether documentation was in order, whether collateral was properly pledged and valued, and whether the borrower had prospective cash flows adequate to service the loan. The stress test was largely top down. It esti-mated the effects that a much slower economy would have on the bank.

On balance, the entry examination has enabled the SSM to start on a positive note. Indeed, the initial announcement that an examination would be conducted prompted many banks across the euro area to raise significant amounts of capital so that they would pass the test. As a result, by the time of the test itself, there were only a few banks that had capital shortfalls still requiring rectification. In addition, the AQR provided the SSM with a granular view of banks' portfolios and their credit procedures. So the SSM starts operation knowing what banks have in place and what banks need to fix.

That should form the core of the supervisory plan that the SSM is developing for each of the 130 institutions that come under its direct supervision.[13] As an input to the supervisory plan the SSM will analyse the bank's business model, identify risks to that model and determine whether the bank needs to take corrective or mitigating action. The bank needs to outline to the supervisor how it will proceed and update the supervisor on progress. If the bank veers from the timetable, or if the bank's condition deteriorates, the supervisor may intervene more forcefully to induce or order the bank to take more immediate measures to improve its condition. If the bank's condition reaches a critical point, the ECB may order the bank to initiate its recovery plan.

So the SSM has set itself up to be a very tough cop indeed. However, the acid test will come when a major bank has major problems: will the SSM be able to identify them and induce the bank to take corrective action?

The SRM aims to make banks 'safe to fail'

The introduction of the SRM greatly increases the likelihood that the SSM will in fact be able to induce troubled banks to take corrective action promptly. If implemented successfully, the SRM will create a credible threat that the ECB could put a bank into resolution without cost to the taxpayer and without wreaking havoc in financial markets or the economy at large. The prospect of death should concentrate the minds of bankers to manage risk more prudently and adhere to supervisory admonitions more readily. In other words, robust resolution fosters strict supervision.

Will resolution in fact be robust under the SRM? In concept, yes, but many details remain to be filled in, and it is these details that will determine whether or not the SRM can fulfil the role assigned to it under banking union.

In essence, the SRM creates a single resolution authority for the euro area under the direction of a Single Resolution Board (SRB). Its mission is to make banks in the euro area resolvable and, if necessary, resolve any euro area bank that does reach the point of non-viability.

Whether the SRM can fulfil this mission depends on three things:

1   how the details of the EU legislative framework for resolution evolve;
2   whether the SRB can build an effective organisation;
3   whether all the relevant authorities can coordinate with one another in the timely and effective manner required to implement resolution.

The legislative framework

The SRM operates within the context of the EU Banking Recovery and Resolution Directive (BRRD). The BRRD implements the key attributes for effective resolution regimes established by the Financial Stability Board. In particular, the BRRD requires that each member state designate a resolution authority and endow this authority with a full range of resolution tools including the ability to transfer the failed institution to a third party, to create a bridge bank, to sell assets to a third party, to transfer deposits and other customer obligations to a third party and to bail in (write down or convert into common equity) some or all of the bank's liabilities. These tools are intended to supplement the authority to liquidate the bank's assets and pay off the creditors (with the deposit guarantee scheme responsible for paying off insured deposits).

In addition, the BRRD requires each member state to establish a resolution fund financed by industry 'contributions' with a target fund level equal to one per cent of insured deposits. The BRRD allows the resolution authority to tap the resources of the fund to recapitalise a failing bank, provided:

- creditors bear losses equal to at least eight per cent of the bank's liabilities;[14] and the assistance from the resolution fund is consistent with state-aid rules.

Although the BRRD runs to over 300 pages, important details remain to be filled in, especially with respect to how bail-in will operate. The BRRD allocates this task to the EBA: by year end 2015 the EBA must develop over 30 binding technical standards. These will be applicable across all 28 member states, not just the members of the SRM. For the SRB, the binding technical standards set the detailed framework in which the SRB will have to work. Accordingly, one of the SRB's first priorities should be to ensure that the binding technical standards do in fact enhance banks' resolvability.

Building an effective organisation

Over the years, the EU and the euro area have become quite effective in creating new organisations – the SSM is the latest evidence of this capability. But the SRM poses new challenges. Unlike supervision, there is no heritage of previous committees or coordination to draw upon. Furthermore, there is no uniformity in the types of organisations that member states have designated as resolution authorities.

The timeframe for the SRM is also more compressed. The SRM began operation on 1 January 2015 and has a significant programme of work to deliver in 2015. In addition to recruiting its staff, the SRM has to begin review of banks' recovery plans and begin to draw up resolution plans for banks. Most importantly, the SRM has to make itself ready to resolve a bank, should it become necessary to do so.[15]

Assuring timely and effective coordination

The most immediate and perhaps the most daunting challenge for the SRM will be to create the basis for timely and effective coordination among all the authorities relevant for a resolution.[16] This starts with the development of resolution plans for banks. The SRB is responsible for drawing up the plan in consultation with the ECB and national resolution authorities in the jurisdictions (within the EU and in third countries) in which the bank has branches or subsidiaries.[17]

The SRB is also responsible, again in consultation with the ECB and relevant national resolution authorities, for making a determination as to whether or not the bank is resolvable.[18] If the SRB determines during its resolvability assessment that there are significant impediments to making the bank resolvable, the SRB shall prepare a report, again in consultation with the relevant authorities, addressed to the bank identifying the impediments and recommending measures to remove such impediments. Within four months, the bank should respond with a plan to remove the impediments. If the SRB does not (again after consultation with the ECB and relevant national authorities) approve the institution's plan, the SRB may order (again after consultation with the ECB and relevant national authorities) the bank to take alternative measures to remove the impediments. The measures that the SRB may order a bank to undertake include the power to order a bank to form a parent holding company and/or to separate certain activities so as to preserve the continuity of critical economic functions.[19]

Effective coordination in the planning stage should promote effective coordination in crisis, especially with respect to 'pulling the trigger' for resolution. In the lead-in to resolution, the SRB effectively has supervisory responsibilities: these will need to be coordinated with the ECB and national authorities. 'In order to ensure rapid resolution action when it becomes necessary,' the SRM Regulation (2014) mandates that: 'the [Single Resolution] Board should closely monitor, in cooperation with the ECB or with the relevant national competent authority the situation of the entities concerned'.[20] In addition, the SRB should be: 'empowered to intervene at an early stage where the financial situation or the solvency of an entity is deteriorating'.[21] Finally, the SRB may on its own initiative make a finding – after giving notice to the ECB – that the bank should enter resolution.[22]

To make this work will require careful coordination as well as consideration of the impact that such measures will have on the ability of the bank in question to be able to finance itself in private markets. Although the SRM Regulation (2014) establishes a process for information sharing and mandates that the relevant authorities conclude a memorandum of understanding that outlines how they will cooperate with one another, there is no guarantee that this will actually work in practice, particularly where the parties disagree about the decision to be taken.

Further complexity arises if the bank in question is receiving emergency liquidity assistance. The mere receipt of such assistance is not per se a reason to initiate resolution, but the decision to end such assistance to a bank that still requires it will surely lead the bank to fail. Both the decision to grant such assistance and the decision to terminate such assistance lie, strictly speaking, outside the purview of the SSM and the SRM.[23] Decisions regarding emergency liquidity assistance (ELA) come under the heading of monetary policy. It is therefore unlikely that either the SSM or the SRB will have a direct voice in deliberations regarding

ELA, even though ELA can have a material impact on the losses that creditors will suffer if the bank does eventually enter resolution.

The coordination challenge is even greater, once the bank trigger is pulled. Although the SRB will have approved a resolution plan in advance of the point at which the bank enters resolution, this still requires the concurrence of the European Commission and potentially the European Council (if the European Commission objects to the plan proposed by the SRB). The SRM Regulation (2014) provides for up to 32 hours for this process to occur (see Figure 2.3).

Such an extended approval process is impractical. If the SRB has to wait until 32 hours of a 'resolution weekend' have elapsed before the resolution plan can start to be implemented, it is unlikely that the SRB will be able to implement an orderly group resolution process, particularly where the bank in resolution has extensive operations in third countries, such as the United States. In the absence of a clear line from the SRB regarding the resolution plan for the bank, authorities in foreign jurisdictions as well as financial market infrastructures are likely to take steps to protect their own interests. These steps may make it difficult, if not impossible, for the SRB to execute resolution in a manner that avoids disruption to financial markets or the economy at large.

Consequently, the SRB will need to assure that it has all the necessary approvals in place prior to placing the bank into resolution. It will also need to assure that the resolution plan provides the bank in resolution with access to liquidity and continued access to financial market infrastructures, not only within the euro area, but across the entire EU and in the third countries in which the bank has material operations.

Achieving such coordination is easier said than done. Although crisis management groups can frame options, when the actual crisis comes, the decision may hinge on the details of the particular case and/or on the political climate prevailing at the time. In sum, the SRM is still very much a work in progress.

The SDGS

In the original proposals for banking union there was a third pillar, the SDGS. This has since been put on the backburner. Instead, a number of measures have been taken to minimise the risk of deposits and strengthen national deposit guarantee schemes.

The BRRD introduced depositor preference. This significantly reduces the risk of deposits, for it gives depositors a first claim on the unencumbered assets of the bank. Revisions to the Deposit Guarantee Schemes Directive have strengthened such schemes. The directive creates a common deposit guarantee limit (€100,000 per depositor per bank), and schemes are now required to be funded up to a level equivalent to 0.8 per cent of covered deposits. That will give schemes the means to pay out depositors if required to do so. Schemes will also have to take measures to assure that such pay-offs can occur within seven days of the bank failing.

However, schemes remain national in scope. Although the directive contains provisions allowing the schemes to borrow from one another, there is no common

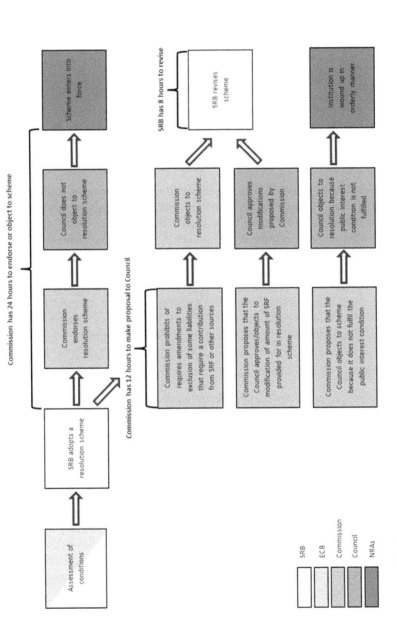

Figure 2.3 Pulling the trigger is a complex process.
Source: EC (2014).

scheme. If bank A fails, its depositors only have recourse to the scheme administered in the member state in which bank A has its headquarters. Hence, protection may be limited to the amount of the scheme's paid-in and available funds plus any credit or support that the national government may provide to its deposit guarantee scheme.

Finally, the deposit guarantee scheme protects only against the risk the bank fails. It does not guarantee against the risk that the government may decide to leave the EU, leave the euro and redenominate the currency in which the deposit is held. This implies that the risk of a deposit may depend on the member state in which the bank is headquartered. That falls short of full banking union.

Protecting banks from governments

The second purpose of banking union is to protect banks from governments, so that the condition of a bank is independent of the member state in which it is head-quartered. Three areas deserve consideration.

The first, concentration risk, is already on the supervisory agenda. As noted above, government bonds are not risk-free, and banks in the euro area invest disproportion-ately in bonds issued by the member state in which they are headquartered (e.g. Italian banks invest in Italian government bonds). Therefore, if a member state has to restructure its debt, the resulting write-off may push the member state's banks into restructuring or resolution as well. Greece is a case in point. To limit this risk Danièle Nouy, the Chair of the Supervisory Board of the SSM, has raised the possibility of placing limits on the amount of government bonds that a bank may acquire.[24]

The second area for consideration is ELA. As noted above, this is a responsibility of national central banks subject to no objection (on monetary policy grounds) from the ECB. Such a division of responsibility increases the likelihood that national authorities will elect to exercise forbearance and delay putting a bank that has reached the point of non-viability into resolution. This potentially aggravates the 'loss given failure' that a bank's creditors may experience, if the bank does ultimately enter reso-lution. It may therefore make sense to shift responsibility for ELA entirely to the ECB, at least for those institutions over which it exercises direct supervision.

The third area for consideration relates to the charter of the bank. At present, banks are headquartered in a specific member state and are subject to the sover-eign risk of that member state, including the risk that the member state will decide to leave the EU and/or the euro. Consideration might be given to creating a truly European charter, which would (in a manner similar to the ECB itself) give a bank legal personality in each of the member states.[25] This would greatly reduce, if not entirely eliminate, the sovereign risk that depositors currently face if a member state were to leave the euro.[26] It would therefore open the door to an SDGS, at least for institutions under such a European charter.

Conclusion

In conclusion, banking union is off to a strong start. The SSM will reduce the probability that banks will fail, and the SRM will potentially contribute to making banks safe to fail. Together that will go a long way to protect governments from banks. But much remains to be done, first to assure that the SSM and SRM work as intended and second, to assure that banks are protected from governments. Only then will banking union fulfil its aims.

Notes

1 The term 'doom loop' stems from Gros (2013). For overall discussions of banking union see (Beck, 2012; Constâncio, 2013; Huertas, 2013).
2 The SSM was created under Regulation (EU) 1024/2013 (hereinafter SSM regulation). For a summary of the ECB's work under the SSM see Nouy (2014).
3 The European Parliament approved the text creating the SRM on 15 April 2014 (hereinafter SRM regulation) and on 21 May 2014 26 member states approved the Intergovernmental Agreement on the transfer and mutualisation of contributions to the Single Resolution Fund.
4 Regarding the SGDS see EC (2014).
5 Opting in to the SSM may provide a means for a member state to improve the quality of its supervision and/or more effectively integrate the supervision of branches and subsidiaries of euro area banks with the supervision of the group as a whole. Although member states entering cooperation agreements have a voice on the SSM Supervisory Board, they have no vote on the ECB Governing Council. To date Romania and Bulgaria have announced the intention to conclude cooperation agreements with the SSM.
6 The provision of ELA is subject to approval by the ECB (and subject to state aid rules).
7 For a discussion of the supervisor as 'monitor' and 'minder' see Huertas (2012).
8 The term 'loss given failure' stems from Moody's Investor Services (2014).
9 The SSM will not replace national supervisory authorities (NSAs). NSAs will continue to exist and will retain responsibility for consumer protection, payment systems and citizens' access to bank accounts and services and other aspects of conduct supervision, as well as for the supervision of smaller institutions not subject to the SSM. The question is what role, if any, the NSAs should continue to play with respect to the supervision of institutions that will be 'directly' supervised by the ECB.
10 The SRB also has the power to recommend that a bank enter resolution (as discussed in the text).
11 The ECB will act as home country supervisor if the group is headquartered in a member state within the SSM. The ECB will act as host country supervisor of subsidiaries headquartered in a member state within the SSM (regardless of where the parent group is headquartered) as well as act as host country supervisor of the branches of entities headquartered in a member state within the SSM. However, NCAs retain responsibility for branches of third country banks (e.g. the Frankfurt branch of a Japanese bank).
12 The organisation of the SSM consists of four directorates general (DG) and a secretariat to support the SSM Supervisory Board (see https://www.ecb.europa.eu/ssm/orga/html/index.en.html, accessed December 2014). DG I supervises the 30 largest banks under direct supervision; DG II the other banks under direct supervision. DG III is responsible for indirect supervision of the remaining banks by the NCAs. DG IV will handle horizontal and specialised services, including authorisation, crisis management, centralised onsite inspections, enforcement and sanctions, internal models, methodology and standard development, planning and coordination of supervisory examination programmes, risk analysis, supervisory quality assurance and supervisory policies.

13 For a summary of the SREP see (ECB, 2014: 23–26).

14 Note that the eight per cent requirement is quite a high bar – it exceeded the losses incurred by practically every bank during the crisis.

15 In addition, the SRM has to make plans on how to administer the Single Resolution Fund. The SRM should also provide input into the EBA as the latter draws up the binding technical standards that will shape what the SRM can and should do, in the event that a bank requires resolution.

16 The SRM regulation (paragraph 54) envisages that: 'The [Single Resolution] Board, the national resolution authorities and the competent authorities, including the ECB, should, where necessary, conclude a memorandum of understanding describing in general terms how they will cooperate with one another in the performance of their respective tasks under Union law. The memorandum should be reviewed on a regular basis'.

17 SRM Regulation, article 8.

18 According to SRM Regulation (article 10): 'An entity shall be deemed to be resolvable if it is feasible and credible for the Board to either liquidate it under normal insolvency proceedings or to resolve it by applying to it resolution tools and exercising resolution powers while avoiding, to the maximum extent possible, any significant adverse consequences for financial systems, including circumstances of broader financial instability or system wide events, of the Member State in which the entity is situated, or other Member States, or the Union and with a view to ensuring the continuity of critical functions carried out by the entity'.

19 According to SRM Regulation Article 10 paragraph 11, the SRB may: 'instruct the national resolution authorities to take any of the following [alternative] measures:

a to require the entity to revise any intragroup financing agreements or review the absence thereof, or draw up service agreements (whether intra-group or with third parties) to cover the provision of critical functions;

b to require the entity to limit its maximum individual and aggregate exposures;

c to impose specific or regular additional information requirements relevant for resolution purposes;

d to require the entity to divest specific assets;

e to require the entity to limit or cease specific existing or proposed activities;

f to restrict or prevent the development of new or existing business lines or sale of new or existing products;

g to require changes to legal or operational structures of the entity or any group entity, either directly or indirectly under their control, so as to reduce complexity in order to ensure that critical functions may be legally and operationally separated from other functions through the application of the resolution tools;

h to require an entity to set up a parent financial holding company in a Member State or a Union parent financial holding company;

i to require an entity to issue eligible liabilities to meet the requirements of Article 12 [minimum requirements for own funds and eligible liabilities];

j to require an entity to take other steps to meet the requirements referred to in Article 12, including in particular to attempt to renegotiate any eligible liability, Additional Tier 1 instrument or Tier 2 instrument it has issued, with a view to ensuring that any decision of the Board to write down or convert that liability or instrument would be effected under the law of the jurisdiction governing that liability or instrument.

20 SRM Regulation paragraph 53.
21 SRM Regulation paragraph 52. Article 13 of the regulation requires the ECB or national competent authority to inform the SRB (and for the SRB to inform the Commission) of measures that they might take under the early intervention power provided for in BRRD. Once the ECB has initiated early intervention, the SRB should finalise the resolution plan that it would employ, if the early intervention measures prove to be unsuccessful. The SRB may also require the institution to seek a third-party purchaser.
22 SRM Regulation Article 18.
23 Initiation and termination of ELA is principally the responsibility of (and for the account of) the national central bank. However, the ECB must not object to its initiation, and the ECB can effectively force the national central bank to terminate the facility.
24 Nouy (2014) commented: 'In my view, there should also be rules for large exposures, meaning that no bank should invest only in one single sovereign bond, in general of its own country'. See also Nouy (2012), Gros (2013) and Huertas (2013).
25 Under Article 282 (3) of the Treaty on the Functioning of the European Union the ECB has 'legal personality' under public international law.
26 If the proposal has economic merit, there is a question of how it might be legally implemented, especially without change to the treaty.

References

Basel Committee on Banking Supervision (2012) *The Core Principles of Effective Banking Supervision*. Available at: http://www.bis.org/publ/bcbs230.pdf (last accessed 3 May 2015).

Beck, T. (2012) *Banking Union for Europe: risks and challenges*, London, UK: CEPR. Available at: http://www.voxeu.org/sites/default/files/file/Banking_Union.pdf (last accessed 3 May 2015).

Constâncio, V. (2013) *The Nature and Significance of Banking Union*. Available at: http://www.ecb.int/press/key/date/2013/html/sp130311.en.html (last accessed 3 May 2015).

EC (2014) *Banking Union: Restoring Financial Stability in the Eurozone*. Available at: http://ec.europa.eu/finance/general-policy/docs/banking-union/banking-union-memo_en.pdf (last accessed 4 May 2015).

ECB (2014) *Guide to Banking Supervision*. Available at: https://www.bankingsupervision.europa.eu/ecb/pub/pdf/ssmguidebankingsupervision201411.en.pdf (last accessed 4 May 2015).

European Council (2012) *Council Agrees Position on Single Supervisory Mechanism*. Available at: http://www.consilium.europa.eu/homepage/showfocus?lang=en&focusID=91265 (last accessed October 2014).

Gros, D. (2013) EZ banking union with a sovereign virus. *Vox Europa*. 14 June. Available at: http://www.voxeu.org/article/ez-banking-union-sovereign-virus (last accessed 3 May 2015).

Huertas, T. F. (2012) *A Race to the Top?* LSE Financial Markets Group Special Paper 208. Available at: http://www.lse.ac.uk/fmg/workingPapers/specialPapers/PDF/SP208.pdf (last accessed 3 May 2015).

Huertas, T. F. (2013) Banking union. *Bank of Spain Financial Stability Review*, May, pp. 31–44. Available at: http://www.bde.es/f/webbde/GAP/Secciones/Publicaciones/InformesBoletinesRevistas/RevistaEstabilidadFinanciera/13/Mayo/Fic/ref201324.pdf (last accessed 3 May 2015).

Moody's Investor Services (2014) *Moody's Proposes Revisions to its Bank Rating Methodology*. Available at: https://www.moodys.com/research/Moodys-proposes-revisions-to-its-Bank-Rating-Methodology--PR_307938 (last accessed 3 May 2015).

Nouy, D. (2012) Is sovereign risk properly addressed by financial regulation? *Banque de France Financial Stability Review* 16: 95–106. Available at: https://www.banque-france.fr/fileadmin/user_upload/banque_de_france/publications/Revue_de_la_stabilite_financiere/2012/rsf-avril-2012/FSR16-article-09.pdf (last accessed December 2014).

Nouy, D. (2014) *Interview with Aripaev*. Available at: https://www.bankingsupervision.europa.eu/press/interviews/date/2014/html/sn 140904.en.html (last accessed 3 May 2015).

SRM Regulation (2014) European Parliament legislative resolution [P7_TA- PROV (2014)0341] of 15 April 2014 on the proposal for a regulation of the European Parliament and of the Council establishing uniform rules and a uniform procedure for the resolution of credit institutions and certain investment firms in the framework of a Single Resolution Mechanism and a Single Bank Resolution Fund and amending Regulation (EU) No 1093/2010 of the European Parliament and of the Council (COM(2013)0520 – C7- 0223/2013 – 2013/0253(COD)). Available at: http://www.europarl.europa.eu/sides/getDoc.do?type=TA&language=EN&reference=P7-TA-2014-0341 (last accessed October 2014).

SSM Regulation (2013) Council Regulation (EU) No 1024/2013 of 15 October 2013 conferring specific tasks on the European Central Bank concerning policies relating to the prudential supervision of credit institutions, OJ 287/63 (29 October 2013). Available at: http://www.europarl.europa.eu/document/activities/cont/201311/20131104ATT73792/20131104ATT73792EN.pdf (last accessed October 2014).

3 Plausible recovery and resolution plans for cross-border financial institutions

Giannoula Karamichailidou and
David G. Mayes[1]

Unfortunately, based on the material so far submitted, in my view each plan being discussed today is deficient and fails to convincingly demonstrate how, in failure, any one of these firms could overcome obstacles to entering bankruptcy without precipitating a financial crisis. Despite the thousands of pages of material these firms submitted, the plans provide no credible or clear path through bankruptcy that doesn't require unrealistic assumptions and direct or indirect public support (Thomas M. Hoenig, Vice Chairman of the Federal Deposit Insurance Corporation (FDIC), 5 August 2014 (FDIC, 2014)).

After the failure of Lehman Brothers, financial authorities around the world, following the recommendations by the Financial Stability Board (FSB), required their systemically important financial institutions (SIFIs) to draft recovery and resolution plans. The US authorities have provided feedback on those plans drawn up by their SIFIs. As is clear from the quotation above, the Board of Governors of the Federal Reserve System and the FDIC are not satisfied with the progress made in this area. Particularly, in their joint release on 5 August 2014, the two agencies reported that there are still significant shortcomings in the living wills submitted by 11 large and complex banking organisations operating in the US, which need to be addressed in the 2015 submissions. These shortcomings relate to resolvability, continuity of functions critical to the financial system, stay of early termination rights of external counterparties and timely production of reliable information (Board of Governors of the Federal Reserve System and FDIC joint release, 2014).[2]

The process in the EU is not so advanced, but one of the key steps to ensuring greater financial stability and the plausible resolution of cross-border financial institutions, namely the proposal for a regulation to place requirements on the structure of these institutions (European Commission, 2014), seems to be encountering major obstacles. Moves to limit contagion of high risk activities to the vital functions of the financial system and moves to ensure that structures of large institutions are not too complex to prevent the speedy resolution of problems without recourse to taxpayers' money, are seen as essential for the success of the regulatory reform of the financial system.

We therefore explore what the difficulties are and whether the approaches that are being used in the US, the UK, the EU, Australia and New Zealand offer ways forward, particularly in the EU. We begin with an overview of the problem before considering the lessons and the way forward.

Introduction

Theoretically, living wills should increase the resilience of banks to adverse idiosyncratic and/or market shocks and, most importantly, solve the too big to fail (TBTF) problem in the sense that functions vital to the stable operation of the financial system can be kept operating without a material break and without the injection of public money (Huertas, 2010).[3]

A *recovery plan* describes ex ante the necessary actions that a large financial institution (FI) in distress is going to undertake in order to recover and regain its viability. Thus, the main objective of a recovery plan is to reduce the likelihood of a failure. The effectiveness of a recovery plan depends on the timeliness and speed of its execution and its credibility to key stakeholders, so confidence in the institution can be maintained (Huertas, 2010). Essentially, the plan involves rapid recapitalising and restructuring of assets and liabilities under conditions when everybody knows the bank has a problem and hence will be reluctant to lend to it. Therefore, guaranteed forms of funding, such as contingent convertibles (CoCos), which do not require discretionary decisions at the time, will be the most plausible.[4] Senior management is responsible for evaluating, updating and promulgating recovery plans, which ideally would improve the understanding of the structure and interconnectedness of the bank the management runs. However, it will be for the authorities to decide whether these are adequate.[5]

If the application of a recovery plan fails to return a distressed FI to soundness, then resolution authorities will apply a *resolution plan*, which they develop in advance with the FI. The purpose of a resolution plan is to resolve a SIFI in an orderly manner that will promote financial stability and minimise the cost to the taxpayer, with the authorities and not the bank's management running the process.

It is highly debatable whether, even in theory, the large cross-border banks could produce recovery and resolution plans that are credible and might not require public support, as they relate to periods of great stress that have not been adequately predicted. A serious problem with a large bank is not likely to be an idiosyncratic event, but a part of a wider malaise. It is more realistic to ask how far the plans can ease the process of adjustment by putting in place much more contingent preparation, so that it is possible to put together a less costly and more rapid recovery or resolution. Public money might be required, first, to act as a guarantee against future loss so the central bank can provide liquidity against adequate collateral if the market is reluctant and, second, to bolster confidence in the rest of the financial system. Furthermore, public money might be required because it is not possible to undertake adequate due diligence for a private sector solution in the time available, and because, for such large institutions, it is difficult to put together the necessary capital in a period of distressed markets that does not bring with it unacceptable structural problems, such as overconcentration and the fear of knock-on problems for the acquirers.

During the recent Global Financial Crisis (GFC) mergers and acquisitions (M&As) were popular options for the authorities to solve FIs failures and avoid the financial system's collapse (for example, the acquisition of Merrill Lynch by Bank of America in the US and that of HBOS by Lloyds in the UK). This has led to more consolidated markets in the post-GFC period exacerbating the TBTF problem (Carmassi and Herring, 2014). Hence, the problems for the future are enhanced. Not only are banks now larger but the chance of being able to use M&A to sort out problems in SIFIs is smaller. So the main private sector route for recovery may not be available. In so far as cross-border mergers have been a solution to previous problems, they have created institutions that are now a bigger cross-border problem.

Norway, Finland and Sweden all successfully resolved the separate banks, which later merged to become Nordea, in the financial crises at the beginning of the 1990s, each applying different methods, while the Danish part of Nordea, Unibank, was itself formed from the merger of three Danish banks in 1990. Next time round, all four countries will have to cooperate as it is now a single banking group. They each have their own currency. Finland alone is part of the euro area, while Norway is not part of the EU but the European Economic Area (EEA). The Swedish government was a part owner until 2013 and the group is headquartered in Sweden. The list of possible contradictions and potential conflicts of interest is long. Where would Nordea look for merger partners in a crisis? Merging with Danske Bank would result in a market share of over 40 per cent and the top two groups would cover over 75 per cent of the market. Merging with DnB NOR would involve the Norwegian government, which owns a third of the bank. Living wills for cross-border FIs have been proposed to deal mostly with the inconsistencies among national legal frameworks, which would be impediments to their resolution (Financial System Policy, 2012). Identifying these impediments in advance via living wills could facilitate their orderly resolution.

However, as soon as it becomes public knowledge that a SIFI is in trouble there will be a much wider impact on confidence in the financial system. The recovery plan therefore has to address these systemic concerns as well. This, therefore, goes beyond what steps the bank itself can set out in advance to make recapitalisation plausible. Even in terms of just recapitalisation, the plan has to offer more than a replenishment of the capital that has been lost and convince people that the revitalised institution has a profitable future. The new capital buffer would need to be clearly above the regulatory minimum. Often in the past, even if the refinancing came from the private sector, some form of government guarantee was required against future loss for this to be successful and for the wider confidence in the system to be restored.[6]

In the case when a resolution plan kicks in, the requirement is even more demanding as it starts from the premise that an 'unassisted' private sector solution has not been found.[7] Such a solution therefore has to be imposed. In the past, getting such an outcome normally required funding, at least in the short run, from somewhere beyond the creditors, such as deposit insurance, even if the funds were repaid eventually through an insolvency process. Now, it is hoped that by augmenting the funds available and by bailing in creditors compulsorily at the time of failure, it will be possible to avoid the direct use of public funds.[8] In the case of the US, the Orderly Liquidation Authority (OLA) may be available for the largest banks and, in the EU, there will be the resolution funds accumulated in advance by levies on the banking system. The discussion has been rather muted over whether such funds might not be needed more broadly in solving the crisis, say by making capital injections available to the whole of the banking system (Gordon and Ringe, 2014). Furthermore, bailing in has not yet been used for any large bank and the examples of Amagerbanken and Fjordbank Mors in Denmark in 2011, as described below, illustrate that the method has problems.

So, current reality stands rather far away from theory. The purpose of this chapter is to explore the problems with the various approaches being used and draw conclusions for the role of recovery and resolution plans in the future. We focus particularly on the progress made in a cross-border context because, as the recent financial crisis has shown, failure of FIs that operate across borders is more likely to lead to contagion and financial instability in a broader region and even be transmitted across continents.

Overall, we conclude that crises with SIFIs are likely to be a system-wide problem, thus, focusing on the resolution of each FI individually cannot guarantee the solution of the problem, as contagion is to be expected. Consequently, it is crucial that there is the ability to access funds in a crisis management framework, as those who are exposed to one FI may simultaneously be exposed to another.

Furthermore, breaking up banking groups or making the vital functions readily separable may well help, but Lehman Brothers was not a retail bank yet its failure was a disaster. So the definition of what is vital may extend so far that it becomes questionable how much dividing up of the bank makes sense.

For cross-border banks, the key difficulty is the coordination of recovery and resolution across the different jurisdictions, where such coordination can only be encouraged but not compelled. Hence, the US and UK focus on resolving a bank at the holding company or parent level (single point of entry) provides a way out as long as adequate resources are available. Where banks are large relative to the home country's ability to borrow (either because the banks are large or the country is heavily indebted already) this will not work as some banks will be too big to save (TBTS). The EU is trying to get round this by establishing a 'banking union', where following the centralisation of supervision – the Single Supervisory Mechanism (SSM) – under the European Central Bank (ECB), there will be a mutualisation of the funds raised from the private sector to assist a bail-in of creditors. However, this leaves many questions unanswered, especially where cross-border banks are not entirely within the centralisation of resolution – the Single Resolution Mechanism (SRM).

It is therefore not surprising if it appears to be very difficult to get something believable in the form of living wills at present.

The cross-border problem

Lessons, recommendations and current approaches

Failures of cross-border FIs have vividly illustrated the problems that need to be addressed for the future. Not that these problems are new or were not addressed before the crisis (Evanoff and Kaufman, 2005; Mayes, 2006). First, the case of Fortis, for example, illustrated that the cross-border crisis management framework needs to be developed to be compatible with the cross-border nature of the operations of those FIs. Second, there need to be mechanisms in place to ensure the continuity of business across all the jurisdictions where a cross-border FI operates. Third, there should be arrangements for information sharing to ensure that critical information is assessed and interpreted in the same way. Finally, financial authorities need to have powers that allow them to override shareholders' rights if financial stability is threatened (Basel Committee on Banking Supervision (BCBS), 2010). The case of Dexia illustrated how important cooperation was between the central banks of the jurisdictions where the FI operated as well as the joint support to the group by both home and host authorities (BCBS, 2010).

Furthermore, the Lehman Brothers collapse showed that structural reforms, which aim to simplify FIs' structure, might be required to align FIs' operations with their legal entities. Also, it made clear that parties involved in the provision of short-term funds will require a guarantee in the interim in order to continue to transact with the firm in trouble until the transaction is completed, implying that government resources might be needed. The Lehman Brothers bankruptcy illustrated clearly that differences in national insolvency regimes impeded the cooperation and coordination among national insolvency officials due to conflicts with the duties of the officials to the creditors of an entity under their jurisdictions. The Icelandic banking crisis shows a further facet of these difficulties, with a clear example of the TBTS problem,[9] which also needs to be resolved in the future structure (BCBS, 2010).

The initial road map for addressing the cross-border problem is now clear. Drawing up a living will is a first step to facilitating such coordinated resolution of a global SIFI (G-SIFI) or regional SIFI (R-SIFI),[10] accompanied by the convergence of national resolution tools as well as mutual recognition of crisis management resolution proceedings across borders, where the resolution regimes should extend from a solo legal entity basis to the consolidated group (BCBS, 2011).

Moreover, the FSB has set out key attributes (KAs) directed at the resolution of G-SIFIs, which are complementing the recovery and resolution planning that is in progress. These include the formation of crisis management groups (CMGs), institution-specific cross-border cooperation agreements (COAGs) and resolvability assessments (FSB, 2011, 2014). All the KAs are interconnected and the successful implementation of one is a precondition for the success of another. Consequently, living wills for cross-border FIs set the steps for cooperation and coordination among the related parties in a crisis that are developed through the CMGs. Furthermore, living wills are developed based on the COAGs assisted by the information provided by the resolvability assessments. This represents a huge task since it is all case specific.

What the GFC re-emphasised was that in a crisis it is more likely that national authorities are going to protect the interests of the local investors and depositors at the expense of the investors and depositors overseas, which might not be the least cost solution as in the case of Fortis and the Icelandic banks. Setting up a crisis management group is one thing. Being confident that it will work well in a crisis when major losses have to be allocated is another. Actions which might restore confidence in one jurisdiction might amplify perceptions of risk in another. Individual authorities may very well feel that in a serious crisis they can renege on previous agreements, which are usually of a soft law character.

Thus, for such a cooperative approach to work there needs to be a fundamental agreement among the participating countries about how such resolutions should proceed. It is already clear that even the Nordic countries, which form one of the most integrated groups internationally, have clear differences of opinion over the tools that should be applied in a crisis, such as government guarantees and the use of asset management companies (Mayes, 2014b). Hüpkes (2013) argues that: 'If authorities do not perceive cooperation to be in their interest, they are less likely to act in a cooperative manner, irrespective of the existence of a binding treaty or non-binding memorandum of understanding to this effect'.

The FSB (2012) has proposed two main resolution strategies that might work in all circumstances.[11] The first resolution strategy is labelled single point of entry (SPOE). According to this approach, the banking group is resolved at a parent or holding company level by a single resolution authority, so no conflicts occur. At the other extreme, in a multiple point of entry (MPOE) approach, where the banking group is separable in each jurisdiction, multiple authorities act independently at a national level. There is no implication here that either outcome is optimal, simply that they are workable and could avoid the use of public funds. The critical argument here is that for MPOE to work, most banks would have to change their structure, separating operations at least on national lines if not along functional lines as well. If one believes that most economies of scale in banking are realised at levels well below the largest banks today, then this may not be a disadvantage (see for example, Davies and Tracey (2014), Schmid and Walter (2009) and Annex 9 of the Commission's impact assessment for the proposed regulation on structural measures improving the resilience of EU credit institutions[12]). Clearly, one would not want the restructuring to reduce the advantages of international risk diversification in reducing the chance of a failure. Although it has been suggested that the more banks that diversify similarly in this way the more the systemic risk (Allen *et al.*, 2011).

To date, the US authorities have entered into bilateral agreements with the UK, the EU, Switzerland and Japan to coordinate the resolution of cross-border SIFIs. The most significant bilateral agreement is that between the US and the UK since four G-SIFIs, as designated by the FSB, are headquartered in the UK and eight in the US. Furthermore, nearly 70 per cent of the foreign activities of the eight US G-SIFIs take place in the UK (FDIC, 2013).

However, for this to work, it is important that the US and the UK parent or holding company has sufficient funds to absorb losses without causing disruption and contagion in the financial markets. In particular, there may not be enough bailinable debt at the group level. Bailing in has two aspects. The first is that external parties have their claims converted into equity. But the more complex idea is that bailing in can be internal within the group as a whole. Thus, a subsidiary in trouble can be resolved by the parent providing extra capital, even though it has to raise that by bailing in some of its own creditors. Similarly, if the parent is in trouble, healthy subsidiaries can provide it with resources. In order to achieve that, the parent and subsidiaries have to be structured appropriately so that they provide the correct form of liabilities for the group. Without restructuring, if debt at the subsidiary level had to be bailed in then one would be back to an MPOE approach. In that case, issues might arise if some creditors in the same category are being bailed in while others are not. Similarly, if the group's problems stem from specific subsidiaries, which are systemic in other countries, the problems may only be resolvable through intervention in those subsidiaries and that will have to be done by the authorities in those jurisdictions.

One reason why SPOE makes more sense in resolving a cross-border bank than MPOE is due to the different insolvency processes and regimes across borders, which comprise an obstacle to an orderly resolution of that cross-border bank (Lastra, 2011). In order to achieve a successful resolution of a cross-border SIFI, it is important that either there is a harmonised or compatible insolvency regime in the countries where the SIFI operates or there is an ex ante arrangement between various national authorities to recognise the actions of one authority (home and/ or host) where insolvency proceedings are initiated in the jurisdiction of the others. This is even without the conflict between 'territorial' and 'universalist' approaches (Baxter *et al.*, 2004).

The Australian and New Zealand example

Australia and New Zealand offer potentially the most straightforward opportunity to sort out the resolution of R-SIFIs. They have the same four banks, headquartered in Australia, that form the large majority of the banking system and hence of systemically important institutions. These same institutions are not normally of systemic importance to other jurisdictions outside some of the Pacific Islands. While the two countries have undertaken some steps to cooperate and coordinate to manage problems in cross-border banks through the Trans-Tasman Council on Banking Supervision (Reserve Bank of Australia, 2012), they have not been able to agree either an SPOE approach or a cooperative (two) MPOE approach, instead opting for separability so each can handle their own problems. Some very simple aspects of their very different approaches to resolution and the safety net explain it. Yet their vigorous solution may represent a realism that others are yet to face.

If a problem originates in the New Zealand banking system, since roughly 15 per cent of operations of Australian banks are conducted in New Zealand, it might be expected that the Australian authorities would solve the problem through the SPE, or that the parent would do so for a lesser problem, for reputational reasons. If the problem originates in Australia, then again it is very likely that the

Australian authorities would apply the SPOE. However, Australia has domestic depositor preference in insolvency. Thus, not surprisingly, New Zealand has required the banks to be structured in a way that facilitates MPOE to protect its depositors, who are not domestic to Australia and hence would otherwise be junior creditors and heavily exposed to losses. Not only would this be patently unfair but it would have substantial systemic implications in New Zealand, where there is no deposit insurance/guarantee scheme.

Since the Australian banks are the owners of the New Zealand subsidiaries, the New Zealand resolution imposes the first losses on the Australian banks thereby increasing the problem in Australia and freezing some of the potential cash flow.[13] A joint resolution or even a resolution applied to the banking group as a whole could be a less costly outcome. This is what the EU tries to achieve through colleges as a joint resolution at a parent level of a cross-border FI. Closer cooperation and coordination is expected to speed up the resolution process and increase the likelihood of success of the actions taken. Nevertheless, if coordination among different authorities across borders does not succeed, the opposite result is expected. Thus, the New Zealand authorities have cut through the problems of coordination among the various countries' authorities of a cross-border bank by making sure they can isolate and control their own systemic problems irrespective of what the home country, i.e. Australia, decides to do.

The case of the EU

The EU has attempted to address the problems of cross-border banks through a 'banking union', which has two parts[14]: the creation of the SSM under the leadership of the ECB and the creation of a resolution authority and all the necessary tools for resolution through the Bank Recovery and Resolution Directive (BRRD) (Directive 2014/59/EU). While the BRRD applies to the whole EU/EEA, the SSM only applies to the euro area and those countries that choose to join and are admitted.[15] Associated with the BRRD is a regulation setting up an SRM with a Single Resolution Fund (SRF) to facilitate resolution for the SSM countries (Regulation (EU) No 806/2014). Resolutions for the SRM will be the responsibility of a new Single Resolution Board (SRB), based in Brussels. The SSM is also backed up by a substantially increased harmonisation of banking regulation under the leadership of the European Banking Authority (EBA), which also applies to the whole of the EU/EEA. The EU had already created colleges for each SIFI that operates in the EU/EEA, both at the supervisory and resolution levels.

With the BRRD and SRM the EU is trying to get a hybrid to work, where resolution may well take place at the national level in an unstructured and highly interdependent cross-border banking group. It hopes that a coordinated MPOE may work. Within the SRM this might eventually be possible as the ECB is responsible for reorganising the structures of FIs while the SRB is to put together resolution plans for each SIFI, but outside the SRM the degree of compulsion required may not be present. The major problem, however, is that not all measures apply to all EU/EEA member states. The full set of measures applies to the euro area. Non-euro area countries may join both the SSM and the SRM, although this will generate some problems of governance. Only euro area central bank governors are members of the Governing Council, so without revision the ECB could not only be taking measures that affected non-euro countries without their being represented but it would be treating euro and non-euro area members differentially, which contradicts the fundamental tenets of how the EU should behave. In the case of the SSM, this is being addressed by having a Supervisory Board on which a representative of each of the supervisory authorities in the participating countries sits. It has a chairman and vice chairman appointed by the Governing Council and four representatives from the ECB itself. However, except where delegated, formal decisions will be taken by the Governing Council of the ECB, which does not include the non-euro area countries.[16]

Consequently, if the problem occurs in the SSM area, it is more likely that it will be solved more swiftly as supervision and decision-making processes will be centralised compared to EU banks outside the SSM/SRM. Resolution of a cross-border FI is expected to be more complicated and conflicted if its operations are expanded to the EU member states that do not participate in the SRM, as it would involve many authorities in the resolution process. Lastly, if the operations of a cross-border FI expand to regions outside the EU, then successful resolution of that FI would require a successful coordination and cooperation among authorities in the EU and the third countries where the cross-border SIFI operates and indeed may be headquartered.[17]

Resolvability

The key to a successful cross-border bank resolution is clearly that ex ante the bank appears 'resolvable' to the authorities. If they cannot work out how they might do the job even in theory, then hope for anything other than a bail-out in practice must be slim. (Of course achieving resolvability in this sense does not ensure success either as there may be unexpected difficulties at the time.)

Resolvability may imply the separation of systemically critical functions of a SIFI from its non-systemically important operations in a crisis. Indeed, this has already been partly mandated by incorporating a version of the Volcker Rule in the Dodd-Frank Act and the Vickers Commission's proposals in the UK into the Banking Reform Act 2013 (Financial Services (Banking Reform) Act (2013)). The EU proposal to require such structural changes, made in January 2014, is currently stalled. Nevertheless, the non-systemic parts of the group may be a source of strength and not the cause of the problem. In this case, the division is counterproductive. Ideally, the continuity of the systemically important parts for the economy will reduce the likelihood of financial instability. One prerequisite for achieving resolvability is, first, to define clearly which functions are considered to be systemically important and, second, to have a clear mapping of legal entities in a SIFI to their operations.

One useful aspect of drawing up living wills lies in the fact that they provide a map of the interconnectedness and complexity of a SIFI, which assists the authorities in identifying the functions that are critical for the stability of the financial system as well as the degree to which these functions can be carved out and protected to be kept going.

The US example

The US has had a considerable head start in this area, because it has already required prompt corrective action (PCA) since the 1990s with the passing of Federal Deposit Insurance Corporation Improvement Act (FDICIA) in 1991 and hence structured intervention in banks before they reach the point of irrecoverable collapse. However, the experience of the application of this approach has been mixed, and many cases were missed in the GFC despite the PCA requirement (see, for example, Garcia (2012)).

According to the Wall Street Reform and Consumer Protection Act (to give the Dodd-Frank Act its proper title) in the US, which passed into law in 2010, large bank holding companies and non-bank financial companies, with total consolidated assets of $50 billion or more, are subject to living wills in which they demonstrate how they will be resolved in an orderly manner under the Bankruptcy Code in the event of distress or failure (Title I). However, if undergoing ordinary bankruptcy procedure jeopardises financial stability, the FDIC is given power by the OLA to resolve the failing FI under special resolution regime (Title II).

In particular, section 166 of Title I on Financial Stability of the Dodd-Frank Act covers recovery plans, which are named as early redemption plans. The purpose of these plans is to minimise the possibility of insolvency of bank holding companies and non-bank financial companies that have total consolidated assets worth $50 billion or above, which are deemed by the authorities as systemically important. At initial stages of financial decline, authorities might require SIFIs covered by the Dodd-Frank Act to limit their capital distributions, acquisitions and asset growth. While at later stages, SIFIs might be asked to sell assets, change their management, hold more capital and limit transactions with affiliates (Dodd-Frank Act, 2010: s166).

Furthermore, section 165(d) of Title I on Financial Stability of the Dodd-Frank Act requires SIFIs to report periodically a plan for rapid and orderly resolution in an event of material financial distress or failure. The main focus is on how insured depository institutions, which are affiliated with the company subject to the new law, are protected from risks arising from activities of its non-bank subsidiaries. For example, full description of ownership structure, assets, liabilities and contractual obligations is required as well as information on cross-guarantees, major counterparties and to whom the collateral of company is pledged.

The authorities need to notify the SIFIs about their resolution plan deficiencies and can demand that SIFIs resubmit plans that address the problems identified. The authorities also have the power to require changes to SIFIs' business operations and corporate structure to facilitate resolution. This implies that the company needs to change its structure to adjust to the new resolution plan. If a SIFI fails to resubmit its resolution plan, the authorities have the power to impose more stringent capital, leverage and liquidity requirements, as well as restrictions on growth and the SIFI's activities and operations. Nevertheless, resolution plans are not binding on bankruptcy courts and receivers (Dodd-Frank Act, 2010: s165(d)).

Additionally, according to Title II on the OLA, creditors and shareholders are the ones that bear losses, not the taxpayers, in the event of financial distress or failure of a company, while at the same time, management is replaced (Dodd-Frank Act, 2010: s204(a)).

The problem in the US seems to be that these living wills are being produced under Title I of the Dodd-Frank Act, which covers recovery, whereas this is just part of the process all the way through to resolution under Title II. The authorities want a feasible way to handle the whole process.

The EU case

The EU setting emphasises the importance of both the recovery and resolution planning of SIFIs at both the EU and euro area (SSM) level as there were no such arrangements before the GFC. According to the BRRD (Directive 2014/59/EU), credit institutions that are not part of a group subject to consolidated supervision should draw up recovery plans and submit them for revision to their competent authorities on an annual basis.[18] When a FI is part of consolidated supervision then the authorities have the discretion to decide whether the group's subsidiaries are also going to be subject to recovery planning at an individual level. The authorities have six months to assess whether the recovery plans submitted are credible and can restore the viability of an institution under stress. Some examples of measures that the competent authorities could require an institution to undertake due to the deficiencies identified in the submitted recovery plan include recapitalisation measures and changes to the governance structure of the institution.

The same institutions and groups are also subject to resolution plans, which are drawn up by the authorities themselves; however, the institutions can be required to assist the authorities in their task. Some of the key elements of a resolution plan are the identification of critical functions, how these functions can be continued without a break and what arrangements an institution should make in order to remove impediments to resolvability. At a group level, the identification of its complexity and interconnectedness is also crucial. Another crucial factor that the Directive incorporates, which will facilitate resolution at a group level, is information sharing and cooperation among various resolution authorities, with the EBA developing procedures and templates for providing and sharing that information.

Under the terms of the BRRD both recovery and resolution plans should not assume any access to public funds nor, in the case of resolution plans, any central bank emergency liquidity assistance.[19] At a group level, if there is a disagreement among the consolidated supervisor and the competent authorities of the subsidiaries, the consolidated supervisor could make its own decision, while the competent authorities can refer it to the EBA, which plays the role of the mediator. If a joint solution is not reached, the measures are taken only in the jurisdictions which reached an agreement.

In order to achieve resolvability, reforms have been proposed. On 29 January 2014 the European Commission published a proposal for a regulation on structural measures (RSM): 'improving the resilience of EU credit', but this measure has not progressed and has attracted a lot of opposition, not just from FIs themselves but also from their regulators, particularly in France and Germany (European Commission, 2014) who have already passed legislation according to which FIs are required to separate their proprietary trading from deposit-taking activities.[20] Although their proposals resemble that of the European Commission, they are more flexible. For example, they allow retail parts of the bank to engage in market-making activities subject to specific conditions. Thus, banks in these countries might be exempted from EU legislation if the European Commission decides that they meet EU standards.[21] Other countries have already made this change with the implementation of the so-called Volcker rule in the Dodd-Frank Act in the US and the ring-fencing and fuller capitalisation of narrow banking functions in the UK following the recommendations of The Independent Commission on Banking (2013) headed by John Vickers.

The US and UK legislation and the Commission proposals (and indeed the recommendations of the 'high-level expert group' (HLEG) chaired by Erkki Liikanen on which the European Commission drew) all come to different decisions about how financial groups should be restructured.[22] Furthermore, we cannot assume that the financial system does not change over time in the light of experience and opportunities, but can most certainly assume that financial firms will react to regulatory requirements to change their structures in ways that the authorities had not envisaged. The idea, therefore, that a reasonably harmonised approach is likely to emerge internationally seems rather distant at present.

For a banking group to be 'resolvable', it needs to be structured in such a way that its vital functions can be kept operating in a resolution in the manner described above. In its justification of its choice of how to split up FIs in the proposed SRM, the European Commission suggests that there are two simple dimensions to consider. The first is where to draw the boundary between the functions of banking that need to be continued and those which can be allowed to enter a more standard insolvency process. The distinction is not simply on the basis of what the functions are but on how important they are in the banking group as a whole. The second is what the nature of the division should be: Do the activities need to be self-standing, ring-fenced units in the organisation? Do they need to be legally separate subsidiaries within the financial group? Does the group itself have to be broken up so that there are no links between the activities at all, although of course people could own shares in all of them?

There is, however, a significant further dimension to this discussion, namely that in the largest FIs, operations run across borders. Hence, resolution is going to involve authorities in a number of countries. Experience in cross-border resolutions shows that they are very difficult. Not only do the different proceedings need to be coordinated but the interests of jurisdictions may conflict. Not only can assets be moved round in a group, so altering the incidence of the losses from one part of the group to another, but typically there is a rush of such reorganisation in the days before the resolution as the group desperately tries to avoid insolvency.

What is surprising about the HLEG report is that there is no detailed discussion of where the boundary between what is labelled 'banking' and 'trading' activities should lie. Trading is thought of as trading in market instruments on the institution's own account rather than that of clients, but is taken to exclude market-making and trading in government bonds. Since 'The use of derivatives for own asset and liability management, as well as sales and purchases of assets to manage the assets in the liquidity portfolio, would also be permitted', it is clear that the definition of trading is narrow (HLEG report, 2012: 101). The report suggests that the decision over what should be included and what should be separated will also depend on the plausibility of the recovery and resolution plans. So, if the EU does not proceed with the RSM, the onus for deciding on how the banking group should be structured will lie with the supervisory and resolution authorities on a case by case basis. Furthermore, the debate over where to draw the boundary between risky and vital activities is still debated. Blundell-Wignall and Roulet (2013), for example, argue that there is empirical evidence that the trading book and available-for-sale securities make a bank safer and not weaker, and that it is the derivatives and wholesale funding that make the bank more vulnerable.

There are two parts to the discussion. The first is the observation that what is vital to financial stability is much larger than might previously have been thought. Thus, letting Lehman Brothers go into a disorderly insolvency was clearly a mistake. AIG needed to be saved and even quite small institutions, such as Northern Rock, were thought too big to fail. Small banks may need to keep operating if they are the only institutions covering a region. Thus, the scale and scope of both bailing in and bailing out may turn out to be larger than thought beforehand. Hence, any ex ante division of institutions into parts that are considered vital and parts that are not is likely to be too conservative, and action will have to be taken to save activities that were not thought vital beforehand. In part, this reflects the expectation that those who will get into difficulty are likely to lie outside the carefully regulated and supervised sector. That leads to the second part of the discussion. The more the authorities seek to regulate part of the financial sector, the more they will tend to drive risky activity out beyond the boundary and into areas where they are relatively less well informed, nicely contributing to raising the chance of a future crisis.

Thus, there is a temptation to include the full range of financial activity within existing groups. An exception here is that banking is a much more important source of business finance in many European countries than in the US or indeed the UK. As a result, banks and financial groups become rather larger compared to the economy. Hence, if they fail, the impact is similarly likely to be bigger. Reducing the relative importance of the banking sector without reducing finance for firms, therefore, might be a more appropriate means of structural change in the sector rather than trying to divide up the existing financial groups into those that are heavily protected and those that are not.

Australia and New Zealand

Australia and New Zealand have also followed different routes with recovery and resolution plans. Australia has decided to proceed with recovery planning for the time being and then continue to resolution planning after satisfactory progress has been made with recovery part of the living wills (Australian Prudential Regulation Authority (APRA), 2011). Initially, recovery planning has affected the large authorised deposit-taking institutions (ADIs) in the country, but there is an indication from the Australian authorities that these arrangements will be extended to smaller ADIs. The lack of eagerness by the Australian authorities to develop and implement living wills could be because their financial system did not suffer large losses in the GFC, as their banks focused mainly on core banking activities rather than the riskier investment banking activities, as happened in the US and the EU (Brown and Ralston, 2013). However, the Australian authorities have received a clear recommendation from the Financial System Inquiry, set up by the new government in 2013, that resolution planning should be pursued as a high priority (Commonwealth of Australia, 2014).

On the other hand, New Zealand has not subjected its Australian-owned SIFIs to living wills, but has focused on establishing viable resolution plans, which are rather different in character from those being pursued in the US and Europe and most importantly from Australia. More specifically, for living wills the Reserve Bank of New Zealand (RBNZ) concluded that they are best suited to deal with globally significant banks with complex structures and cross-border interactions. The scheme would be less beneficial in New Zealand, because banks generally are stand-alone domestic institutions or subsidiaries of Australian banking groups (Lee, 2013). Moreover, while it is still not clear what comprises a vital function and what not in the US and the EU, in New Zealand there is an explicit definition of what is deemed as systemically important operation and what not, which is a prerequisite for its resolution regime, labelled Open Bank Resolution (OBR), to work (RBNZ, 2013).

The large New Zealand-registered banks are required to have technical and operational arrangements in place in advance to facilitate OBR, which is a form of bail-in, and they need to disclose to the authorities all the steps they have undertaken in order to achieve those arrangements. In more detail, each bank must be a locally incorporated and separately capitalised subsidiary[23] so that the New Zealand authorities can have the legal power to resolve it; each bank must be able to operate on its own overnight, independently of its parent or other key supplier, so that it has the practical basis for resolution; and each bank must implement and regularly test the detailed procedures necessary to be able to separate out accounts and other claims into their frozen and unfrozen parts overnight (Chetwin, 2006; Hoskin and Javier, 2013; Hoskin and Woolford, 2011; RBNZ, 2013). These large banks are almost entirely retail and indeed three operate their wholesale activities through a separate branch of the Australian parent. Thus, New Zealand offers as near a 'vanilla' solution as one can expect, assisted by the fact that the country is small and hence the absolute scale limited, although similar to many European countries.

OBR operates overnight so that the window during which the resolution takes place does not constitute a material break in the operation of the vital functions. If a SIFI is in trouble, authorities under the OBR have the power to appoint a statutory manager (similar in concept to a receiver or perhaps more literally a conservator as the bank is to be kept open) and temporarily close the bank. Consequently, the customers stop having access to the bank and all liabilities are frozen. The statutory manager determines customers' liability account balances according to a conservative valuation and applies a partial freeze to customers' liability accounts based on estimated losses in order to return the bank to balance – recapitalisation comes later. At the same time, government issues guarantees for the unfrozen funds. The bank reopens at the start of business on the next day for core transaction business. As new information emerges, the statutory manager determines future operations and potential restructuring of the failed bank and might release additional frozen funds, if available (Hoskin and Woolford, 2011). The bank will exit statutory management when a suitable acquirer can be found who provides the necessary recapitalisation, or by winding down or dismembering the bank while maintaining the core transaction function over a longer period of time.

Nevertheless, as mentioned above, one consequence of those resolvability proposals is that more risky activities are likely to move to the less supervised parts of the financial sector, the so-called shadow banking, where less supervised entities such as hedge funds, structured investment vehicles and money market funds can also provide banking-like activities (Lybeck, forthcoming). It is thus debatable in the light of the problems caused by the failure of Lehman Brothers, whether this separation will lead to a more or less stable financial system. Without doubt the ring-fenced narrow banking operations will become safer (the tighter the fence the safer) as riskier operations are excluded and capitalisation increased. However, those outside the fence may now become more fragile without the banking resources. There is no equivalent of deposit insurance to buy time and with relatively better informed creditors, who might get bailed in, the temptation to exit at the first sign of trouble will become larger. Thus, these institutions may be pushed into crisis resolution earlier than before.

Ways forward

In order to improve SIFIs resolvability, there are some important problems that need to be addressed.

Funding

Providing funding for resolution in advance represents a dead weight cost that has to be borne irrespective of whether the funds are ever needed. However, attempting to raise such funds from a distressed banking sector in a crisis is unlikely to be possible and so recourse would have to be made (temporarily) to the state – assuming, that is, that the state itself has the resources, which has not been the case in some European examples. There is thus a good case for having some ex ante resources available, and this has been a long standing argument for deposit guarantee/insurance funds. However, such funds have usually been aimed at the short-run costs of resolving small institutions, where the failures are idiosyncratic and not part of a general distress across the economy.

While such funds would also be required if there were insufficient loss-absorbing capacity in a resolution, much of the debate has revolved around requirements for funds that either could not or should not be the responsibility of the creditors. All this assumes of course that future resolutions are orderly, and, hence, that cases like Lehman result in relatively small losses, as the FDIC avers it could have achieved with the appropriate powers (FDIC, 2011).

The first issue is associated with the size of the value of the derivative contracts on and off the balance sheet of the SIFIs as well as the short-term nature of their other liabilities, which may reach trillions of dollars. Hellwig (2014) distinguishes the need to fund operations as long as they are ongoing from the need to allocate or absorb losses. He argues that resolution funds might be sufficient to absorb losses; however, these funds are not sufficient to keep the systemically important operations going, at least in the short run. Consequently, establishing interim funding is also crucial.

The position varies across countries. There are no ex ante arrangements for resolution funds in Australia and New Zealand. In Australia, the expectation is that the government will provide the funding in the short run and will recoup any losses from the resolution. In New Zealand it is assumed that guarantees will be sufficient, but in so far as any funding is required it will come straight from the government budget. In the US the FDIC could receive Treasury support through the OLA. The EU decided to go for establishing funds to facilitate resolution rather than rely on ex post resources. In particular, member states need to set up ex ante resolution funds. But before eligible FIs can have access to those funds, a minimum level of losses equal to eight per cent of total liabilities including own funds will have to be imposed on shareholders and creditors (Council of the European Union, 2014).

According to the BRRD, the national resolution funds will have to reach a target level of at least one per cent of covered deposits of all credit institutions authorised in their country raised by the industry. FIs have to contribute annually based on their liabilities (excluding own funds and covered deposits), adjusted for risk (Directive 2014/59/EU, Article 103). Resolution funds can provide temporary support to FIs under resolution via loans, guarantees, asset purchases or capital for bridge banks. However, the contribution of the resolution funds should not exceed five per cent of a bank's total liabilities (Directive 2014/59/EU, Article 44).

Under SRM, the decisions are made centrally in order to enhance the functioning of the Single Market. More specifically, resolution decisions will be prepared and monitored centrally by the SRB, which will apply the Single Rulebook on the FI's resolution specified in the BRRD. Moreover, the SRF established under the SRM regulation will be composed of separate national compartments, which will be merged during a transitional period of eight years (Regulation (EU) No 806/2014, Article 77).

However, the resolution funds are relatively small, just one per cent of covered deposits, and hence might get exhausted in a crisis. It is possible that it may be very difficult to recapitalise problem banks by creditor funds alone. There is a second reason why funds are needed in that because resolution of SIFIs takes into account the wider public interest and not just the private interests of the creditors, someone else should bear that extra cost. Making it the whole of those involved in the banking industry seems appropriate. Deposit guarantee funds will be bailed in to the extent that covered depositors would have been bailed in had they been treated equally with other creditors in the same class.[24] Nevertheless, currently, there may not be access to sufficient interim funding under the BRRD.[25] Hence, other sources of funds might be needed. A medium-term solution could be a further integration in the EU via establishing a fiscal union (Moro, 2014).

Furthermore, intra-group financing cannot be used in some cases as part of a resolution process. For example, the UK, which has one of the largest financial markets, is outside SSM and SRM. This could have an impact on intra-group financing if there is no ex ante agreement or close cooperation between the involved parties. Furthermore, the UK and the US are considering taking more responsibilities for host countries in terms of supervising foreign-owned banks' branches and subsidiaries and requiring foreign banks to operate as independent subsidiaries subject to the UK and US law, similar to the arrangement in New Zealand (FDIC and the Bank of England, 2012).

Again, this implies that using intra-group financing arrangements to resolve the problem at a cross-border level might not be an option. If this is the case, then setting out those arrangements explicitly in the living wills of the SIFIs at a group and subsidiary level might ameliorate the uncertainty around the resolution of a cross-border bank. Nevertheless, the lead authority can apply transfers within the parts of the group which lie within its jurisdiction.

Under OBR in New Zealand, it is assumed that with the statutory management and the involvement of the state, probably as a guarantor against future losses, the wholesale and other funding markets would immediately reopen. The costs of the resolution process itself would be charged to the subject bank and hence fall on the creditors. Clearly, the costs of running the saved part of the bank should be a charge on the new institution, while the costs of resolving the problems will effectively be a charge on the insolvency. In the OBR case, the lender of last resort (LOLR) function would presumably work because the bank is now solvent and should have adequate collateral to place with the central bank. In any case, if a government guarantee has been issued, then this could stand in lieu of collateral with inadequate quality. In the EU it appears that these guarantees are to be discouraged and only applied through the limited resolution funds, which might leave the banks with continuing liquidity problems. It is thus the EU case where one might worry that adequate funding will not be available. However, it makes obvious sense for the rhetoric against taxpayer funding to be as strong as possible, if only to minimise the moral hazard, while at the same time being prepared, without stating it, to be able to provide at least interim finance for the wider costs of maintaining confidence in the financial system in the event of the failure of a major bank.

The plausibility of bailing in

In resolving a cross-border FI, the first question is: 'Who is going to pay?' In order to achieve the financial stability objective of a recovery/resolution framework, it is crucial that the decisions are made very rapidly, which implies very extensive preparation, of which living wills form part. However, if there are no legally binding arrangements for burden-sharing agreed in advance, then it is less likely that resolution will succeed and achieve its objectives.[26] This is where the attractiveness of bailing in comes in – there is no public debt burden to be shared. However, the national composition of those being bailed in and that of the protected depositors and indeed borrowers may be completely different. For example, Nordic and Baltic countries, having financial groups operating in their region, made ex ante burden-sharing arrangements in their Cooperation Agreement (CA, 2010). This is an important first step. However, in a crisis, it is likely that national authorities will protect domestic interests first before pursuing resolution at a cross-border level, which might require their funding support. One possible solution for the living wills of cross-border SIFIs to be credible is to establish a common resolution and insolvency regime across borders with explicit burden-sharing arrangements.[27]

Another important problem that needs to be addressed is the credibility of the bail-in tool as a resolution measure. Bail-in measures have been introduced in part to reduce moral hazard. These measures are expected to eliminate the implicit public subsidy problem, i.e. the cheaper funding that has existed for those SIFIs whom the market expects will be bailed out, which thereby gives them an advantage over other smaller FIs (see for example, Baker and McArthur, 2009). This in turn is expected to increase the cost of funding as investors are aware that they will not be bailed out. An increase in funding costs as well as compliance costs can be passed on to the non-financial sectors and ordinary people, who borrow money from FIs subject to these costs. Nevertheless, the removal of this distortion should not represent a social cost to the economy. However, the requirement simply for all banks to hold more capital in future, especially the largest banks, which may be subject to a special surcharge, is a different issue. Admati and Hellwig (2013) argue that because banks are required to hold more capital and liquid assets, this might lower the costs of funding as the likelihood of failure falls along with the risk to the investors or lenders.

The EU, New Zealand and US authorities made it clear that shareholders and creditors will also bear losses in an event of failure. Currently, there is no such explicit arrangement in Australia, but the authorities have made it clear that they expect to recoup the cost of their intervention, which amounts to much the same thing, but without a clear indication of how the loss will be distributed across the same group. It is also clear that the EU, New Zealand and US authorities do not believe the Admati and Hellwig (2013) argument, as their impact studies include a clear allowance for an increase in bank funding costs. However, the social cost is lower than the bank funding cost as the social benefit from losing the element of subsidy for the TBTF banks has to be offset against the cost.

Although living wills appear to be useful in resolving individual failures, they are of less value in dealing with systemic crises. When there is an unexpected change in the economy that affects the whole financial industry, rather than an individual FI, it is difficult to predict how all the SIFIs are going to acquire additional capital or apply the measures they developed in their living wills to recover from the market shock or be resolved in an orderly manner at the same time (Pakin, 2013). (Indeed one might well argue that serious idiosyncratic problems in SIFIs are unlikely to lead to failures unless there are general problems in the financial system. Hence, most problems in SIFIs are likely to be part of a more general crisis.) This is a version of what Robert Eisenbeis (2006) described as the Hurricane Katrina problem. All hospitals and rest homes in New Orleans had to have contracts with bus companies to shift their patients in the event of a serious problem, such as a fire. But, of course, these contracts were all with the same bus companies, so when the hurricane affected all the hospitals and rest homes at the same time the contracts did not work. Individual plans will assume saleability of subsidiaries or successful capital injections. Taken jointly this will not work, which may explain some of the unenthusiastic response of the FDIC and the Federal Reserve to the initial living wills quoted at the beginning of the chapter.

Goodhart and Avgouleas (2014) illustrate a further facet of the problem by emphasising that bailing in may generate a collateral crunch with widespread impact. They argue that as soon as the first bail-in starts, prices of other bailinable debt will fall and the market will dry up. Preliminary research shows that bailing in would have been technically feasible during the recent financial crisis in the sense that there were enough eligible liabilities to be bailed in. For example, Bagus *et al.* (2014) look at the feasibility of bail-in for Spain and find that, although many liabilities are excluded, bail-in would be feasible in Spain. Conlon and Cotter (2014), who also examine the feasibility of bail-in across some European countries, find that equity and subordinated bondholders would bear most of the impairment losses realised by European banks if they were bailed in. (They develop this argument further in chapter 5 in this book.) Losses to senior debtholders, however, would have been small while there would not have been losses for depositors. In the cases of Greece, Austria and Ireland, senior debtholders would have suffered significant losses too, along with the shareholders and subordinated bondholders. The Vickers Report suggests that a bailinable capacity of 16 per cent of total liabilities would have been sufficient to cover the losses of all the major failures in the GFC, except Anglo-Irish Bank where the losses were much larger, and hence recommended that the desirable buffer should be 17 per cent for the UK banks, a number that was then embodied in the legislation.

Since some liabilities are excluded from the bail-in,[28] living wills would explicitly disclose and show sufficient eligible liabilities to ensure that, if the bail-in tool were to be applied, losses could be absorbed and thus enhance the credibility of that tool (Directive 2014/59/EU, Article 45).

Denmark was the first country in the EU to impose the bail-in tool on senior unsecured creditors after the shareholders and subordinated debtholders, in the case of its two medium-sized banks that operate mainly domestically, Amagerbanken and Fjordbank Mors, which failed in 2011. In particular, in the case of Amagerbanken, the initial haircut for subordinated creditors whose claims were not covered by the Deposit Guarantee Scheme was set at 41 per cent, but after a subsequent assessment the final payout was increased from 59 per cent to 84.4 per cent. While in the case of Fjordbank Mors holders of senior unsecured claims reportedly faced a 26 per cent loss (14 per cent according to a Danske Bank report (Danske Bank, 2012)) (European Commission, 2012).

Nevertheless, the implementation of the bail-in tool on the senior unsecured bondholders was deemed as an inferior solution by the chief executive officer of the Danish state resolution agency, Henrik Bjerre-Nielsen. As he stated: 'Denmark is freeing itself of the bail-in stigma that shut most of its banks out of international funding markets' (Schwartzkopff, 2012).

The bailing in of creditors in Denmark led to the repricing of Danish bank debt compared to other Scandinavian/Nordic banks. Danish banks had to pay an additional 100–200 basis points, making it harder for the banking system to survive (Lybeck, forthcoming).

The resolution of the banking crisis in Cyprus in March 2013 also illustrated the problem of who should be bailed in and is an important contributor to the EU's decision to try to exclude depositors in future and to have a proper legal basis. In the Cyprus case, both insured and uninsured depositors were made to bear losses to contribute to the recapitalisation, ahead of senior bondholders. Simply introducing the uncertainty over whether depositors in other countries might be bailed in increased the fragility of banks in Europe.

The New Zealand system approaches recovery indirectly. RBNZ argues (RBNZ, 2012) that the main gains from bailing in occur not because they are cheaper. They estimate that bailing in will have as big an adverse impact on GDP as a 'bad' bail-out. The gain comes because banks themselves will want to make sure that they are resolvable/recoverable through the private sector. This is a straightforward moral hazard argument. Because shareholders will be wiped out and the senior management can expect to lose their jobs under OBR, they will have a strong incentive to make sure that an OBR never occurs. This incentive rests firmly on the belief that, should they get into difficulty, they will not be bailed out.

New Zealand arrangements show how one can put together a resolution plan that would work in most circumstances without any resort to public money, unless either a guarantee is required and called upon or if the dividing line between the frozen and unfrozen balances undervalued the losses. (OBR assumes that it is not possible to apply the writing down process a second time.) One of the reasons the New Zealand arrangements could work in theory is that there is plenty of bailin-able debt as deposits can be bailed in. But this same exposure makes the chances of the scheme being applied in practice quite low, as the government of the time would be imposing losses directly on a large portion of electors.

Bailing out would be a far less obvious way of imposing the same losses on ordinary people and hence is likely to be more attractive politically even if it is not so 'fair', in not putting responsibility on those who took the risks. Furthermore, bailing in is likely to cause much greater instability, because at the first sniff that a bank might be in trouble it would be sensible for depositors to withdraw their money from the whole banking system. If one of the large four banks is in trouble it is unlikely to be in circumstances where there are not worries about the viability of the financial system more generally. Since deposits are on call, the system could be destabilised immediately.

In general, bailing in does not imply that those bailed in can survive the losses. If the same pension funds are bailed into several banks, then the risk becomes more concentrated and the impact on the funds more dramatic, spreading the crisis to them rather than allowing them to act as risk absorbers and reduce the overall impact of the crisis on GDP in the short run. Loss-absorbing capacity recommendations required by the FSB for bailing in are silent on their wider economic consequences. Loss-absorbing capacity in the FSB sense simply means that there are funds available against which the losses can be offset. There is no discussion of any consequent actions by those then making the losses, which in turn might lower economic activity and expand the financial crisis through a different channel.

It is important to distinguish between the direct cost to the taxpayer, which financial authorities aim to minimise through the recovery and resolution planning, and other economic costs. For example, the BRRD talks about minimising the impact on the taxpayer, but this is a narrow view of direct costs and takes no account of the impact on GDP, unemployment and hence tax revenues and welfare expenditures in the economic downturn that a crisis or failure in a systemic bank will cause. Simply being able to resolve a bank without a taxpayer bail-out does not reduce the economic cost of the resolution.

The FDIC (2011) estimates that had an orderly resolution been performed on Lehman Brothers, the loss to general unsecured creditors could have been just $5 billion, once equity and subordinated debtholders had been wiped out. To use the FDIC's words it would have been able to 'preserve financial stability'. However, the FDIC did not consider the hugely costly knock-on effects around the world.

It is worth reflecting on the RBNZ's (2012) estimate of the cost to GDP of a bail-in of one of the four main banks. Their rough estimate is 25 per cent. Thus, any need to resolve a major bank through OBR will constitute a crisis. Indeed, they expect even private sector solutions to result in a 12.5 per cent reduction in GDP compared to what it would otherwise have been. While the exact numbers are open to question, the main point stands. Any event which threatens to bring down one of the four main banks must be so large that it constitutes a crisis for the economy however it is resolved. The idea that losses on this scale to a well-capitalised SIFI can somehow occur in a vacuum seems unlikely. Even though some frauds have reached staggering proportions, a failure on this scale is likely to be associated with a serious downturn in the economy or a natural disaster.

Complying with living wills does not exclude the possibility that SIFIs will not be bailed out, although the main objective of the introduction of living wills is to reduce the possibility of a failure and potentially of a bail-out of a SIFI subject to the requirements of those living wills. Again, a crucial factor is the market's perception of what the financial authorities are going to do.

What is more, bail-outs are not always the best way to go especially in cases where the country in which a SIFI operates has fiscal problems. A bail-out under these circumstances can lead to a sovereign default. Consequently, recovery and resolution planning should be assessed and updated hand in hand with fiscal and macroeconomic developments at a national and international level. Overall, while bail-ins seem fairer than bail-outs, because those who knowingly run the risks bear the direct costs in the same order of priority as in an insolvency, the impact on the wider economy and society at large is not necessarily lower. Therefore, there can be a trade-off between impact and fairness in that a bail-out may enable some creditors to avoid or reduce their losses. In the EU case, where there is the European Stability Mechanism available to stand behind countries and their banks in some circumstances, this will increase the chance of a less enthusiastic use of bailing in.

Concluding remarks

It is obvious that it will take some time for the recovery and resolution framework to be improved and strengthened. First, living wills are not sufficient on their own to tackle a systemic crisis. However, they are valuable if just so that the authorities get a better and more complete picture of each individual FI and the financial system as a whole. Understanding the complexities and interdependencies among different parts of the system will facilitate the identification of weaknesses in the system and activate a process of resolving these problems before they mount. Second, resolution of G-SIFIs needs more elements to it apart from living wills. It will be a continuing process of interaction among living wills, CMGs, COAGs and resolvability assessments.

At present, living wills are imposed on SIFIs with an emphasis on deposit-taking institutions. While a comprehensive recovery and resolution framework is also needed for smaller banks, as irrespective of their size they are very sensitive to public confidence, anything equivalent to a living will would be a much more straightforward plan. Even a failure of a small bank can lead to contagion, and experience such as Northern Rock suggests that political intervention will, in practice, be at rather lower levels of possible crisis than current new regulation implies. Moreover, living wills could expand to other parts of the financial system, such as insurance and market infrastructure as well as shadow banking, which is opaque and not subject to the same regulations as the banking sector, although it performs bank-like functions (European Systemic Risk Board, 2012).

There is a systemic component beyond resolvability that can occur even in the recovery phase, which should not be ignored, and that is restoration of confidence in the financial system as a whole. This chapter illustrates several reasons why public money might be needed such as with government guarantees to other banks, which have not entered a recovery or resolution regime.

Some of the main problems associated with plausible cross-border recovery and resolution frameworks will be addressed steadily over coming years, such as the nature of resolvability, the exact definition of functions whose continuing operation is critical for the economy and the information that needs to be shared among authorities. The move towards banking union in Europe will help address areas such as the inconsistent insolvency regimes and mutual recognition of recovery and resolution procedures across borders, inconsistent definition of vital functions and disagreement on the structural reforms of FIs and improved credibility of the bail-in tool. However, major obstacles remain and it does not seem likely on present progress that large financial groups will become neatly structured with the vital functions for each jurisdiction, each organised in separate subsidiaries that are capable of functioning on their own overnight.

Some restructuring is clearly needed and living wills will help identify that need. However, the sheer size and market dominance of many of the larger institutions means that the restructuring of the industry, common in past crises, namely through mergers, is not so likely in the future. Just simply making banks smaller might address this, but requiring it would be politically difficult.

The recapitalisation of banks that is progressing towards much higher levels, including limiting leverage, and the requirements to have sufficient liquidity to weather short-run shocks, will make banks more resilient in the first place. Coupled with bailinable capital and other options for PCA at an earlier stage, this should make the chance of the authorities having to perform speedy and efficient resolutions smaller. Similarly, the agreements on the tools needed and the considerable level of planning should make the chance of such orderly resolutions greater. However, the history of crises suggests that problems will not be recognised in the future and that the next crisis will involve aspects of the system that were not appreciated. So, despite all the planning, we can expect the normal panic and the need to take extraordinary actions, some of which are likely to involve taxpayers' money. At the very least, bailing in on a large scale across several institutions simultaneously has not been attempted, and the consequences in practice may be rather different from those anticipated in theory.

Notes

1   We are grateful to Santiago Carbo-Valverde, Andrew Hewitt and participants at the conference on 'European Banking Union: Prospects and Challenges' at the University of Buckingham and at the IBEFA session at the WEAI International Conference in Wellington in January 2015 for their comments.

2   The text of living wills is confidential, so it is not possible for the outside observer to form a judgement. There is a public version available for each bank as part of the Dodd-Frank Act requirements, but these are not very informative and hence unlikely to enhance either public confidence or market discipline (Carmassi and Herring, 2013).

3   The full speech can be read at: http://www.fsa.gov.uk/pages/Library/Communication/Speeches/2010/0212_th.shtml.

4   Calomiris and Herring (2011) set out how CoCos can be designed to encourage the existing shareholders to recapitalise the bank without triggering the bail-in.

5   In the case of the EU, the assessment process is complex as it involves agreement not just among the supervisory authorities in each relevant country but with the resolution authorities as well (Directive 2014/59/EU, Articles 6–9).

6   See Mayes (2014b) for an analysis of this in the case of the Nordic experience since 1990.

7   Unassisted in the sense that no resolution tools have been used. The bank will have been subject to close surveillance, possibly some restrictions on actions and solutions will have been 'encouraged' with prospective investors and partners.

8   This bail-in would be in addition to any 'voluntary' bail-in of CoCos and other convertible liabilities as part of the unsuccessful recovery procedure.

9   Where large banks are headquartered in small countries it may be impossible to raise adequate financing in that country alone to resolve a troubled bank – even more so if it is the entire banking system that is in trouble, as was the case in Iceland.

10 The G (R) global (regional) modifiers relate to whether the failure of the institution is likely to affect financial stability globally (regionally) rather than just in its home country.

11 Very much along the lines suggested in Mayes (2006).

12 Available at http://www.cdep.ro/afaceri_europene/CE/2014/SWD_2014_30_EN_ DOCUMENTDETRAVAIL_f.pdf (accessed 25 July 2015).

13 See Mayes (2014a) for an exposition of the New Zealand 'Open Bank Resolution' scheme and its implications for other jurisdictions with cross-border banks.

14 In the original design there was to be a third part in the form of an EU-wide deposit guarantee scheme, but this has proved too difficult to agree. The EU system thus looks very different from the US as there is no FDIC equivalent.

15 Sweden and the UK, for example, have made it clear that they do not propose to join the SSM. To be literal, non-euro countries cannot 'join' the SSM, per se. They can enter a 'close cooperation agreement' with the ECB, which will have much the same effect but, as discussed below, they cannot enter fully into the governance of the system as they do not have a seat on the ECB's Governing Council.

16 The Supervisory Board is to be distinguished from the Board of Supervisors in the EBA and the SRB, which are both different organisations.

17 It is not as yet clear how the ECB and the SRB will work together. The assessment of whether a financial institution subject to SSM is failing, or is likely to fail, is made by the ECB, while the assessment of whether there are no alternative private sector measures that would prevent a financial institution's failure within a reasonable timeframe is made by the SRB. The SRB can also make an assessment on whether an FI is failing or is likely to fail, but: 'only after informing the ECB of its intention and only if the ECB, within three calendar days of receipt of that information, does not make such an assessment' (Regulation (EU) No 806/2014, Article 18(1)). In practice, one would expect that the ECB will recommend the implementation of a resolution scheme as it is the main supervisor and regulator, but that it will be the SRB that determines what the form of resolution will be.

18 By 'competent authorities' the EU means the supervisory authorities that have jurisdiction in each specific case.

19 It is worth noting that in the US as well there has been some tightening up of the ability of a solvent bank with liquidity problems to borrow from the Federal Reserve under Federal Article 13(3) or the lender of last resort (LOLR) arrangement (Scott, 2012).

20 Loi 2013-672 du 26 juillet 2013 de séparation et de régulation des activités bancaires, J.O. n°173 du 27 juillet 2013, p. 12,530 and Gesetz zur Abschirmung von Risiken und zur Planung der Sanierung und Abwicklung von Kreditinstituten und Finanzgruppen v. 7.8.2013, BGBl. 2013 I p. 3090. See Lehmann (2014) for a discussion.

21 http://www.europarl.europa.eu/RegData/etudes/BRIE/2014/542145/EPRS_ BRI(2014)542145_REV1_EN.pdf (last accessed 25 July 2015).

22 The January 2014 proposal from the European Commission alters the Liikanen proposals in a number of respects. First, it widens what can be included in banking activities – government bond trading, for example, Second, it is permissive rather than compulsive and authorities have the discretion to decide whether a separation is needed, and last, the nature of the separation is harshened, so that the non-banks have to be legally separate and not just different subsidiaries within the same banking group. Lehmann (2014) offers a comparison of the Volcker, Vickers, Liikanen and European Commission proposals. See also Gambacorta and van Rixtel (2013).

23 With clear separation of assets and liabilities from those of the parent (RBNZ, 2014).

24 All depositors have preference in the insolvency proceedings, but the Deposit Guarantee Scheme has first claim ahead of the uncovered depositors.

25 Deposit guarantee funds and resolution funds will be separate in many countries, for example, Finland, where the deposit funds are private and controlled by the banks themselves, the Bankers Association in the Finnish case, and are therefore not subject to direction by the resolution authority. The case is different in Germany where private funds have historically been used to facilitate resolution, without access to state funding. In the UK, funding has been ex post. Hence, considerable variety can be expected in the actual arrangements in the future despite the uniformity implied by the directive.

26 While a memorandum of understanding (MoU) exists (for example the MoU among Nordic countries), in a crisis it is not clear that they would necessarily be followed, especially if a state was finding it difficult to raise sovereign debt or felt that the responsibility for the problems lay in another jurisdiction.

27 Avgouleas *et al.* (2013) propose incorporating burden-sharing agreements in the living wills. The authors recognise that living wills will reveal the inconsistencies of resolution regimes, which subsequently can be dealt with. They argue that this is a good start to developing a common legal framework for resolving SIFIs across the G20.

28 Typically, all secured debt, liabilities to other parts of the banking system, derivatives and related contracts and all short-term funding (Directive 2014/59/EU, Article 44).

References

Admati, A. and Hellwig, M. (2013) *The Bankers' New Clothes*. Princeton NJ: Princeton University Press.

Allen, F., Beck, T., Carletti, E., Lane, P. R., Schoenmaker, D. and Wagner, W. (2011) *Cross-Border Banking in Europe: Implications for Financial Stability and Macroeconomic Policies*. London, UK: Centre for Economic and Policy Research.

APRA (2011) *Apra's Regulatory Priorities – An Update*. Available at: http://www.apra. gov.au/Speeches/NewDocLib2/Finsia Financial Services Conference-25 October 2011. pdf (last accessed 30 October 2014).

Avgouleas, E., Goodhart, C. and Schoenmaker, D. (2013) Bank resolution plans as a catalyst for global financial reform. *Journal of Financial Stability* 9(2): 210–218.

Bagus, P., Julián, J. R. R. and Neira, M. A. A. (2014) Bail-in or bail-out: The case of Spain. *CESifo Economic Studies* 60(1): 89–106.

Baker, D. and McArthur, T. (2009) The value of the 'too big to fail' big bank subsidy. *Issue Brief*. London, UK: Centre for Economic and Policy Research.

Baxter, T. H., Hansen, J. M. and Sommer, J. H. (2004) Two cheers for territoriality: An essay on international bank insolvency law. *American Bankruptcy Law Journal* 78(1): 57–91.

BCBS (2010) *Report and Recommendations of the Cross-Border Bank Resolution Group*. Available at: http://www.bis.org/publ/bcbs169.pdf (last accessed 30 October 2014).

BCBS (2011) *Resolution Policies and Frameworks – Progress So Far*. Available at: www. bis.org/publ/bcbs200.pdf (last accessed 30 October 2014).

Blundell-Wignall, A. and Roulet, C. (2013) Bank business models, capital rules and structural separation policies: an evidence-based critique of current policy trends. *Journal of Financial Economic Policy* 5(4): 339–360.

Board of Governors of the Federal Reserve System and FDIC joint release (2014) *Agencies Provide Feedback on Second Round Resolution Plans of 'First-Wave' Filers*. Available at: https://www.fdic.gov/news/news/press/2014/pr14067.html (last accessed 30 October 2014).

Brown, C. and Ralston, D. (2013) The poor performance of compulsory saving in Australia. Superannuation and corporate governance. In Mayes, D. G. and Wood, G. (eds) *Reforming the Governance of the Financial Sector*. New York: Routledge, pp. 54–79.

CA (2010) *Cooperation Agreement on Cross-Border Financial Stability, Crisis Management and Resolution Between Relevant Ministries, Central Banks and Financial Supervisory Authorities of Denmark, Estonia, Finland, Iceland, Latvia, Lithuania, Norway and Sweden*. Available at: http://www.sedlabanki.is/lisalib/getfile.aspx?itemid=1207b563-c75f-11e1-b050-001ec9ed78b2 (last accessed 30 October 2014).

Calomiris, C. and Herring, R. (2011) *Why and How to Design a Contingent Convertible Debt Requirement*. Wharton School. Available at: http://fic.wharton.upenn.edu/fic/papers/11/11-41.pdf (accessed 17 July 2015).

Carmassi, J. and Herring, R. J. (2013) Living wills and cross-border resolution of systemically important banks. *Journal of Financial Economic Policy* 5(4): 361–387.

Carmassi, J. and Herring, R. J. (2014) *Corporate Structures, Transparency and Resolvability of Global Systemically Important Banks*. Available at: http://www.systemicriskcouncil. org/2015/01/new-paper-finds-little-progress-in-reducing-the-complexity-of-global-systemically-important-banks/ (last accessed 24 April 2015).

Chetwin, W. (2006) The Reserve Bank's local incorporation policy. *Reserve Bank of New Zealand Bulletin* 69(4): 12–21.

Commonwealth of Australia (2014) *Financial System Inquiry Final Report*, November. Available at: http://fsi.gov.au/files/2014/12/FSI_Final_Report_Consolidated20141210. pdf (last accessed 22 April 2015).

Conlon, T. and Cotter, J. (2014) *Anatomy of a Bail-In*. UCD Geary Institute, Discussion Paper Series, University College Dublin. Available at: http://dx.doi.org/10.2139/ssrn.2294100 (last accessed 17 July 2015).

Council of the European Union (2014) *Council Adopts Rules on Bank Recovery and Resolution*. Available at: http://www.consilium.europa.eu/uedocs/cms_data/docs/press-data/en/ecofin/142492.pdf (last accessed 30 October 2014).

Danske Bank (2012) *Danish Support Packages for the Financial and Corporate Sectors*. Available at: http://danskebank.com/da-dk/ir/Documents/Presentations/2012/201203-Danish-Support-Packages.pdf (last accessed 31 October 2014).

Davies, R. and Tracey, B. (2014) Too big to be efficient? The impact of too big to fail factors on scale economies for banks. *Journal of Money, Credit and Banking* 46(s1): 219–253.

Directive 2014/59/EU of the European Parliament and of the Council of 15 May 2014 establishing a framework for the recovery and resolution of credit institutions and investment firms and amending Council Directive 82/891/EEC, and Directives 2001/24/EC, 2002/47/ EC, 2004/25/EC, 2005/56/EC, 2007/36/EC, 2011/35/EU, 2012/30/EU and 2013/36/EU, and Regulations (EU) No 1093/2010 and (EU) No 648/2012, of the European Parliament and of the Council. Available at: http://eur-lex.europa.eu/legal-content/EN/TXT/?uri=uri serv:OJ.L_.2014.173.01.0190.01.ENG (last accessed 30 October 2014).

Dodd-Frank Act (2010) Available at: https://www.sec.gov/about/laws/wallstreetreform-cpa.pdf (last accessed 30 October 2014).

Eisenbeis, R. (2006) Agency problems and goal conflicts in achieving financial stability. In Mayes, D. and Wood, G. (eds) *The Structure of Financial Regulation*. Abingdon, UK: Routledge, pp. 232–256.

European Commission (2012) Commission staff working document on impact assessment accompanying the document proposal for a directive of the European Parliament and of the Council establishing a framework for the recovery and resolution of credit institutions and investment firms and amending Council Directives 77/91/EEC and 82/891/

EC, Directives 2001/24/EC, 2002/47/EC, 2004/25/EC, 2005/56/EC, 2007/36/EC and 2011/35/EC and Regulation (EU) No 1093/2010. Available at: http://ec.europa.eu/internal_market/bank/docs/crisis-management/2012_eu_framework/impact_ass_en.pdf (last accessed 31 October 2014).

European Commission (2014) *Proposal for a Regulation of the European Parliament and of the Council on Structural Measures Improving the Resilience of EU Credit Institutions.* Available at: http://eur-lex.europa.eu/legal-content/EN/TXT/?uri=CELEX: 52014PC0043 (last accessed 30 October 2014).

European Systemic Risk Board (2012) Response to the European Commission Consultation on a possible recovery and resolution framework for financial institutions other than banks. Available at: https://www.esrb.europa.eu/pub/pdf/other/121220_ESRB_response. pdf?9d06ec4d54865700b5eb3459c9486fbe (last accessed 22 January 2015).

Evanoff, D. and Kaufman, G. (2005) *Systemic Bank Crises: Resolving Large Bank Insolvencies.* Amsterdam, The Netherlands: Elsevier.

FDIC (2011) The orderly liquidation of Lehman Brothers Holdings Inc. under the Dodd-Frank Act. *FDIC Quarterly* 5(2): 1–19.

FDIC (2013) *Statement of James R. Wigand, Director, Office of Complex Financial Institutions on Improving Cross Border Resolution to Better Protect Taxpayers and the Economy to the Subcommittee on National Security and International Trade and Finance.* Speeches and Testimony. Available at: https://www.fdic.gov/news/news/ speeches/archives/2013/spmay1513_2.html (last accessed 30 October 2014).

FDIC (2014) *Statement by Vice Chairman Thomas M. Hoenig. Credibility of the 2013 Living Wills Submitted by First Wave Filers.* Available at: https://www.fdic.gov/news/ news/speeches/spaug0514a.pdf (last accessed 30 October 2014).

FDIC and the Bank of England (2012) *Resolving Globally Active, Systemically Important, Financial Institutions.* Joint paper. Available at: https://www.fdic.gov/about/srac/2012/ gsifi.pdf (last accessed 30 October 2014).

Financial Services (Banking Reform) Act (2013) Available at: http://www.legislation.gov. uk/ukpga/2013/33/contents/enacted (last accessed 31 October 2014).

Financial System Policy (2012) *Alternatives and Complements to OBR.* Available at: http://www.rbnz.govt.nz/regulation_and_supervision/banks/oia-obr/5229392.pdf (last accessed 30 October 2014).

FSB (2011) *Key Attributes of Effective Resolution Regimes for Financial Institutions.* Available at: http://www.financialstabilityboard.org/publications/r_111104cc.pdf (last accessed 30 October 2014).

FSB (2012) *Resolution of Systemically Important Financial Institutions Progress Report.* Available at: www.financialstabilityboard.org/publications/r_121031aa.pdf (last accessed 30 October 2014).

FSB (2014) *Key Attributes of Effective Resolution Regimes for Financial Institutions.* Available at: http://www.financialstabilityboard.org/publications/r_141015.pdf (last accessed 30 October 2014).

Gambacorta, L. and van Rixtel, A. (2013) *Structural Bank Regulation Initiatives: Approaches and Implications.* BIS Working Paper no. 412. Available at: http://www. bis.org/publ/work412.pdf (last accessed 17 July 2015).

Garcia, G. G. H. (2012) Missing the red flags. In Mayes, D. G. and Wood, G. E. (eds) *Improving the Governance of the Financial Sector.* Abingdon, UK: Routledge, chapter 10.

Goodhart, C. and Avgouleas, E. (2014) *A Critical Evaluation of Bail-Ins as Bank Recapitalisation Mechanisms.* Centre for Economic Policy Research. Discussion Paper 10065. Available at: http://papers.ssrn.com/sol3/papers.cfm?abstract_id=2478647 (last accessed 30 October 2014).

Gordon, J. N. and Ringe, W-G. (2014) *Bank Resolution in the European Banking Union: A Transatlantic Perspective on What It Would Take*. University of Oxford Legal Research Paper 18/2014. Available at: http://dx.doi.org/10.2139/ssrn.2361347 (last accessed 17 July 2015).

Hellwig, M. (2014) *Yes Virginia, There is a European Banking Union! But it May Not Make Your Wishes Come True*. Max Planck Institute for Research on Collective Goods, Bonn, Germany. Available at: http://www.coll.mpg.de. (last accessed 17 July 2015).

HLEG (2012) *High-Level Expert Group on Reforming the Structure of the EU Banking Sector*. Available at: http://ec.europa.eu/internal_market/bank/structural-reform/index_en.htm (last accessed 30 October 2014).

Hoskin, K. and Woolford, I. (2011) A primer on Open Bank Resolution. *Reserve Bank of New Zealand Bulletin* 74(3): 5–10. Available at: http://www.rbnz.govt.nz/research_and_publications/reserve_bank_bulletin/2011/2011sep74_3HoskinWoolford.pdf (last accessed 30 October 2014).

Hoskin, K. and Javier, N. (2013) Open Bank Resolution – the New Zealand response to a global challenge, *Reserve Bank of New Zealand Bulletin* 76 (1): 12–18. Available at: http://www.rbnz.govt.nz/research_and_publications/reserve_bank_bulletin/2013/2013mar76_1hoskinjavier.pdf (last accessed 30 October 2014).

Huertas, T. F. (2010) *Living Wills: How Can the Concept Be Implemented?* Speech at the Financial Services Authority. The full speech by Thomas F. Huertas can be read at: http://www.fsa.gov.uk/pages/Library/Communication/Speeches/2010/0212_th.shtml (last accessed 30 October 2014).

Hüpkes, E. (2013) Lines of defense against systemic crises: Resolution. In Caprio, G. and Bacchetta, P. *Handbook of Safeguarding Global Financial Stability Political, Social, Cultural, and Economic Theories and Models*. London, UK and Waltham, MA: Academic Press.

Lastra, R. M. (ed.) (2011) *Cross-Border Bank Insolvency*. New York: Oxford University Press.

Lee, A. (2013) *NZ's Open Bank Resolution: A New Option for Bank Reform?* Available at: http://www.iflr.com/Article/3196161/NZs-Open-Bank-Resolution-a-new-option-for-bank-reform.html (last accessed at 30 October 2014).

Lehmann, M. (2014) *Volcker Rule, Ring-Fencing or Separation of Bank Activities: Comparison of Structural Reform Acts Around the World*. LSE Law, Society and Economy Working Paper 25/2014. Available at: http://www.lse.ac.uk/collections/law/wps/WPS2014-25_Lehmann.pdf (last accessed 17 July 2015).

Lybeck, J. A. (forthcoming) *Bail-Out or Bail-In? Into Whose Hands Shall We Entrust Ailing Banks*? Cambridge, UK: Cambridge University Press.

Mayes, D. G. (2006) Financial stability in a world of cross-border banking: Nordic and Antipodean solutions to the problem of responsibility without power. *Journal of Banking Regulation* 8(1): 20–39.

Mayes, D. G. (2014a) Bank resolution in New Zealand and its implications for Europe. In Goodhart, C., Gabor, D., Vestegaard, J. and Erturk, I. (eds) *Central Banking at a Cross-Roads*. London, UK: Anthem Press, pp. 123–139.

Mayes, D. G. (2014b) *Top-Down Restructuring of Markets and Institutions: The Nordic Banking Crises*. Paper presented at the SAFE conference on Reorganisation and Resolution of Transnational Institutions, Bad Homburg, Germany, 10 October. Available at: http://safe-frankfurt.de/fileadmin/user_upload/editor_common/Events/TT_2014/David_G_Mayes_paper.pdf (last accessed 4 April 2015).

Moro, B. (2014) Lessons from the European economic and financial great crisis: A survey. *European Journal of Political Economy* 34(Supplement): S9–S24.

Pakin, N. (2013) The case against Dodd-Frank Act's living wills: Contingency planning following the financial crisis. *Berkeley Business Law Journal* 9(1): 29 – 93.

Regulation (EU) No 806/2014 of the European Parliament and of the Council establishing uniform rules and a uniform procedure for the resolution of credit institutions and certain investment firms in the framework of a Single Resolution Mechanism and a Single Resolution Fund and amending Regulation (EU) No 1093/2010. Available at: http://eur-lex.europa.eu/legal-content/EN/TXT/?uri=CELEX:32014R0806 (last accessed 30 October 2014).

RBNZ (2012) *Regulatory Impact Assessment of Pre-Positioning for Open Bank Resolution.* Available at: http://www.rbnz.govt.nz/regulation_and_supervision/banks/policy/5014272.pdf last accessed 20 October 2014).

RBNZ (2013) *Open Bank Resolution (OBR) Pre-Positioning Requirements Policy.* Prudential Supervision Department. Document BS17. Available at: http://www.rbnz.govt.nz/regulation_and_supervision/banks/banking_supervision_handbook/5341478.pdf (last accessed 30 October 2014).

RBNZ (2014) *Statement of Principles. Bank Registration and Supervision.* Prudential Supervision Department. Document BS1. Available at: http://www.rbnz.govt.nz/regulation_and_supervision/banks/banking_supervision_handbook/3272066.pdf (last accessed 17 July 2015).

Reserve Bank of Australia (2012) Developments in the financial system architecture. *Financial Stability Review.* Available at: http://www.rba.gov.au/publications/fsr/2012/mar/pdf/dev-fin-sys-arch.pdf (last accessed 30 October 2014).

Schmid, M. M. and Walter, I. (2009) Do financial conglomerates create or destroy economic value? *Journal of Financial Intermediation* 18(2): 193–216.

Schwartzkopff, F. (2012) *Danish Bail-In Trauma Consigned to History in Merger Wave.* Available at: http://www.bloomberg.com/news/2012-04-26/danish-bail-in-trauma-con-signed-to-history-in-merger-wave.html (last accessed 31 October 2014).

Scott, K. (2012) A guide to the resolution of failed financial institutions: Dodd-Frank Title II and proposed Chapter 14. In Jackson, T. H., Scott, K. E., Summe, K. A. and Taylor, J. B. *Resolution of Failed Financial Institutions: Orderly Liquidation Authority and a New Chapter 14.* Studies by the Resolution Project at Stanford University's Hoover Institution Working Group on Economic Policy, chapter 1. Available at: http://www.federalreserve.gov/SECRS/2011/June/20110620/OP-1418/OP-1418_061511_81311_5 44434921739_1.pdf (last accessed 30 October 2014).

The Independent Commission on Banking (2013) *The Vickers Report.* Available at: http://www.parliament.uk/business/publications/research/briefing-papers/SN06171.pdf (last accessed 31 October 2014).

4   The Cyprus debacle

Implications for the European banking union

Kate Phylaktis

The Cyprus levy plan has been described by some officials as a bleak day for banking union – the grand and unfinished project to shore up the Eurozone through a single supervision, resolution and deposit insurance system. The most immediate effect is on the credibility of the deposit insurance regime, that is the promise to protect savings under 100,000 Euro that the EU rushed through to build confidence after the 2008 crisis (*Financial Times*, 2013).

The events of March 2013 made Cyprus a household name around the world. The haircut of deposits in the country's two largest banks was unprecedented in conception and scale and had a huge impact on the island's economy. Such events can be traced back to market distortions and inefficiencies over a number of years and to various actions by many players, which created the collapse of the economy. The collapse is spectacular for an economy that withstood the impact of the Turkish invasion back in 1974, which displaced a large part of the population, and recovered to become a thriving economy again in subsequent years. Since its recovery from the Turkish invasion and up until the start of the crisis, the average rate of GDP growth had been four per cent and the unemployment rate 3.5 per cent.[1]

The purpose of this chapter is first to discuss the events of March 2013, second to put these events in a broader historical perspective, concentrating on the economic developments in Cyprus, especially those related to the banking sector, and finally, to discuss the crisis and its resolution in relation to the European banking union. The whole issue is multifaceted, but the emphasis of this chapter is on the banking sector.

The events of March 2013

In March 2013, after 30 years of uninterrupted economic prosperity on the island, economic growth came to an end. The problems, however, started much earlier. In May 2011 Cyprus was cut off from international markets. This marked the start of the Cyprus crisis. More than a year later, in June 2012, the government applied to the International Monetary Fund, European Commission and European Central Bank (IMF-EC-ECB, the 'troika') for assistance. Cyprus was unique in that it refused to finalise a memorandum of understanding (MoU) after it asked for assistance. In contrast, Spain, which also asked for assistance on the same day, completed its agreement three weeks later on 20 July 2012. Cyprus, on the other hand, agreed a programme 271 days afterwards, when a new government was elected.[2] This delay by the communist government to avoid short-term political cost before the election in February 2013 made the crisis deeper and the impact on the economy more severe.

It was only on 16 March 2013 that Nicos Anastasiades, the President of Cyprus, the newly elected right-wing government and the Eurozone finance ministers agreed a rescue plan, which would include the bail-in of uninsured and insured depositors in all Cypriot financial institutions. The bail-out Cyprus needed to cover government debt expiration, projected government deficits and financial system support was calculated to be €17 billion, out of which €7 billion was for the recapitalisation of the financial sector. The troika was willing to fund €10 billion, which was relatively big for the size of the economy (56 per cent of GDP in 2012).[3]

The troika's willingness to fund only €10 billion rested on two reasons. First, Germany and the other Eurozone finance ministers believed that a high proportion of the banking sector's deposits belonged to wealthy non-EU depositors, attracted to Cyprus by the high interest rates paid by the banks. Since these depositors had been receiving three to four per cent higher interest for a few years (inflation was also higher than in these other countries, implying that some of the differential was justified), it considered it justifiable for the depositors to contribute to the recapitalisation of the banks. Secondly, the IMF would not participate in a programme that would result in the debt of Cyprus becoming unsustainable. The Cyprus banking system was much larger than the country's GDP and was funded by depositors (€66.7 billion), which made up 71 per cent of the liabilities. Of the deposits, 40 per cent belonged to Cypriot residents, 34 per cent to non-residents domiciled in Cyprus, 19 per cent to residents from Greece, 2 per cent to residents from Russia and 5 per cent to the rest of the world (PIMCO, 2013).

Thus, Cyprus had to find the €7 billion needed for the banking sector from its own resources. The Cyprus government suggested plans, such as to have pension funds contributing to the funding gap, which would avoid the bail-in of depositors, but on 15 March it was made clear to the Cypriot delegation that only proposals where depositors would be affected would be considered.

Junior bond holders would lose €1.2 billion, but there was disagreement on how to raise the remaining €5.8 billion from the depositors. An agreement was reached on an across-the-board shares for deposits swap on all depositors of all banks, in order not to have a bail-in above ten per cent for any depositor. That implied that all Cypriot financial institutions were going to be affected. Depositors with over €100,000 would have 9.9 per cent of their deposits converted into shares of the troubled institutions that would have received their deposits in order to recapitalise. At the same time, insured depositors would have 6.75 per cent of their deposits similarly affected.

The Eurozone finance ministers immediately regretted their decision to bail in even insured depositors and the euro area was only saved embarrassment, because the bail-out was rejected by the Cypriot Parliament. However, the damage had been done that insured depositors were not safe. Small depositors should not expect to believe that their savings were safe from overnight taxes to avert bank collapse.

While a deal was being negotiated, the banks in Cyprus remained closed to avoid bank runs. The economy of Cyprus was transformed into a cash only exchange economy as no one was allowed to withdraw more than €300 a day from ATMs.[4] The banks opened again on 25 March after a 12-day banking holiday, when a deal was agreed with an increase of the bail-out amount from €17 billion to €20.6 billion to take account of the impact on the economy caused by the capital controls. Further capital controls had been imposed to prevent capital flight.[5] The new deal required Cyprus to bail in the uninsured depositors of the two largest banks on the island, Marfin-Laiki Bank and the Bank of Cyprus (BOC). It was decided not to close down either of them, but to restructure them instead. Marfin-Laiki's insured depositors would be transferred to the BOC, along with all the performing assets. The uninsured depositors of Marfin-Laiki were bailed in and would become the shareholders of 'bad Marfin-Laiki', which had an undisclosed amount of non-performing assets. In the process Marfin-Laiki shareholders and junior bondholders were wiped out.

The BOC would partially bail in uninsured depositors at an unknown percentage and take the insured depositors and good assets of Marfin-Laiki. The BOC board refused to sign and the bank was taken over by the Central Bank of Cyprus (CBC) who sacked the board. CBC initially cancelled all shareholders, but reversed its decision after the local courts put a halt to the proceedings, questioning the legality of cancelling existing property rights. The CBC responded by creating four categories of shares, placing the new, bailed-in shareholders in the first category, with junior bondholders and existing shareholders in lower categories. Several individual cases have been filed in the Supreme Court, as well as in the district courts, claiming that the bail-in is unconstitutional. Cyprus, as an ex British colony, has followed the British legal system and adopted the common law system, which respects property rights and protects minority shareholders.

The new deal also entailed the sale of Cypriot bank branches in Greece. The bank branches of all Cypriot banks, irrespective of whether they were in trouble, were to be sold to Piraeus Bank in Greece, by the order of the CBC. The deal was very bad. The CBC sold €16 billion of assets for a mere €0.525 billion, which was effectively funded by the Hellenic Financial Stability Fund. Cyprus had to recapitalise the Greek branch losses prior to the sale, which was estimated just for Marfin-Laiki to be €2.8 billion. Thus Cyprus was obliged to cover the liquidity gap created by the withdrawal of Greek deposits from Cypriot banks, despite being guaranteed on Greek assets, which were in any case sold. Marfin-Laiki executors refused to sign, so the CBC signed on their behalf.

The troika insisted on the sale of the Cypriot branches in Greece to cut off any channel of contagion to the rest of the euro area. Depositors in Greece avoided the bail-in, but at the same time Cypriot depositors were to be bailed in much more as a result.

Historical developments in Cyprus prior to the crisis

The bailout conditions above, together with an array of additional conditions to consolidate fiscal balances to enable Cyprus to service its loans, left Cyprus facing an unprecedented economic recession and a banking system in disarray. The European Commission estimated the cumulative fall of nominal GDP to be 15 per cent over 3 years, while the IMF suggested a fall of more than 12 per cent in 2013 alone. In this section I provide a background to the deterioration of the fiscal balances and the developments of the banking sector, which led to the twin fiscal and banking crises.

Public finances

Cyprus had historically sustained a fiscal deficit, which reached 6.5 per cent of GDP in 2003, while its public debt rose to 70 per cent of GDP following a major tax reform in 2003. However, in order to meet the criteria for entering the euro area, Cyprus adopted a policy of fiscal discipline, which resulted in reversing the deficit into a surplus of 3.5 per cent and reducing the debt to GDP ratio to 48.9 per cent by 2008. This improvement was, however, due to a tax amnesty and capital gains tax from real estate transactions, which were high due to the real estate bubble.[6]

In 2008 the new government, which was positioned politically to the extreme left, embarked on a spending spree, with rapid increases in social spending and government employees, which together with a fall in tax revenue resulted in cumulative deficits over the period 2009–2013 of about 30 per cent of 2013 GDP.[7] The generous increases in pensions and other retirement benefits, without taking steps to ensure their funding, generated serious sustainability concerns. The deterioration of fiscal imbalances eventually led to the government losing access to the international markets in May 2011.

The financial system

The problems of the banking sector had their roots in the protected environment of the past before Cyprus joined the European Union on 1 May 2004. Cyprus had a tightly controlled and profitable banking system, which supplied the economy with sufficient credit. It was stable and had not experienced any major crises in the commercial banking sector (apart from the co-operative sector crisis in the early 1980s). The allocation of credit was not however, optimal. Interest rate regulation encouraged lending on the basis of collateral value and personal guarantees.[8] Thus, credit went to sectors, where collateral was available. So Cyprus overinvested in real estate, which was amenable to collateral, and underinvested in machinery and equipment, which are important factors for economic growth. Personal loans took an increasing share of the credit. Cyprus's private sector credit as a percentage of GDP rose to 298 per cent in 2011, surpassed only briefly by Iceland in 2006.[9] Local institutions, not being able to compete on price, adopted non-price competition through the provision of quality of service and extended branch networks. They became inefficient, with little expertise in project appraisal and risk management, which were very important skills when the financial environment opened up with Cyprus's accession to the EU and the euro.

The integration of Cyprus into the euro area facilitated significant growth in professional services activity in Cyprus during the 2000s, which helped Cyprus to emerge as a leading regional provider of international banking services, along with related accounting, legal and other professional services. This was accompanied by rapid growth of foreign financial flows, which in turn led to substantial expansion of the balance sheets of Cypriot banks. Total assets of the Cyprus banking sector stood at €143 billion in March 2012, while the GDP was €17.8 billion (PIMCO, 2013). As a result, the banking system became far greater than the monetary authorities' ability to monitor and support it.

The substantial capital inflows financed Cyprus's current account deficit, which had deteriorated to an average of 10.5 per cent of GDP for the 5-year period prior to the crisis from an average of 5.7 per cent of GDP in the previous 10 years – making Cyprus vulnerable to a reversal of inflows at times of global uncertainty. This capital was not directed towards productive investments and continued to go into consumption and real estate investment. The result was the development of a property bubble especially in the period 2006–2008, which eventually burst with the global economic crisis.

The more open environment encouraged the banks to become more outwardly orientated institutions, expanding their operations in Greece and other countries. When the Greek economy ran into problems in 2009, it dealt a huge blow to the Cypriot banks' exposure in Greece. Holders of Greek government bonds sustained large losses through the private sector involvement (PSI). The Cypriot government did not attempt to ensure that the losses of the Cypriot banks would be accommodated, which amounted to €3.5 billion. Naively it was believed that the Eurozone finance ministers would not take kindly to the bailing out of banks, which speculated on such bonds. The restructuring of the Greek debt in October 2011 created a disproportionately large burden for the Cypriot banks relative to other member states in the euro area. The impact of PSI as a percentage of GDP was 23 per cent for Cyprus, compared to 18.28 per cent for Greece and 0.14 per cent for Germany.[10] The decision created an additional capital requirement of about 25 per cent of Cypriot GDP for the Cypriot banks. The banks had extra capital to cover 15 per cent of GDP. For the remainder, the banks, especially the second largest bank, Marfin-Laiki, needed temporary support from the sovereign. However, the sovereign could not provide that by issuing long-term public debt as it had lost market access. This was the beginning of the problems, which led to the crisis in March 2013.

The blow was magnified by the failure of the Cyprus government to act promptly to the oncoming crisis,[11] and the failure of the CBC to control the deteriorating financial position of the banks.

The Cyprus banking sector had total liabilities of about 800 per cent of GDP and was dominated by two banks, which were 'too big to fail' and 'too big to save'. At the same time, the Cyprus authorities did not realise the risks of running a big banking industry, paying insufficient attention to the fact that the banks were acting imprudently and how potential shocks may be handled. They gave low priority to monitoring banking risks and supervising the banks (Independent Commission on the Future of the Cyprus Banking Sector, 2013).

What insights does the Cyprus crisis hold for European banking union?

The European banking union has three pillars: the Single Supervisory Mechanism (SSM), bank resolution and deposit insurance. Some progress has been made with regard to SSM with the ECB beginning its role as a supervisory authority by starting an asset quality assessment review of European banks. However, progress has not been made with regard to the other two pillars in spite of proposals by the European Commission.

The Cyprus crisis brought to light two issues, which have implications for the formation of the European banking union, which need to be addressed. First, the EU banking sector has become interconnected as banks have found it easy to expand their operations across countries, so that problems in the banking sector of one country can spill over to other countries, making national banking supervision ineffective; and second, the link between the sovereign and banking risks, which increases the risk for a country to sustain a crisis.

Interconnected banking sector

Cypriot banks, having outgrown the Cyprus market, expanded to Greece and other countries. The two biggest banks had large exposures to both the Greek public and private sectors on their loan portfolios. According to S&P, total exposure to Greece of BOC and Marfin-Laiki was €30.4 billion, 168 per cent of GDP. It should be noted that both of these banks are domestic, implying that national authorities will bear the support in the event of a crisis.

The problems in the banking sector and generally in the economy of Greece highlighted how easy it is for problems to spill over to another country. In addition, it highlighted the difficulties that a national supervising authority will have in supervising its banks in such an environment, due to either inexperience or frictions between the central bank and the government (i.e. the Ministry of Finance). It seems that the national supervisory authority of Cyprus, the CBC, made several mistakes, actual or perceived, which either contributed to the crisis, or failed to stop it. The major mistake was to allow the banks to pay above market interest rates prevailing in the rest of the euro area, which attracted huge deposits and boosted the growth of the banking sector. The banks then invested the funds in high-yielding Greek bonds, which carried a zero-risk weight against capital for regulatory purposes, but which in reality were very risky. There was failure on the part of the Cyprus authorities (the Ministry of Finance and CBC) to understand the risks of running a banking sector, which was eight times the size of the economy.

As early as 2006 the IMF raised warning lights about Cyprus's inadequate financial sector supervision and regulation. It recommended an expansion of supervisory resources, an enhancement of supervision skills, supervision of banks' internal risk systems and models and a strengthening of cross-border supervision arising from bank expansion. The IMF recommended that the CBC should consider requiring banks to set formal limits for country risk (IMF, 2006).

However, the most controversial issue with regard to the crisis relates to the CBC's treatment of Marfin-Laiki and to governor, Panicos Demetriades's, policy of allowing Marfin-Laiki to stay operational by providing it with Emergency Liquidity Assistance (ELA) while the bank was insolvent. The CBC, with ECB agreement, had provided €9.8 billion of ELA by June 2012. The holes in the balance sheets of the Cypriot banks had, however, become obvious as far back as 2011 when the Greek sovereign debt was restructured. There is little doubt that Marfin-Laiki was insolvent by the end of 2012.[12] If that is the case, then the continued provision of ELA by the CBC was in violation of the ECB rule that an institution receiving ELA must be solvent. The governor supported his view by saying that he was expecting the government to agree a programme quickly.[13] As was mentioned earlier, an agreement was only signed when there was a change of government and after 271 days of approaching the European Commission for assistance.

Thus, the need for a single supervisor, not captured by local interests, is underlined. Had there been a supra-national supervision system the crisis might not have taken place. An SSM with the ECB at the centre and responsible for the health of all major banks, or indeed all banks including smaller ones within the EU, would have been able to intervene early on and perhaps not allow the high interest rates, which encouraged the growth of the banking sector.

Furthermore, had there been a Single Resolution Mechanism, which would govern the resolution tools to banks within the banking union, the crisis might not have been averted, but might have been less deep. The problems of the Cypriot banks became obvious in 2011 when the Greek sovereign debt was restructured but, given the political inertia of the Cyprus government to do something about it and the lack of resources to undertake any restructuring, the problems were not assessed until it was too late. Had there been a euro area wide resolution authority with the necessary powers and resources the intervention could have taken place earlier, with less economic costs. As it happened, the ECB was injecting money to keep insolvent banks alive, because the Cyprus government was unwilling to resolve the failing banks due to the forthcoming election.

The link between the sovereign and banking risks

The second insight that the Cyprus crisis has highlighted with regard to the establishment of a viable European banking union is the implications of the close ties between sovereign and banking risks. According to Angeloni and Wolff (2012), there was a high positive correlation between sovereign and bank credit default (CDS) during 2011 for a number of euro area countries, in both the periphery and stronger economies such as France and Germany.

Evidence shows that banks of the European periphery have been investing more heavily than before in domestic government bonds. The banks in the euro area have been doing that, because of the zero-risk weights for government bonds on their balance sheet within the EU. The proportion of sovereign debt that was held by the banks in the EU in the form of the country's own bonds was on average close to 60 per cent and has been particularly higher for banks of troubled sovereigns – Greece, Ireland, Spain, Portugal and Italy (Acharya *et al.*, 2012).

During a crisis this link between sovereign and bank solvency deepens as the economy falls into recession, worsening the government's fiscal balance and increasing sovereign risk, which in turn puts pressure on the balance sheets of banks that hold government bonds, but who also depend on the same government for possible recapitalisation.

This is exactly what happened in the case of Cyprus. In 2008, when the new government was elected and embarked on a spending spree, fiscal balances deteriorated and the debt to GDP ratio gradually increased from 48.9 per cent to 71 per cent by 2011. This led to a series of sovereign credit rating downgrades,[14] and, as a result, the Cyprus government lost access to the international markets in May 2011 and the ability to support the banks. This obliged the government to borrow short term, with the result that 71 per cent of total debt was maturing during the period 2013–2016. It should be noted that part of the short-term borrowing was through the use of Euro Medium Term Notes (EMTN) – €3.5 billion – which had a hard deadline and delays repaying it would have led to default. Thus, the newly elected government in February 2013 had no choice but to agree with the troika and the Eurozone finance ministers' programme.

The Cyprus case has highlighted another implication of the link between sovereign and banking solvency. It has shown that when the solvency of the sovereign is in doubt, depositors lose faith in a deposit insurance scheme and start withdrawing their deposits, thus defeating one of the main objectives of deposit insurance, which is to prevent bank runs. That was the idea behind the increase of deposit insurance limits across the EU to €100,000, following the global financial crisis. The lack of confidence can only be overcome by a euro area wide deposit scheme, whose credibility will depend on having the ability to cope with large-scale banking failures. National deposit insurance schemes are typically designed for idiosyncratic bank failures, not for systemic crises where public funding is required. The credibility of the public backing depends on whether the sovereign is solvent.

A unified deposit guarantee scheme will have many benefits. It will ensure that decisions that are taken at the supra-national level affect depositors in all countries in the same way. Thus, depositors would be treated in a uniform way across countries, independently of their location and the location of the bank with which they have entrusted their savings.

This issue of the link between sovereign and banking solvency needs to be addressed, because in the long term it increases the risks and the links between banks and sovereigns (Acharya *et al.*, 2012). This will put the currency union on a more sustainable footing.

Conclusion

The Cypriot crisis has underlined the need for a supra-national supervision system, a euro area wide resolution mechanism and for a euro area wide deposit insurance scheme. I have outlined what would have been different if these pillars of the European banking union had been in place.

One might say that the Cyprus crisis originated with the business model adopted for the banking system. The significant expansion of the Cypriot banking system and of the big domestically owned banks in particular, has been part of the broader objective of promoting the island as an international business centre, contributing to the growth of the financial services sector, to employment and GDP. The main problem was that the banking sector and the two biggest banks were too big for the economy, carried systemic risk and were domestically owned, requiring the support of the national authorities in times of crisis. The CBC failed to understand the importance of supervising and monitoring more closely such a big banking sector and its cross-border activities.[15] The sovereign failed to understand the importance of strong macroeconomic fundamentals when adopting such a model. In addition, party political considerations got in the way. As Beck *et al.* (2013) have shown, a large financial system might stimulate growth in the short term, but this comes at the expense of higher volatility. Furthermore, a recent study by Sahay *et al.* (2015) on the relationship between financial deepening and growth finds that when financial development proceeds too quickly, deepening financial institutions can lead to economic and financial instability as it encourages greater risk-taking and high leverage if poorly regulated and supervised.

Although there were many issues with the business model of the Cypriot banking sector, the banks' approach of pursuing deposit-funded balance sheets was the envy of many banks around the world after the Lehman Brothers collapse. The banks, realising that in times of crisis bond markets dry up leaving long-term lending commitments potentially unfunded, tried to boost deposits as their core funding mechanism. The drive has been underpinned by policymakers who have endorsed the push for deposits. In addition to the EU's pro-deposit stance, there has been a clear favouring of deposit funding by regulators around the world. The Basel Committee on Banking Supervision, which oversees global bank rules on liquid finance reserves, made it clear in January 2013 that it thought deposits were far less likely to flee in times of trouble than earlier drafts of the rules predicted, and as part of the Basel 3 package of reforms will require lenders to increase their highest-quality capital – such as equity and cash reserves – gradually from two per cent of the risky assets they hold to seven per cent by 2019.

The business model for the banking sector was already in place in 2004 when Cyprus joined the EU and in 2008 when it joined the euro. Had there been a European banking union along proposed lines in place during that time, there might have been greater scrutiny when Cyprus joined the EU and recommendations would have been made on how to put the banking sector on a better footing. European banking union has come too late for Cyprus.

Notes

1 For a historical overview of the Cyprus economy see Orphanides and Syrichas (2012).
2 The communist government secured a bilateral loan from the Russian government that allowed it to circumvent its inability to access markets and postpone meaningful negotiations until after the election of February 2013. This side-tracked attention from sorting out the deteriorating fiscal balances. The government even ignored the repeated ECB warnings about its fiscal imbalances.
3 For an account of the events in March 2013 see Apostolides (2013).
4 That implied that a Cypriot euro was not the same as a German or a Dutch euro, as they could not be freely exchanged via the banking system; a contradiction to the idea of a banking union.
5 The imposition of capital controls contravened the premise of free capital movement in the monetary union.
6 For a detailed review of the public finances see Zenios (2013).
7 It should be noted that in July 2011 there was an explosion, which destroyed the island's largest power station and half of its electricity supply with a catastrophic impact on the economy and the rate of unemployment, adding to the deteriorating economic situation.
8 See Phylaktis (1995) for a comprehensive history of the banking system in Cyprus from its inception in the nineteenth century to the mid-1990s; and Clerides (2014) for developments in more recent times.
9 World Bank Data.
10 Zenios (2013), which was based on calculations by the EBA.
11 For an account of the government's inertia to act promptly to the deteriorating banking situation, which aggravated the situation, see Orphanides (2014).
12 Although it is not easy to establish when Marfin-Laiki became insolvent, it seems that in response to a request for an opinion on the government's plan for recapitalising Marfin-Laiki, the ECB stated on 2 July 2012 that: 'the objectives pursued by the support measures may be better achieved through bank resolution tools'. See Clerides (2014).
13 According to Orphanides (2014), the governor explained the rationale for his decision in an interview on 26 March 2013 as follows: 'This was not something pleasant, but we had to sustain the bank. It was required to sustain the bank in order for the elections to take place, a new government to come to power, take its decisions, reach an agreement with our European partners, to avoid bankruptcy of the bank and the state'.
14 S&P downgraded Cyprus from A in March 2011 to CCC in 2013.
15 Several studies at the time raised these issues. See Stephanou (2011a, 2011b).

References

Acharya, V., Drechsler, I. and Schnabl, P. (2012) *A Tale of Two Overhangs: The Nexus of Financial Sector and Sovereign Risks*. 15 April. Available at: http://www.voxeu.org/article/tale-two-overhangs-nexus-financial-sector-and-sovereign-credit-risks (last accessed 19 July 2015).
Angeloni, C. and Wolff, G. B. (2012) *Are Banks Affected By Their Holdings of Government Debt?* Bruegel Working Paper 2012/07. Available at: http://www.bruegel.org/publications/publication-detail/publication/717-are-banks-affected-by-their-holdings-of-government-debt/ (last accessed 19 July 2015).
Apostolides, A. (2013) Beware of German gifts near elections: How Cyprus got here and why it is currently more out than in. *Capital Markets Law Journal* 8(3): 300–318.

Beck, T., Degryse, H. and Kneer, C. (2013) Is more finance better? Disentangling inter-mediation and size effects of financial systems. *Journal of Financial Stability* 10(C): 50–64.

Clerides, S. (2014) The collapse of the Cypriot banking system: A bird's eye view. *Cyprus Economic Review* 8(2): 3–45.

Financial Times (2013) 18 March. Available at: http://www.ft.com/intl/cms/s/0/16fbd550-8ff9-11e2-9239-00144feabdc0.html#axzz3gJoV5B5G (last accessed 19 July 2015).

IMF (2006) *Cyprus Assessment of Financial Supervision, Including Reports of the Observance of Standards and Codes on the Following Topics: Banking Supervision, Insurance Supervision and Securities Regulation.* IMF Country Report, October. Available at: http://www.imf.org/External/Pubs/FT/SCR/2006/cr06347.PDF (last accessed 19 July 2015).

Independent Commission on the Future of the Cyprus Banking Sector (2013) *Final Report and Recommendations.* Available at: http://www.icfcbs.org/wp-content/uploads/2013/10/ICFCBS-Final-Report.pdf (last accessed 27 May 2015).

Orphanides, A. (2014) *What Happened in Cyprus? The Economic Consequences of the Last Communist Government in Europe.* 2014 FMG Special Paper 232. Available at: http://www.lse.ac.uk/fmg/workingPapers/specialPapers/PDF/SP232-Final.pdf (last accessed 19 July 2015).

Orphanides, A. and Syrichas, G. (eds) (2012) *The Cyprus Economy: Historical Review, Prospects and Challenges.* Nicosia, Cyprus: CBC.

Phylaktis, K. (1995) *The Banking System of Cyprus: Past, Present and Future.* Basingstoke, UK: Macmillan.

PIMCO (2013) *Independent Due Diligence of the Banking System of Cyprus.* Available at: http://ftalphaville.ft.com/files/2013/04/reportasws.pdf.pdf (last accessed 27 May 2015).

Sahay, R., Čihák, M., N'Diaye, P., Barajas, A., Bi, R., Ayala, D., Gao, Y., Kyobe, A., Nguyen, L., Saborowski, C., Svirydzenka, K. and Yousefi, S. (2015) *Rethinking Financial Deepening: Stability and Growth in Emerging Markets.* IMF Staff Discussion Paper, May. Available at: http://www.imf.org/external/pubs/ft/sdn/2015/sdn1508.pdf (last accessed 27 May 2015).

Stephanou, C. (2011a) Big banks in small countries: The case of Cyprus. *Cyprus Economic Policy Review* 5(1): 3–21.

Stephanou, C. (2011b) The banking system of Cyprus: Time to rethink the business model. *Cyprus Economic Policy Review* 5(2): 123–130.

Zenios, S. A. (2013) The Cyprus crisis and a way forward. *Cyprus Economic Policy Review* 7(1): 3–13.

5 Euro area bank resolution and bail-in

Intervention, triggers and writedowns

Thomas Conlon and John Cotter[1]

The global financial crisis and subsequent European sovereign debt crisis have yielded strong evidence for the dangerous links between bank failure and sovereign distress. Historically, a persistent increase in government debt has been shown to be a consequence of banking crises (Reinhart and Rogoff, 2013). In an attempt to sever the link between banks and the sovereign, the EU has introduced a formal framework of procedures to deal with bank resolution. Under this framework, banks on the precipice of failure may be subject to resolution, with investors suffering writedowns before public funds may be called upon. The aim of this study is to examine retrospectively the implications of the resolution framework for euro area banks and their creditors during the global financial crisis.

The Bank Resolution and Recovery directive (BRRD) has been introduced to provide a consistent set of rules surrounding bank failure in the 28 countries of the EU. In this chapter we focus on the Single Resolution Mechanism (SRM), the means by which the BRRD will be implemented in euro area countries. In order to understand the scale of the problem for euro area banks during the crisis, we first detail the level of impairments realised due to losses over the period 2008–2012. Under the SRM guidelines, these losses would have been applied to investors, motivating our examination of the balance sheet liabilities of euro area banks with particular focus on the largest systemically important institutions. In this context, we then retrospectively apply the bail-in[2] rules mandated by the EU to euro area banks during the crisis and examine their impact on differing bank creditors.[3] Finally, given the somewhat subjective nature of the resolution triggers mandated under the European resolution framework, we examine the benefits of a range of market- and balance sheet-based resolution triggers.

Our findings are generally supportive of the resolution framework. Total impairment charges for euro area banks over the period 2008 to 2012 are measured at €621 billion. In our retrospective analysis, we make the assumption that bail-in is applied to all banks and examine the impact this would have had on banks of different sizes and listed banks. Our findings suggest that equity holders would have been the most impacted by bail-in, especially for the largest 30 banks accounting for 81 per cent of total euro area bank assets. However, additional conversion to equity for subordinated and senior debt investors would have been required to ensure banks were adequately capitalised post bail-in. Depositors would not have required bail-in for any of the institutions examined. We conclude the study by examining a range of market- and balance sheet-based triggers for resolution, but find weak evidence in support of quantitative resolution triggers.

Many of the previous studies considering the European framework for bank resolution have primarily focused on the legislative details or potential structure of the policy (Kudrna, 2012; Dermine, 2013; Ignatowski and Korte, 2014). Others have outlined the commonalities between the resolution methodologies adopted during this crisis and previous crises (Mayes, 2009a, 2009b). Zhou *et al.* (2012) considered potential benefits and risks concerning implementation of a bail-in mechanism. Schoenmaker and Siegmann (2013) simulated the impact of national coordination of bank bail-outs on the efficiency of the resolution, finding maximum efficiency for a supranational approach. In the context of U.S. bank resolution legislation, Ignatowski and Korte (2014) developed a framework to test the impact of recent regulatory changes on banking risk. Our chapter differs in many ways from the extant literature on banking resolution, applying the resolution framework retrospectively to euro area banks. While Conlon and Cotter (2014) also examine the impact of the European resolution framework, the current study focuses only on euro area banks governed by the SRM. Moreover, additional novel contributions to the literature on bank resolution are provided here, such as the consideration of the bail-in mechanism for the largest systemically important banks, listed versus unlisted institutions and an examination of potential resolution triggers.[4] The focus on large systemically important financial institutions (SIFIs) is of particular value to regulators, as it informs the potential outcome of SRM resolution during a period of severe market stress.

A large literature documents the propensity of fundamental and accounting-based data to predict banking failure. Techniques employed by these early warning models vary considerably, but tend to focus either on prediction of systemic crisis events in countries or failure of specific banks (Davis and Karim, 2008). Betz *et al.* (2014) use a combination of macro-economic and micro bank specific variables to predict distress in individual European banks, while Poghosyan and Cihak (2011) identify a set of indicators predicting European bank failure over the period 1990 to 2008. Various studies have attempted to improve the ability of early warning models to predict banking distress by incorporating market information (Flannery, 1998; Evanoff and Wall, 2001; Sironi, 2003; Gropp *et al.*, 2006). In particular, evidence that equity market information may be of value in predicting bank distress has been well documented (Krainer, 2004; Distinguin *et al.*, 2006; Curry *et al.*, 2008). In this chapter we contribute to the literature on bank resolution by examining, in a univariate framework, whether equity and fundamental information could act as a trigger for bank resolution. The addition of a quantitative trigger to the framework on bank resolution and recovery might help provide market participants with further clarity in light of the somewhat subjective nature of the proposed resolution triggers.

The next section outlines the forthcoming European framework for bank resolution. The data used in the empirical analysis are described in the section that follows. Empirical results relating to writedowns, bail-in and resolution triggers are then detailed. The final section provides some concluding remarks.

European bank resolution

Throughout the global financial crisis, many euro area banks required public intervention in the form of bail-outs to avert potential failure and associated financial disruption. The approaches adopted in the implementation of bail-outs varied substantially across jurisdictions, perhaps contributing to contagion and financial turmoil. Common across many bail-outs was a considerable level of state support.[5] To reduce the social and economic costs associated with bail-outs and to mitigate the dangers of financial contagion, the European Commission has introduced a common bank resolution policy. The process of resolution refers to the restructuring of a bank that is failing or likely to fail by a resolution authority. The BRRD provides a set of comprehensive arrangements to deal with failing or failed banks at a national level, in addition to a set of supranational rules to resolve cross-border banking failures. The SRM complements the BRRD by setting out the architecture for applying the BRRD in member states participating in the banking union. In contrast, the BRRD provides rules for the whole EU single market. Although this study only applies the SRM to euro area banks, both the SRM and BRRD are detailed here as the SRM is contingent on a number of facets of the BRRD.

The EU BRRD

The BRRD came into force on 1 January 2015, apart from rules on creditor write-downs which are due to take effect from 1 January 2016 (The European Parliament and the Council of the European Union, 2014). The key pillars of the BRRD are preparation and prevention, early intervention, resolution and cooperation, and coordination. The primary aims of resolution, as listed by the directive, are to:

- safeguard the continuity of essential banking services;
- protect depositors, client assets and public funds;
- minimise risks to financial stability;
- avoid the unnecessary destruction of value.

Some consequences of the BRRD are that banks and authorities will need to prepare recovery and resolution plans for a variety of scenarios, supervisors will be given the means to intervene in troubled banks at a sufficiently early stage and coordinated resolution tools will be available to national authorities.

The directive further lists the following range of circumstances, which would lead to the triggering of a resolution for an individual institution:

- if it has reached a point of distress such that there are no realistic prospects of recovery over an appropriate timeframe;
- if all other private sector or supervisory intervention measures have proved insufficient to restore the bank to viability;
- if winding up the institution under normal insolvency procedures would risk prolonged uncertainty or financial instability and, therefore, resolving the bank would be better from a public interest perspective.

In order to achieve the aforementioned objectives, the resolution authorities will have a range of tools available to them. These include facilitating private sector acquisitions, transferring institutions to a temporary bridge bank, separation into a 'good' and 'bad' bank and, finally, bail-in of creditors.

This final bail-in option refers to the ability to recapitalise a bank through the writedown of liabilities and/or their conversion to equity, thus allowing the bank to continue as a going concern. By following the process of bail-in, the authority should be able to avoid, or at least minimise, the requirement for public funds in stabilising a financial institution. The process of bail-in should result in equity investors being wiped out or diluted and management replaced. Moreover, should circumstances dictate, authorities will further have powers to impose a writedown or conversion to equity of liabilities held by higher-ranked creditors.

Under the BRRD, bail-in will apply to any bank liability not backed by assets or collateral. Exclusions from bail-in include short-term inter-bank lending (under seven days), client assets, salaries, taxes and pensions. Moreover, deposits protected by a deposit guarantee scheme will not be bailed in, but the guarantee scheme will be liable to assume corresponding losses. Exceptionally, authorities may choose to exempt other liabilities from bail-in to prevent financial disruption or contagion. Bail-in is to be applied to liabilities in order of capital structure ranking, with equity absorbing losses in full before any debt liabilities may be written down. Once equity is completely written down, holders of subordinated debt and then senior debt holders will be bailed in. Finally, deposits from natural persons and SMEs (including those over €100,000) are to be preferred over senior creditors. To assure the credibility of the BRRD framework, the regulator will prescribe that banks hold a certain level of securities not excluded from bail-in.

The BRRD bail-in rules will apply to all outstanding and newly issued securities from 1 January 2016. Individual member states may also choose to apply the tool prior to 2016.

The SRM

The BRRD provides guidelines to deal with distressed banks at a national level across all 28 EU countries, in addition to provisions to resolve cross-country bank failures. The SRM was introduced by the European Council in order to ensure that member states that share the same currency or are supervised by the same bank regulator, the European Central Bank (ECB), adhere to the same resolution policy (Howarth and Quaglia, 2014). Moreover, negative perceptions about individual member states' ability to withstand large banking failures could amplify potential financial contagion between banks and the sovereign. An SRM will help to sever the negative relationship between individual countries and banks, limiting taxpayer exposure. The legal basis for the SRM regulation is Article 114 of the Treaty on the Functioning of the European Union (The European Parliament and the Council of the European Union, 2008). Under the terms of the SRM, decisions regarding resolution will be made by a Single Resolution Board (SRB), which will apply the single rulebook on bank resolution provided for in the BRRD.⁶ The SRM regulation further establishes a Single Resolution Fund (SRF), to be financed by contributions from the banking sector. Once established, the SRB will be responsible for resolution decisions surrounding about 6,000 banks in participating member states.

Decisions relating to the determination of whether an institution is failing or is likely to fail will be the responsibility of the regulator, the ECB. The SRB further retains the discretion to adjudge an institution as failing or having the potential to fail and may request information from the ECB. The target size of the SRF will equal one per cent of all covered deposits in banks in participating member states, or about €55 billion based on 2011 balance sheets. The objective of the SRM is to achieve resolution without recourse to taxpayers in individual member states. While the SRB is responsible for decisions relating to which banks are to be resolved, the national resolution authorities retain responsibility for implementation of resolution actions.

Under the SRM, entities shall be deemed to be failing or likely to fail if any of the following conditions hold (The European Commission, 2014):

- the entity infringes or there are objective elements to support a determination that the institution will, in the near future, infringe the requirements for continuing authorisation in a way that would justify the withdrawal of authorisation by the ECB, including but not limited to the fact that the institution has incurred or is likely to incur losses that will deplete all or a significant amount of its own funds;
- the assets of the entity are, or there are objective elements to support a determination that the assets of the entity will, in the near future, be less than its liabilities;
- the entity is, or there are objective elements to support a determination that the entity will, in the near future, be unable to pay its debts or other liabilities as they fall due;
- extraordinary public financial support is required except where, in order to remedy a serious disturbance in the economy of a member state and preserve financial stability, that extraordinary public financial support takes any of the following forms:

  i   a state guarantee to back liquidity facilities provided by central banks in accordance with the central banks' conditions;
  ii   a state guarantee of newly issued liabilities;
  iii an injection of own funds or purchase of capital instruments at prices and on terms that do not confer an advantage upon the entity.

While the SRM provides for bail-in of institutions, national regulatory authorities shall decide on and implement any bail-in, if the SRB mandates resolution. The order of priority of claims to be written down is to be in accordance with the BRRD. As with the BRRD, the relevant deposit guarantee scheme will be responsible for losses that would have been imposed on guaranteed depositors. Next, we turn our attention to the data used in the analysis and the empirical results relating to impairments, bail-ins and triggers.

Data

Fundamental accounting data relating to European banks is sourced from Bankscope for the period 2006 to 2012. The dataset covers the largest 12 euro area countries for which banks fall under the supervision of the ECB under the single supervisory mechanism (SSM). The specific countries included are Austria, Belgium, Finland, France, Germany, Greece, Ireland, Italy, Luxembourg, Netherlands, Portugal and Spain. Bankscope provides data on both listed and unlisted banks, resulting in a total of 701 banks.

In selecting the data, banks at the highest level of the business were selected, often resulting in the holding company level. This ensures no double counting, removing multiple aggregation across both holding and subsidiary institutions. An additional selection criterion, to ensure banks are deposit-taking, excludes banks with a deposit to total asset ratio of less than 20 per cent (Beltratti and Stulz, 2012).

Market-related data for each listed bank is obtained from Datastream, a division of Thompson-Reuters. Using the monthly market prices of each listed bank, returns, total volatility, idiosyncratic volatility and systematic risk are calculated for 2006, 2007 and 2008. Surviving banks, nationalised banks and banks requiring government capital are identified by drawing on a number of official and published sources, (Goddard *et al.*, 2009; Petrovic and Tutsch, 2009; Laeven and Valencia, 2010; Molyneux *et al.*, 2014).

Empirical results

Writedowns

The global financial crisis was the largest single catastrophe to hit banks worldwide since at least the 1930s. In Europe, the crisis resulted in public bail-outs of banks in a majority of jurisdictions. These bail-outs took various forms, including capital injections and nationalisation.[7] To get some perspective on the potential size of losses experienced by euro area banks (those that will come under the supervision of the ECB under the SSM), we examine total impairment charges experienced by banks in the period 2008 to 2012. To calculate impairments, we aggregate loan writedowns and non-recurring expenses for each euro area bank. Total impairment charges for euro area banks over the period 2008 to 2012 are measured at €621 billion.

Figure 5.1 details the total impairment changes for each euro area country over the period 2008–2012. While Spain was not at the epicentre of public bail-outs during the primary crisis years of 2007 to 2009, the total impairment charges experienced by Spanish banks were nominally the largest in the euro area. Moreover,

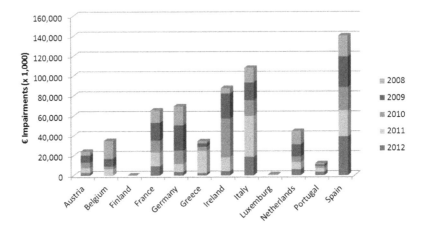

Figure 5.1 Euro area bank impairment charges by country and year (2008–2012).

Source: All data is sourced from Bankscope and stated in thousands of euros.

Notes
Total euro area bank impairment charges are calculated from 2008 to 2012 and broken out by country and year. Total realised impairments are calculated as the sum of loan writedowns and non-recurring expenses.

these losses were distributed relatively uniformly by year. Italian banks had total impairments of €108 billion. Irish banks had the next largest writedowns over the sample, with the majority of impairments accounted for in the years 2009 and 2010.[8] German, French and Dutch banks further experienced large impairments, while aggregate impairments in the remaining countries were limited to €35 billion.

Total euro area impairment charges are further broken out by year and bank status in Figure 5.2. Banks requiring public injections of capital accounted for the majority of impairments during the years 2008–2012. However, losses experienced by surviving banks are also found to be a large proportion of total losses. Finally, while the number of nationalised banks was small, impairments experienced by these institutions were non-negligible. In summary, we have shown that losses experienced by euro area banks over the global crisis were large and distributed across the majority of countries. We later use these impairments as a benchmark when testing the retrospective performance of the SRM bail-in framework.

Euro area bank balance sheet

Table 5.1 details a cumulative proportional bank balance sheet calculated for banks from all 12 euro area countries examined for the years 2006 to 2008. For

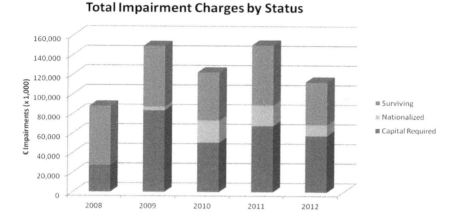

Figure 5.2 Euro area bank impairment charges by bank status (2008–2012).

Source: All data is sourced from Bankscope and stated in thousands of euros.

Notes

Total euro area bank impairment charges are calculated from 2008 to 2012 and categorised as surviving, government capital required and nationalised. Total realised impairments are calculated as the sum of loan writedowns and non-recurring expenses.

each year, the cumulative balance sheet is presented for banks requiring government recapitalisation, nationalised banks, banks surviving without recapitalisation, the largest 20 banks by total assets and all banks. Considering first the pre-crisis period of 2006, we see that nationalised banks had smaller proportions of equity (3.1 per cent) than all other classifications. Moreover, the top 20 banks had lower equity than average, likely related to their 'too big to fail' status. Surviving banks tended to use a larger proportion of customer deposits in their funding and a smaller amount of less sticky bank deposits. Contrasting the levels of long-term debt, nationalised banks are the largest outlier using senior debt to fund 33.8 per cent of their balance sheet, more than double that of all other classifications.

Similar analysis is performed for 2007 and 2008, but it is worth noting that balance sheets may, by this time, have become impacted by difficult funding conditions. With the exception of nationalised banks from 2006 to 2007, the proportion of equity held by banks dropped year on year. Considering customer deposits, little change is observed for most bank classifications from 2006 to 2008, with the exception of nationalised banks where customer deposits dropped from 25.3 per cent to 19.4 per cent. This drop in deposits for nationalised banks is largely accounted for by falls in current deposits, with some of these funds replaced by a corresponding increase in term deposits. Moreover, nationalised banks increased

Table 5.1 Cumulative liabilities from euro area bank balance sheets (2006–2008)

Liability Type	2008					2007					2006				
	Capital	Nat.	Surv.	All	Top 20 banks	Capital	Nat.	Surv.	All	Top 20 banks	Capital	Nat.	Surv.	All	Top 20 banks
Total customer deposits	29.1	19.4	35.8	32.0	27.7	29.6	20.1	36.1	32.3	28.8	29.9	25.3	37.1	33.2	30.2
Deposits – current	14.6	5.9	16.0	14.9	12.6	14.7	6.5	18.0	15.9	13.4	16.3	18.1	17.1	16.7	15.2
Deposits – savings	5.9	0.9	6.9	6.2	5.8	6.4	0.9	6.8	6.4	5.8	7.0	1.7	9.4	8.0	8.1
Deposits – term	8.6	12.7	12.9	10.9	9.3	8.5	12.7	11.3	10.0	9.5	7.7	6.2	10.7	9.1	7.8
Deposits from banks	16.7	25.5	10.1	13.8	12.8	18.5	22.4	12.2	15.7	14.8	18.8	19.5	13.1	16.0	15.2
Total long-term debt	13.9	33.4	18.3	16.8	15.6	16.5	32.9	19.5	18.7	17.5	18.0	35.4	21.1	20.1	18.8
Senior debt	11.2	31.2	14.0	13.3	12.6	13.8	30.9	16.3	15.8	14.9	15.6	33.8	16.5	16.6	15.1
Subordinated debt	1.5	1.5	1.3	1.4	1.4	1.5	1.8	1.5	1.5	1.4	1.4	1.6	1.5	1.4	1.4
Other funding	1.2	0.8	3.0	2.1	1.6	1.2	0.1	1.7	1.4	1.2	2.4	0.0	4.6	3.4	3.9
Other liabilities (Derivatives, non-interest, repos etc.)	37.3	20.3	31.2	33.7	41.0	31.4	20.4	27.0	28.8	35.2	29.3	16.7	24.1	26.4	32.4
Derivatives	15.1	6.4	15.7	15.0	19.9	7.6	3.3	8.1	7.7	10.2	6.2	2.4	6.6	6.3	8.5
Total liabilities	97.0	98.6	95.4	96.3	97.0	96.0	95.7	94.8	95.4	96.3	95.7	96.9	94.8	95.3	96.1
Total equity	3.0	1.4	4.6	3.7	3.0	4.0	4.3	5.2	4.6	3.7	4.3	3.1	5.2	4.7	3.9

Notes

A cumulative euro area bank balance sheet is determined by summing all liabilities. Proportions (detailed in percentage terms) are then found as a percentage of total balance sheet liabilities for each year from 2006 to 2008. Banks are categorised as: 'Capital' – bank required government re-capitalisation; 'Nat.' – bank was nationalised by government; 'Surv.' – survived without assistance from government; 'All' – all banks; 'Top 20 banks' – cumulative balance sheet for 20 largest banks. Banks are included from 12 euro area countries listed in the data section of this chapter. Other liabilities include derivatives, non-interest, repos and trading liabilities.

their proportion of deposits from banks from 19.5 per cent to 25.5 per cent, probably as a consequence of government underwriting. The proportion of long-term debt used by banks is found to have decreased over time for all banks. Finally, the proportion of liabilities accounted for by derivatives, non-interest liabilities and repos, among others, are noted to have increased substantially over time. This is predominantly driven by an increase in the proportion of derivatives, which increased from 6.3 per cent of balance sheet liabilities for all banks in 2006 to 15 per cent in 2008.

Large banks account for a substantial proportion of total bank assets. For example, the largest 20 banks accounted for 71.1 per cent of all bank assets in the euro area during 2006. Given their systemic importance, we examine the funding position of the largest 20 banks in isolation. Across all years, the equity held by the top 20 banks is lower than the average level. The proportion of customer deposits, bank deposits and long-term debt held by these institutions is also smaller than average. This suggests that, under a potential bail-in, these banks would have less available resources for the purposes of bail-in than the average euro area bank, a result that is borne out in our later analysis. Finally, the proportion of derivatives on the balance sheet of the top 20 banks is larger than the average. Given the less than clear position regarding derivatives in the BRRD, large banks holding derivatives accounting for an extensive proportion of total liabilities may be of concern to regulators. Moreover, the smaller quantities of liabilities available for bail-in in these large banks may impact the credibility of the resolution framework. Given the funding background detailed, we next consider the application of bail-in to euro area banks according to asset size.

Bail-in – a retrospective analysis

We now investigate a retrospective application of the bail-in tool provided for in the BRRD and SRM. To arrive at a required level of bail-in for each bank, the impairment charges accounted for over the period 2008–2012 are taken as the baseline losses experienced.[9] In each case, we determine the proportion of each balance sheet liability required to be written down in order to cover actual losses experienced. The aggregate level of writedown and equity conversion required to achieve the 3 per cent leverage ratio mandated under the Basel III accord is also calculated.[10]

The analysis is presented for writedowns and equity conversions relating to bank balance sheets from 2006, although little qualitative variation in results is found for 2007 or 2008. The order in which bail-in is applied is structured in the same manner as that mandated by the BRRD. Importantly, this requires senior debt to be written down prior to any losses being imposed on depositors, which would not have been possible in all countries during the crisis.[11] One restriction on our analysis is the paucity of information relating to the proportion of balance sheet liabilities backed by assets or collateral.[12]

The first analysis, shown in Table 5.2, considers the proportion of balance sheet liabilities required for bail-in according to bank size. Previously, governments found themselves taking responsibility for liabilities of very large banks that were a significant proportion of GDP. As this ultimately impacted the sovereign, it is vital to understand the impact of bail-in on banks that are systemically important. Considering the largest 10 banks, we note that these account for 51 per cent of total euro area bank assets in 2006. Under the bail-in rules, the total impairments experienced by these banks would have required writedowns of 80.4 per cent of book equity, with no impact on subordinated or senior debt. The next 10 largest banks account for 20 per cent of all euro area bank assets and would have required a writedown of equity amounting to 52.2 per cent. Similar results are found for the next ten banks, accounting for ten per cent of total assets. These findings for large banks are reassuring, suggesting that writedowns associated with bail-in for the largest European banks would not have any impact on depositors or long-term debt holders.

Considering the size cohorts, only banks ranked from 30 to 50 would have required writedowns of subordinated or senior debt on aggregate. Losses in these two cohorts are dominated by Irish bank, Anglo Irish Bank, and Greek banks, Eurobank Ergasias SA and Alpha Bank AE. Considering smaller banks, those outside the top 50 only account for 10.7 per cent of all assets. In all cases, writedowns would have been confined to equity holders. For the very smallest banks examined, impairments were limited, even relative to book equity. Table 5.2 also details the levels of writedowns and equity conversion required to achieve a leverage ratio of three per cent post bail-in.[13] For the largest ten euro area banks, 19.57 per cent of equity would have remained after writedowns. The remaining equity requirement would have come from full conversion of subordinated debt into equity, in addition to a conversion of 3.76 per cent of senior debt. Across the 50 largest euro area banks, at least some proportion of subordinated debt would have been converted into equity. The largest proportion of senior debt that would have required conversion is 15.26 per cent, well below the level of depositors. For the smallest banks, no equity conversion would have been required, as these maintained high levels of equity capital prior to the crisis.

Large numbers of small, unlisted banks exist in Europe, which account for a minority of total bank assets. In Table 5.3 we apply the bail-in rules to listed and unlisted European banks in turn. While only 62 of the 701 euro area banks considered are listed, they account for 64.5 per cent of all assets. Moreover, the total proportion of writedowns required to cover losses was 4.32 per cent of total liabilities and equity, compared to 1.65 per cent for unlisted banks.

We further split the results into banks that survived, those that were nationalised and those that required government capital. Considering listed banks, equity would have been completely written down for surviving and nationalised banks. Moreover, 7.64 per cent of subordinated debt would have been written down for surviving banks and 100 per cent for nationalised banks. Finally, listed nationalised banks would also have required a modest writedown of senior debt. For unlisted banks, the situation is less severe, as only the three nationalised unlisted banks would have required writedowns of subordinated debt or equity.

To achieve a three per cent leverage ratio, listed banks would have required all subordinated debt to be either written down or converted to equity across all

Table 5.2 Retrospective bail-in writedowns and equity conversion by bank size for euro area banks

Ranking	Prop. total bank assets	Total liab. and equity	Writedown only			Equity conversion			Total writedown and equity conversion	
			Total equity writedown	Subord. debt writedown	Senior debt writedown	Equity remaining after writedown	Subord. debt conversion	Senior debt conversion	Subord. debt total	Senior debt total
1–10	51.13	3.03	80.43	0	0	19.57	100.00	3.76	100.00	3.76
11–20	19.99	2.16	52.24	0	0	47.76	51.91	0	51.91	0
21–30	10.07	4.55	69.37	0	0	30.63	30.56	0	30.56	0
31–40	5.02	9.22	100.00	100.00	6.66	0	0	15.26	100.00	21.92
41–50	3.06	6.15	100.00	57.53	0	0	42.47	4.94	100.00	4.94
51–70	3.00	4.98	68.62	0	0	31.38	0	0	0	0
71–100	2.14	1.97	17.93	0	0	82.07	0	0	0	0
101–150	1.89	1.51	17.36	0	0	82.64	0	0	0	0
151–200	1.16	1.78	27.47	0	0	72.53	0	0	0	0
201+	2.53	0.64	9.56	0	0	90.44	0	0	0	0

Notes

This table retrospectively measures the proportion of writedown losses and equity conversion that would have been imposed on liability holders of banks in the event of bail-in. Bail-in proportions (detailed in percentage terms) are calculated for banks ranked and aggregated according to asset size. Bank balance sheets from 2006 are used as the basis for the bail-in analysis. Bail-in costs are calculated using total realised impairment charges, calculated as the sum of loan writedowns and non-recurring expenses between 2008 and 2012. Equity conversion assumes a required three per cent leverage ratio post resolution. For each liability type, the proportion of remaining equity after writedowns and the proportion of subordinated and senior debt to be converted to equity are calculated. The data comprise euro area banks from 12 countries, which are covered by the EU bank resolution framework.

Table 5.3 Retrospective bail-in writedowns and equity conversion for listed and unlisted euro area banks

Status	No. banks	Prop. total bank assets	Total liab. and equity	Writedown only			Equity conversion			Total writedown and equity conversion	
				Total equity writedown	Subord. debt writedown	Senior debt writedown	Equity remaining after writedown	Subord. debt conversion	Senior debt conversion	Subord. debt total	Senior debt total
Listed Banks											
All	62	64.5	4.32	97.95	0	0	2.05	100.00	5.95	100	5.95
Surviving	25	37.6	4.79	100.00	7.64	0	0	92.36	4.78	100	4.78
Capital	32	57.7	3.6	82.20	0	0	17.80	100.00	3.89	100	3.89
Nationalised	5	4.7	9.66	100.00	100.00	15.71	0	0	7.01	100	22.72
Unlisted Banks											
All	639	35.5	1.65	31.16	0	0	68.84	100	0	100	0
Surviving	611	62.1	1.51	25.32	0	0	74.68	100	0	100	0
Capital	25	36.8	1.61	38.75	0	0	61.25	100	0	100	0
Nationalised	3	1.1	11.03	100.00	100.00	11.73	0	0	5.39	100	17.12

Notes

This table retrospectively measures the proportion of losses that would have been experienced by liability holders of banks in the event of bail-in both for listed and unlisted banks. Bank balance sheets from 2006 are used as the basis for the bail-in analysis. Bail-in costs are calculated using total realised impairment charges, calculated as the sum of loan writedowns and non-recurring expenses between 2008 and 2012. Equity conversion assumes a required three per cent leverage ratio post resolution. For each liability type, the proportion of remaining equity after writedowns and the proportion of subordinated and senior debt to be converted to equity are calculated. The data comprises euro area banks from 12 countries, which are covered by the EU bank resolution framework.

classifications. Moreover, a small proportion of senior debt would have been converted to equity for surviving and recapitalised banks. For nationalised banks, 7.01 per cent of senior debt would have been converted in addition to the 15.71 per cent of senior debt written down. While this is a comparatively large proportion, it suggests that bail-in would have protected depositors even for banks with the largest losses. In the case of unlisted banks, the slight impact of equity conversion would have been limited to the small number of recapitalised and nationalised banks. In summary, our results show that bail-in writedowns would largely have been imposed on equity investors. In particular, the largest systemically important banks would have required equity writedowns exclusively in order to cover impairments. Some debt to equity conversion would have additionally been required to ensure solvency post bail-in. However, writedowns experienced by listed banks are found to be large relative to equity held, in some cases resulting in writedowns of senior and subordinated debt. These results are primarily driven by a small number of banks which experienced very heavy losses, both relative to their size and to the GDP of their domiciled state. These include Fortis Bank, Anglo Irish Bank, Permanent TSB, Hypo Real Estate, EBS Building Society and Irish Nationwide Building Society. Common to all analysis detailed is an absence of writedowns imposed on depositors even after equity conversion requirements, fulfilling one of the main objectives of the BRRD.

Bail-in triggers

Under the framework provided by the BRRD and SRM, the triggers for bank resolution may be viewed as somewhat subjective. Troubled banks are deemed to be failing or likely to fail if they are expected to infringe the requirements for authorisation, if the assets are likely to be less than liabilities, if they are likely not to be able to meet debt repayments or if public intervention is required. However, the lack of a single definitive trigger or set of triggers could result in uncertainty, potentially leading to a spiral of doubt surrounding an institution or unnecessary resolution. In the retrospective study of bail-in outlined, we have considered the actual bail-out of banks as the trigger. We next investigate a range of potential quantitative market and balance sheet triggers to determine characteristic differences between failed and surviving banks.[14] Market-based triggers are forward-looking, capturing the markets perception of a bank's position. Balance sheet triggers are backward-looking, revealing the reported financial position of the bank. Each of these has been extensively linked in the literature to the prediction of future banking distress and failure (Distinguin *et al.*, 2006; Männasoo and Mayes, 2009; Betz *et al.*, 2014). Market-based triggers are considered in Table 5.4 for listed European banks.

Four different equity-related triggers are contrasted for bailed-out and surviving banks, namely equity returns, total volatility, systematic risk and idiosyncratic risk.[15] Equity returns, which are not risk adjusted, reveal small significant differences between failed and surviving banks until 2008, by which time the crisis had already manifested. Bailed-out banks had higher equity volatility or total risk

Table 5.4 Bail-in analysis – market triggers

Year	Bailed out	Surviving	Difference	t-value	p-value	Number bailed out	Number surviving
Equity Return							
2006	0.312	0.325	-0.013	-0.24	0.815	22	20
2007	-0.041	0.019	-0.061	-1.32	0.196	24	21
2008	-0.682	-0.378	-0.304	-4.71	0.000	24	21
Equity volatility							
2006	0.193	0.155	0.038	2.04	0.048	22	21
2007	0.184	0.181	0.003	0.13	0.900	24	21
2008	0.596	0.390	0.206	2.55	0.016	24	21
Equity systematic risk							
2006	0.873	1.121	-0.248	-1.25	0.219	22	21
2007	0.896	0.530	0.366	2.40	0.021	24	21
2008	1.308	0.910	0.398	2.15	0.038	24	21
Idiosyncratic risk							
2006	0.170	0.118	0.052	3.09	0.004	22	20
2007	0.134	0.164	-0.029	-1.31	0.200	22	21
2008	0.400	0.250	0.150	2.07	0.048	24	21

Notes

The potential of market-based triggers to indicate potential bail-in requirement is examined retrospectively in the case of euro area banks. Equity returns are calculated as the average monthly return and total volatility as the standard deviation of monthly returns. Systematic risk is measured using a market model, $r_i = \alpha_i + \beta r_m + \varepsilon_{i}$, where β gives the systematic or market risk and the average value of the squared residual, ε_{i}^2, measures idiosyncratic or firm specific risk. A difference-in-means test is performed for failed and surviving banks before and including the global financial crisis period. The Satterthwaite approximation for the standard errors is applied, which does not assume equal variances of the two samples.

during 2006, but consistent evidence is not found during 2007. Systematic risk for bailed-out banks is greater during 2007, but not significantly so different during 2006. Finally, considering idiosyncratic risk, bailed-out banks were significantly riskier during 2006, but not during 2007. While some specific evidence concerning the ability of market-based triggers to differentiate between failed and surviving banks is provided, the inconsistency of results over time suggest they may be unsuitable as definitive triggers of resolution.

We next examine the ability of balance sheet-based triggers to differentiate between failed and surviving banks before and during the global financial crisis. Table 5.5 details changes in a range of balance sheet fundamentals. For instance, the total book equity of bailed-out banks increased by 20.3 per cent between 2005 and 2006, while that of surviving banks increased by 9.1 per cent. During 2006, only subordinated debt, total equity and total liabilities and equity were found to be significantly different between surviving and failed banks.[16] A number of significant differences between surviving and failed banks are found during 2007, including total liabilities, total deposits, senior debt, subordinated debt and customer deposits, with no significant differences in total equity. Increases in total equity during 2006 are likely the result of retained earnings, a consequence of profitability, and would be unlikely to act as a sensible trigger. Restricted access to subordinated debt markets may be an indicator of financial troubles. However, our findings suggest that failed banks actually increased their proportions of subordinated debt, while surviving banks decreased their dependence, counter to our intuition. Similar findings are shown for customer deposits and bank deposits, with failed banks increasing their dependence on each of these by more than their surviving counterparts. Thus, failed banks did not experience difficulties in raising funds from depositors. Considering the other metrics detailed, little evidence of significant differences between failed and surviving banks emerges.

A paucity of viable information regarding liquidity and asset quality for banks during the global financial crisis led to investors withdrawing funding when banks were most in need. With the introduction of creditor bail-in, investors may be forced to withdraw funding from institutions perceived to be in difficulty. The current resolution triggers provide little guidance regarding the metrics that regulators will apply in order to trigger bail-in. To provide investor clarity and prevent safe institutions from suffering liquidity crises, a defined quantitative trigger would help prevent a withdrawal of funding from banks not suffering distress. However, our univariate findings demonstrate the difficulties involved in identifying appropriate triggers.[17] While weak evidence exists for the ability of equity market-based triggers to differentiate between failed and surviving banks, the evidence for balance sheet triggers is not intuitive in the sample of euro area banks examined. These findings do not altogether preclude the application of early warning type models in triggering resolution, as regulators would likely have access to better, more detailed and up-to-date information than may be garnered from historic balance sheets.

It is important to note that our findings, while providing little evidence as to the benefits of quantitative triggers, do not rule out the use of contingent liabilities. For example, a number of banks have begun to introduce contingent convertibles,

Table 5.5 Bail-in analysis – balance sheet triggers

Year	Bailed out	Surviving	Difference	t-value	p-value	Number bailed out	Number surviving
Total liabilities							
2006	0.363	0.050	0.313	1.270	0.210	63	631
2007	0.134	0.061	0.073	2.700	0.009	64	636
2008	0.055	0.067	−0.012	−0.860	0.395	65	636
Total deposits, money market and short-term funding							
2006	0.480	0.036	0.445	1.160	0.253	63	631
2007	0.204	0.062	0.142	2.640	0.010	64	636
2008	0.077	0.077	0.000	0.000	0.996	65	635
Senior debt							
2006	1.115	2.863	−1.748	−0.840	0.403	55	94
2007	0.538	0.021	0.518	1.770	0.081	60	100
2008	−0.002	0.024	−0.026	−0.260	0.797	58	92
Subordinated debt							
2006	0.156	−0.063	0.219	2.970	0.004	56	385
2007	0.180	−0.108	0.287	4.560	0.000	58	371
2008	5.063	−0.021	0.084	0.800	0.427	60	340
Total long-term funding							
2006	1.201	0.571	0.630	1.020	0.311	62	552
2007	0.436	0.284	0.152	0.500	0.619	64	558
2008	0.122	−0.016	0.138	0.960	0.341	65	551

Customer deposits

2006	0.542	0.050	0.492	1.180	0.242	62	626
2007	0.148	0.064	0.084	3.550	0.000	64	634
2008	0.040	0.074	−0.034	−1.660	0.099	65	635

Bank deposits

2006	0.327	0.104	0.223	0.950	0.347	61	623
2007	0.349	0.191	0.158	0.990	0.324	63	630
2008	0.266	0.199	0.068	0.060	0.553	64	629

Total equity

2006	0.203	0.091	0.112	1.150	0.041	63	631
2007	0.116	0.068	0.049	0.850	0.398	64	636
2008	−0.225	0.032	−0.257	−7.770	0.000	65	636

Total liabilities and equity

2006	0.201	0.053	0.148	1.890	0.063	63	631
2007	0.124	0.061	0.063	2.350	0.022	64	636
2008	0.031	0.063	−0.032	−2.410	0.018	65	636

Notes

The potential of balance sheet based triggers to indicate potential bail-in requirement is examined retrospectively in the case of euro area banks. A difference-in-means test is performed for failed and surviving banks before and including the global financial crisis period. The Satterthwaite approximation for the standard errors is applied, which does not assume equal variances of the two samples.

securities which are convertible into equity if a pre-specified trigger occurs. For some securities issued, the triggers have been backward-looking accounting and fundamental measures such as capital ratios (Glasserman and Nouri, 2012). Forward-looking market-based triggers may be more appropriate, easing the dangers of market manipulation or conversion errors (Sundaresan and Wang, 2015). Moreover, by incorporating securities providing for bail-in directly into the capital structure of banks, market participants have clear guidance before providing capital to institutions.

Concluding remarks

This chapter contributes to the literature by considering the retrospective application of the recent European rules on banking resolution. Specifically, we focus on how resolution under the SRM would have impacted euro area banks during the global financial crisis. Our results indicate that euro area banks experienced total impairment charges of €621 billion over the period 2008 to 2012. Had the bail-in mechanism been in place during this period, these losses would have been primarily imposed on equity investors. For the largest, systemically important financial institutions, bail-in writedowns would have exclusively applied to equity investors. However, to ensure adequate capitalisation post bail-in, the majority of large, listed banks would have required conversion to equity for all subordinated and some senior debt creditors. Depositors would not have required bail-in under any of the analyses detailed, fulfilling one of the major objectives of the BRRD.

We augment the retrospective analysis of bail-in for European banks with further analysis of resolution triggers. While a variety of studies have detailed the importance of market-related information in predicting bank failure, this is the first study to examine their importance in the context of triggering bank resolution via bail-in. While our findings suggest some differentiation between the triggers considered for failed and surviving banks, the evidence is somewhat weak. This demonstrates the difficulty in mandating specific quantitative triggers of bank resolution and is supportive of the more subjective approaches outlined in the BRRD and SRM.

Notes

1   The authors acknowledge the financial support of Science Foundation Ireland under Grant Number 08/SRC/FM1389. We are grateful to Juan Castañeda, Giannoula Karamichailidou, David Mayes, Geoffrey Wood, the discussant Alessandro Roselli and participants at the European Banking Union: Prospects and Challenges conference (University of Buckingham, 21–22 November 2014) for helpful and informative comments.
2   Bail-in refers to recapitalisation of banks through the mandatory writedown of liabilities or, alternatively, the conversion of liabilities to equity.
3   For an outline of developments in European banking over recent decades, see Goddard *et al.* (2007).
4   Moreover, the BRRD and SRM frameworks have been finalised since the publication of Conlon and Cotter (2014) and findings here, especially those regarding the treatment of senior debt holders and depositors, reflect this.

5 Some examples of banks requiring substantial public support during the crisis include Anglo Irish Bank, nationalised by the Irish government on 15 January 2009, Fortis Bank, formerly one of the largest financial institutions in the world, but partially nationalised by the Belgian, Dutch and Luxembourg governments on 28 September 2008, and Hypo Real Estate, fully nationalised by the German state on 5 October 2009.

6 In other non-participating countries, the BRRD will be applied by national resolution authorities. For example, in the UK the Prudential Regulation Authority has proposed changes to their rules to implement the BRRD.

7 Moreover, other forms of bail-out including guaranteed debt issuance took place in numerous states. This ubiquitous form of bail-out is not considered in this study.

8 The timing here corresponds largely to the transfer of impaired assets from banks to the Irish 'bad bank', the National Asset Management Agency.

9 It is important to note that definitions of loan impairment are heterogeneous throughout the EU, and there has been a move to a more harmonised definition, which may result in an increase in impaired assets. However, Conlon and Cotter (2014) perform stress tests, which demonstrate that depositors would not have been impacted by writedowns, even for much larger levels of impairments. We are grateful to our discussant, Alessandro Roselli, for pointing out this issue.

10 Without further information regarding which assets were written down, accurate estimation of other risk-weighted capital requirements, such as tier 1 capital to risk-weighted assets, is problematic.

11 It is worth noting that this nuance would not have impacted our results, as depositors would not have required bail-in based on the realised impairment charges from 2008 to 2012.

12 The results detailed suggest that senior creditors would have been little impacted, negating somewhat the importance of information regarding collateral or asset-backed liabilities.

13 It is possible that resolution authorities would have mandated a higher leverage ratio than three per cent for bailed-in banks in order to reassure markets, but no details regarding this are suggested in the BRRD or SRM.

14 Banks requiring nationalisation and public capital injections are both considered as failed in the analysis to follow.

15 Equity returns are calculated as the average monthly return and total volatility as the standard deviation of monthly returns. Systematic risk is measured using a market model, $r_i = \alpha_i + \beta r_m + \varepsilon_i$, where β gives the systematic or market risk and the average value of the squared residual, εi^2, measures idiosyncratic or firm specific risk.

16 While large differences are evident between bailed-out and surviving banks for characteristics such as total liabilities, total deposits, money market and short-term funding, senior debt and customer deposits, the differences were not found to be significant once the Satterthwaite approximation, accounting for unequal variances in the standard errors, was applied.

17 Moreover, given the weak results using univariate models, it is less than likely that multivariate models would glean any additional information.

References

Beltratti, A. and Stulz, R. M. (2012) The credit crisis around the globe: Why did some banks perform better? *Journal of Financial Economics* 105(1): 1–17.

Betz, F., Opric, S., Peltonen, T. A. and Sarlin, P. (2014) Predicting distress in European banks. *Journal of Banking & Finance* 45(August): 225–241.

Conlon, T. and Cotter, J. (2014) Anatomy of a bail-in. *Journal of Financial Stability* 15: 257–263.

Curry, T. J., Fissel, G. S. and Hanweck, G. A. (2008) Equity market information, bank holding company risk, and market discipline. *Journal of Banking & Finance* 32(5): 807–819.

Davis, E. and Karim, D. (2008) Comparing early warning systems for banking crises. *Journal of Financial Stability* 4(2): 89–120.

Dermine, J. (2013) Bank regulations after the global financial crisis: Good intentions and unintended evil. *European Financial Management* 19(4): 658–674.

Distinguin, I., Rous, P. and Tarazi, A. (2006) Market discipline and the use of stock market data to predict bank financial distress. *Journal of Financial Services Research* 30(2): 151–176.

Evanoff, D. D. and Wall, L. D. (2001) Sub-debt yield spreads as bank risk measures. *Journal of Financial Services Research* 20(2/3): 121–145.

Flannery, M. J. (1998) Using market information in prudential bank supervision: A review of the U.S. empirical evidence. *Journal of Money, Credit and Banking* 30(3): 273–305.

Glasserman, P. and Nouri, B. (2012) Contingent capital with a capital-ratio trigger. *Management Science* 58(10): 1816–1833.

Goddard, J., Molyneux, P. and Wilson, J. O. S. (2009) The financial crisis in Europe: Evolution, policy responses and lessons for the future. *Journal of Financial Regulation and Compliance* 17(4): 362–380.

Goddard, J., Molyneux, P., Wilson, J. O. S. and Tavakoli, M. (2007) European banking: An overview. *Journal of Banking & Finance* 31(7): 1911–1935.

Gropp, R., Vesala, J. and Vulpes, G. (2006) Equity and bond market signals as leading indicators of bank fragility. *Journal of Money, Credit and Banking* 38(2): 399–428.

Howarth, D. and Quaglia, L. (2014) The steep road to European banking union: Constructing the Single Resolution Mechanism. *Journal of Common Market Studies* 52(Special issue: The JCMS annual review of the European Union in 2013): 125–140.

Ignatowski, M. and Korte, J. (2014) Wishful thinking or effective threat? Tightening bank resolution regimes and bank risk-taking. *Journal of Financial Stability* 15: 264–281.

Krainer, J. (2004) Incorporating equity market information into supervisory monitoring models. *Journal of Money, Credit and Banking* 36(6): 1043–1067.

Kudrna, Z. (2012) Cross-border resolution of failed banks in the European Union after the crisis: Business as usual. *Journal of Common Market Studies* 50(2): 283–299.

Laeven, L. and Valencia, F. (2010) *Resolution of Banking Crises: The Good, the Bad, and the Ugly*. IMF Working Paper, WP/10/146. Available at: https://www.imf.org/external/pubs/ft/wp/2010/wp10146.pdf (last accessed 19 July 2015).

Männasoo, K. and Mayes, D. (2009) Explaining bank distress in Eastern European transition economies. *Journal of Banking & Finance* 33(2): 244–253.

Mayes, D. G. (2009a) Banking crisis resolution policy – different country experiences. *Norges Bank Staff Memo no. 10*. Available at: http://static.norges-bank.no/Pages/77285/Staff_memo_09_10.pdf (last accessed 19 July 2015).

Mayes, D. G. (2009b) Did recent experience of a financial crisis help in coping with the current financial turmoil? The case of the Nordic countries. *Journal of Common Market Studies* 47(5): 997–1015.

Molyneux, P., Schaeck, K. and Zhou, T. M. (2014) Too systemically important to fail in banking – evidence from bank mergers and acquisitions. *Journal of International Money and Finance* 49(B): 258–282.

Petrovic, A. and Tutsch, R. (2009) *National Rescue Measures in Response to the Current Financial Crisis*. ECB Legal Working Paper Series, 8. Available at: https://www.ecb.europa.eu/pub/pdf/scplps/ecblwp8.pdf (last accessed 19 July 2015).

Poghosyan, T. and Cihak, M. (2011) Determinants of bank distress in Europe: Evidence from a new data set. *Journal of Financial Services Research* 40(3): 163–184.

Reinhart, C. M. and Rogoff, K. S. (2013) Banking crises: An equal opportunity menace. *Journal of Banking & Finance* 37(11): 4557–4573.

Schoenmaker, D. and Siegmann, A. (2013) Can European bank bailouts work? *Journal of Banking & Finance* 48(November): 334–349.

Sironi, A. (2003) Testing for market discipline in the European banking industry: Evidence from subordinated debt issues. *Journal of Money, Credit and Banking* 35(3): 443–472.

Sundaresan, S. and Wang, Z. (2015) On the design of contingent capital with market trigger. *Journal of Finance* 70(2): 881–920.

The European Commission (2014) Regulation of the European Parliament and the Council establishing uniform rules and a uniform procedure for the resolution of credit institutions and certain investment firms in the framework of a Single Resolution Mechanism and a Single Resolution Fund. *Official Journal of the European Union*. Available at: http://eur-lex.europa.eu/legal-content/EN/TXT/PDF/?uri=OJ:L:2014:225:FULL&from=EN (last accessed 19 July 2015).

The European Parliament and the Council of the European Union (2008) Consolidated versions of the Treaty on European Union and the Treaty on the Functioning of the European Union. *Official Journal of the European Union*. Available at: http://eur-lex.europa.eu/legal-content/EN/TXT/PDF/?uri=CELEX:12012E/TXT&from=EN (last accessed 19 July 2015).

The European Parliament and the Council of the European Union (2014) EU Directive establishing a framework for the recovery and resolution of credit institutions and investment firms. *Official Journal of the European Union* 173/190. Available at: http://eur-lex.europa.eu/legal-content/EN/TXT/PDF/?uri=CELEX:32014L0059&from=EN (last accessed 19 July 2015).

Zhou, J., Rutledge, V., Bossu, W., Dobler, M., Jassaud, N. and Moore, M. (2012) From bail-out to bail-in: Mandatory debt restructuring of systemic financial institutions. *IMF Staff Discussion Note* SDN/12/03. Available at: http://www.imf.org/external/pubs/ft/sdn/2012/sdn1203.pdf (last accessed 19 July 2015).

Comment

Alessandro Roselli

The chapter by Thomas Conlon and John Cotter is an elegant contribution and is supportive of the idea that, in a very difficult crisis such as the one experienced recently, which is, in a way, still with us, bail-in provisions may be a valid alternative to taxpayer money in dealing with distressed banks.

In short, according to the authors, rather than having spent a huge amount of public money for nationalisation or recapitalisation of European banks in the period 2008–2012, the entire bank losses might have been covered by shareholders and, to a limited extent, by investors in some debt instruments. Depositors would have remained unscathed, even for the part exceeding the national guarantee schemes. The authors' exercise has been carried out in a counterfactual way: what would have happened if bail-ins could have been activated during the crisis, using the actual bail-outs as triggers?

With reference to triggers, the authors complain about the subjective character of the triggers as specified in the Bank Recovery and Resolution Directive (BRRD), but add that the adoption of triggers based on objective, quantitative data (related to banks' market performance or balance sheet) would rest on weak evidence.

Reasons for bail-ins and scope of their application

The introduction of bail-ins for troubled institutions following the global financial crisis is not necessarily related to the sovereign issue. There is indeed a strong correlation between banking and sovereign solvency crises in Europe, but outside Europe the adoption of bail-in provisions is generally linked to the moral hazard issue and the consequent need to make bank creditors/investors less 'relaxed' in their monitoring of financial institutions of systemic importance. For instance, in the US, the Orderly Liquidation Authority regime, introduced by the Dodd-Frank Act, makes bail-ins possible in the case of creditors of financial companies of systemic relevance (so-called SIFIs), without the US having experienced the 'doom loop' banks/sovereigns we are witnessing in Europe. Similarly, the Financial Stability Board (2014) in its recent consultation paper on the subject, deals with a: 'total bank loss-absorbing capacity–TLAC', for: 'global systemically important banks–GSIBs', regardless of the origin of the distress. It is in Europe that the case for bail-ins does not need the systemic risk scare connected to the 'moral hazard'. The recovery and resolution procedure, including bail-ins, is envisaged any time a public interest issue arises as the alternative to the ordinary liquidation of the institution. This would imply, in principle, a more extended, and more severe, use of bail-ins. In this last regard, it should be noted that according to the BRRD shareholders and eligible creditors have to absorb their bank's losses for not less than eight per cent of total liabilities, a provision that seems not to exist elsewhere.

Total impairment charges over the 2008–2012 period

In the chapter Italian bank impairments appear as the third highest, after Spain and Ireland. The issue of the high level of Italian impairments has been discussed elsewhere, but it is worthwhile remembering that:

1   The definitions of loan impairment within the EU are highly heterogeneous and only very recently, in 2014, have they been harmonised. The definition adopted in Italy was particularly wide. In recent years, Italian banks have requested higher guarantees from their borrowers and reduced the loan-to-value ratio. According to that definition, impaired assets are assessed on the basis of the borrower's creditworthiness, even if the exposure is fully guaranteed. If guaranteed positions were excluded, the stock of impaired assets would be much lower, by 32 per cent, according to some calculations (see Gualandri, 2013).
2   In Italy judicial procedures are notoriously long, and banks tend to set aside bigger amounts in view of that; consequently, the NPL/total loans ratio is structurally high.

Moving to the new harmonised definition implies a substantial increase of impairments for European banks in general, but a minor one for Italian ones. On the basis of the new definition, as the Bank of Italy (2014) observes, the stock of impaired assets at the end of 2013 would increase by 7.4 per cent for European banks in general and only by 0.2 per cent for the Italian ones. By taking into account also the analysis carried out in relation to the asset quality review, asset impairments have been adjusted upwards by 18.3 per cent for EU banks in general, and by 9.6 per cent for Italian institutions (see Table 5.6).

Impairments and government interventions

Starting from a solid balance sheet position, the Italian banking system has faced the global financial crisis, the instability of the sovereign market and two important recessions without a meaningful recourse to public bail-out. There has been a huge discrepancy in Italy between the amounts of impairments and government interventions in banking crises. Interventions have been drastically lower in Italy than in other European countries. As reported by the Bank of Italy (2014), according to Eurostat (2014), at the end of 2013 state aid to the financial sector

Table 5.6 Prudential reclassifications of positions from performing to non-performing exposures

(billions of euro and basis points in terms of RWA)

	Stock of non-performing exposures (end-2013 nat. definition)	New non-performing exposures						Stock of non-performing exposures (based on the AQR)	
		Portion owing to new harmonized definition		Portion owing to asset analysis		Total			
	billions	billions	basis points	billions	basis points	billions	basis points	billions	percentage change on 2013
SSM banks	743	55	81	81	120	136	201	879	18.3
Italian banks	198	0.4	4	18.6	194	19	198	217	9.6

Source: ECB, *Aggregate Report on the Comprehensive Assessment*, October 2014.
(reproduced from Banca d'Italia *Financial Stability Report*, no. 2, 2014, p. 27 with permission.)

amounted to €250bn in Germany, almost €60bn in Spain, around €50bn in Ireland and the Netherlands and more than €40bn in Greece. In Italy the support was around €4bn, of which €3bn was repaid in 2014 (see Figure 5.3; the lines show the amount of support and the bars show the impact of the support on GDP).[1]

It might be interesting if the authors were to show the breakdown of impairments by country as shown in Figure 5.1 – a huge difference between impairments and government expenditure in troubled institutions would appear for Italy. Impairments have been high in Italy, but have been covered almost entirely by the banks' balance sheets, without substantial support from the state.

Counter-factuality of the exercise

The 'what if' analyses are widespread in economics and are gaining increasing popularity in economic history. However, they have to rely heavily on deterministic assumptions ('other things being equal'), and tend to neglect that societies, and economic and financial systems, are more related to the dynamics of chaos.

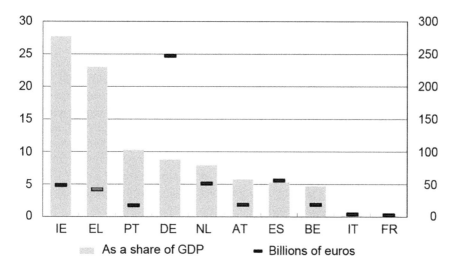

Figure 5.3 Impact of public support to national financial systems on government liabilities (left-hand scale %, right-hand scale €bn).

Source: Eurostat, *Eurostat Supplementary Tables for the Financial Crisis: Background Note*, October 2014.

Note
Data shown are collected by Eurostat according to its decision of 15 July 2009 (further clarified in 2012 and 2013) on 'The statistical recording of public interventions to support financial institutions and financial markets during the financial crisis'. They include liabilities of entities that have been reclassified into general government, and of newly established government defeasance structures. Contingent liabilities (mainly government guarantees on financial institutions' assets and liabilities) are not included.

(reprinted from Banca d'Italia, *Financial Stability Report*, no. 2, 2014, Figure 3.5, p. 31, with permission.)

A change in initial conditions can lead to different outcomes. In our case, what if bail-in enactment clauses, or simple announcements or triggers provoke sudden shifts in investment preferences, such as a sell off of hybrid securities or a shift of interbank deposits at potentially troubled institutions, as examples of instruments that might be affected? Bail-ins might deepen the crisis, multiply losses, increase the costs involved and perhaps expand the haircuts to customers' deposits. Disclosure requirements for banks with regard to the amount, maturity and composition of securities used to absorb potential losses (as mentioned in Financial Stability Board, 2014) are, on the one hand, relevant for market discipline, but, on the other, may generate unwanted consequences in terms of market reactions to a perceived inadequacy of what is set aside as a 'buffer'.

According to the authors the losses of the period in question would have wiped out around 80 per cent of the equity of the main banks (ranked 1–10). This may be far from a tranquillising outcome. After having witnessed the panic of the past few years, with the states that had to guarantee bondholders and depositors, it is difficult to think that in a future crisis one may just look at the bail-ins doing their own job. Realistically, states will again have to extend guarantees to depositors and senior bondholders.

Aggregate versus individual calculations

The authors detail a cumulative balance sheet for Eurozone banks. The breakdown in Table 5.2 is by asset ranking of banks and its findings are necessarily related to asset groups. We may conceivably assume that asset impairments are concentrated in a few specific institutions (a case of idiosyncratic risk), and that impairments (losses) cannot be fully bailed in by equity and debt instruments, therefore necessarily affecting depositors and, finally, the public purse (of whatever kind: national or supranational entity). What may be true at a macro level is not necessarily true at a single institution level. Again, the consequences might be much larger and become systemic.

Triggers

Market-based or balance sheet triggers, the chapter suggests, may be unsuitable according to the available evidence and luckily so, I dare say. It is true that, as I argue below, regulators have over-reacted in terms of always increasing layers of regulation, but, if a decision has to be taken about the very life of an institution, human judgement, flawed as it may be, is preferable to purely objective quantitative indicators.

Cost of subordinated debt

An issue not considered in the chapter, but worthy of attention in commenting on bail-ins, regards the cost of debt instruments. It has been stressed that creditors facing greater risk will either demand a higher return or place funds with banks in the form of deposits in order to be immune from, or less exposed to, bail-ins. According to the *Financial Times* (Thompson, 2014), issuance of subordinated debt, which suffers losses before senior debt in a capital's hierarchy, had risen by 80 per cent year on year thus far in 2014. In fact, investors have been attracted by the higher yield of subordinated instruments, given the 'search for yield' in the current environment. The resulting, decreasing spread vis-à-vis other securities may appear now as a minor problem, because it is possible that investors are forgetting the higher risk of the bonds they are purchasing. But, should crises re-emerge, we may see a sell off of subordinated debt and a thinner cushion to absorb losses. Problems of contagion may arise if banks hold bail-in securities of other banks: as noted by Avinash Persaud (2014): 'trouble at one bank would instantly spread to other banks'.

Structural issues

It is questionable whether – as observed by Binder in chapter 7 – issues related to resolution planning and structural banking reform are being discussed separately at a policy level. The costs of additional layers of regulation should be balanced against the benefits in terms of an efficient banking system and of its overall stability. The regulatory response to the financial crisis has been, so far, the result of a basic loss of confidence in how banks behave, and this has translated into the most complicated, convoluted, sometimes incomprehensible, regulatory regime. Authorities have created an intrusive set of regulations, a sort of micromanagement of institutions, even extended to what sort of compensation managers should receive, which risk they might assume, how risks should be weighted and so on. While it is pretty sure that the system is becoming more costly and cumbersome and, therefore, that the balance tilts towards inefficiency, it remains to be seen whether this regulation has created a more stable financial system.

In this regard, it is worthwhile observing that we are witnessing a generalised shrinking of banking systems. While this trend may be due to the recession or weak recovery, it is a widespread and probably correct opinion that it has to do, at least in part, with the aforementioned costs of regulation. There is the risk that borrowers in the 'real economy' – the business and household sectors – will be partly deprived of banking credit. This may not be an overwhelming danger in countries where capital markets are large and efficient and can be an alternative to bank loans, as in the US, but the situation is different in most of the European countries, which rely heavily on banks for credit. In addition, on a transatlantic basis, just because of this shrinking, an increasing role is being taken by shadow banking, and risks to stability may also come from this sector.

In the discussion of a specific chapter on bail-ins, it is not appropriate, I think, to dwell on large structural issues, even important as they are. But there is a strong conceptual link between the two, which may help to put in focus some basic choices of the regulators, and I shall try to schematise this link as follows.

To reduce or avoid potentially huge costs for the taxpayer coming from enormous bail-outs, it is useful to look at the balance sheet structure of financial intermediaries.[2] Either – on the liabilities side – we have to convert creditors into equity holders, who by definition run the full risk of an unstable asset structure (in this way the translation of costs from the taxpayer to the creditors would be complete); or – on the asset side – we need perfectly safe instruments, which maintain a stable balance sheet and do not endanger the intermediaries' liabilities.

As we know, the first alternative is, to a certain extent, the one pursued internationally by regulators, partly by increasing capital (equity) requirements and partly by envisaging a panoply of instruments, subscribed by investors, which should bail in the institution in case of crisis. It is unclear what would be the optimal level of equity, or quasi-equity, which would be sufficient to protect the safety of the intermediary. It is telling that Vickers, the chair of the UK independent banking commission that in September 2011 proposed a stricter banking regulation, later doubled the already high percentage of equity capital (*tier one*) that a bank should maintain, deemed as appropriate to the bank's safety (Vickers, 2013). The difficulty comes mainly from the instability of the value of the asset side of the balance sheet. As further evidence of uncertainty about the appropriate figures, the Financial Stability Board (2014) consultation paper proposed a 'minimum pillar' for the total loss-absorbing capacity–TLAC requirement for big institutions (GSIBs). It goes up to the range of 16 to 20 per cent of risk-weighted assets, at least 33 per cent of which should be made up of debt instruments to be written down or converted into equity.

In the extreme, this approach would end up by radically resolving the leverage issue of banks, by transforming the liabilities side of a bank's balance sheet from an externally funded institution with a high leverage, into an equity investment, at full risk of the investors. The bank, or better, the intermediary, would radically change its nature into an asset management company or a mutual fund, or a number of mutual funds that would permit sharing the aggregate risk, according to different degrees of riskiness (Kotlikoff, 2010).

The most serious flaw in this kind of structure is that it cannot survive on a stand-alone basis in the financial system, because it would be devoid of the core business of banks, which is to work at the centre of the payment system. The only money – as a credit unconditionally backed by the state – would be made up of currency in circulation: an impossible limit in the context of a modern monetary system.[3] This core business, the 'monetary' business, given its nature of public utility, must of course be preserved. To avoid the implicit danger of leverage, it should be conducted by a separate entity.

The second alternative leads us to the 'narrow banking' concept. The narrow bank has on the liability side what we call 'bank money', deposits. It would not admit other creditors of any kind, the 'investors'. On the asset side, it has just 'safe assets': in the extreme, balances at the central bank. Similarly to the first alternative, it has never been brought into existence, even though broadly discussed in financial literature (Fisher (1935); Simons (1936); Friedman (1965); Litan (1987); Tobin (1987); Phillips (1995); Kay (2009), just to name a few; and, lately, Wolf (2014)). The narrow bank cuts the 'Gordian knot' of deposit-taking and lending (Litan, 1987) by severely restricting the scope of permissible assets, therefore limiting the government's guarantee to instruments that are totally safe and free from any credit or market risk. To my knowledge, the closest attempt to putting it into practice was in the 1930s with the proposals of a prominent New Dealer, Adolf Berle, limiting deposit-taking banks' investments to government securities and commercial paper discountable at the central bank. He lost to the Glass-Steagall legislation that he even saw as a 'public underwriting of risky credit activities' (Phillips, 1994).

These alternatives complement each other, because the structure of the 'banking' system would have two basic components: the narrow bank and a series of mutual funds (if we take the Kotlikoff (2010) scheme) with a substantial 'equity' nature, but with a wide range of different degrees of risk.

Notes

1 According to another statistical source (the EU–DG Competition, available at: http://ec.europa.eu/dgs/competition/index_en.htm (last accessed 3 August 2015)), we have the following figures for state recapitalisation and asset relief measures in the euro area in 2008–2014 (for state interventions in excess of €10bn): Germany €144.1bn, Spain €88.1bn, Ireland €65.4bn, Belgium €40.4bn, Greece €37.3bn, France €26.2bn, Holland €23.9bn and Denmark €10.8bn. Italy stays at €6.0bn. (Interventions totalled €591.9bn.)

2 It will be noticed that in this discussion I do not refer to insurance intermediation, which is characterised by long-term maturities on both sides of its balance sheet. Not by chance, only banks are included in the official statistics in the monetary sector of the economy, together with the central bank.

3 Kotlikoff proposes a 'cash mutual fund', whose liabilities would be demand, chequable deposits (his 'limited purpose bank' is substantially the equivalent of the narrow bank).

References

Bank of Italy (2014) *Financial Stability Report*, No. 2. November. Available at: http://www.bancaditalia.it/pubblicazioni/rapporto-stabilita/2014-2/index.html?com.dotmarketing.htmlpage.language=1 (last accessed 4 May 2015).

Eurostat (2014) *Eurostat Supplementary Tables for the Financial Crisis: Background Note*. October. Available at: http://ec.europa.eu/eurostat/web/government-finance-statistics/excessive-deficit/supplemtary-tables-financial-crisis (last accessed 28 July 2015).

Financial Stability Board (2014) *Adequacy of Loss-Absorbing Capacity of Global Systemically Important Banks in Resolution*. November. Available at: http://www.financialstabilityboard.org/wp-content/uploads/TLAC-Condoc-6-Nov-2014-FINAL.pdf (last accessed 4 May 2015).

Fisher, I. (1935) *100% Money*. New York: Adelphi.

Friedman, M. (1965) A program for monetary stability. In Kendall, L. and Ketchum, M. (eds) *Readings in Financial Institutions*. Boston, MA: Houghton Mifflin, pp. 189–209.

Gualandri, E. (2013) Sofferenze, ogni paese le conta a modo suo. 11 June. Available at: http://www.lavoce.info/archives/9932/sofferenze-ogni-paese-le-conta-a-modo-suo/ (last accessed 19 July 2015).

Kay, J. (2009) *Narrow Banking: The Reform of Banking Regulation*. Centre for the Study of Financial Innovation. Available at: http://www.johnkay.com/wp-content/uploads/2009/12/JK-Narrow-Banking.pdf (last accessed 4 May 2015).

Kotlikoff, L. J. (2010) *Jimmy Stewart Is Dead. Ending the World's Ongoing Financial Plague with Limited Purpose Banking.* Hoboken, NJ: John Wiley & Sons.

Litan, R. E. (1987) *What Should Banks Do?* Washington, DC: The Brookings Institution.

Persaud, A. D. (2014) *Why Bail-In Securities Are Fool's Gold.* Peterson Institute for International Economics, PB 14–23. Available at: http://www.iie.com/publications/pb/pb14-23.pdf (last accessed 19 July 2015).

Phillips, R. (1994) *The Chicago Plan & New Deal Banking Reform.* Armonk, NY: M. E. Sharpe.

Phillips, R. (1995) *Narrow Banking Reconsidered.* Levy Institute, Public Policy Brief no. 18. Available at: http://estes.levy.org/pubs/ppb17.pdf (last accessed 19 July 2015).

Simons, H. C. (1936) Rules versus authorities in monetary policy. *Journal of Political Economy* 44(1): 1–30.

Thompson, C. (2014) EU banks' risky debt deal volume soars. *Financial Times,* 9 November. Available at: http://www.ft.com/intl/cms/s/0/a7735396-669a-11e4-91ab-00144feabdc0.html#axzz3gJoV5B5G (last accessed 19 July 2015).

Tobin, J. (1987) The case for preserving regulatory distinctions. In Federal Reserve Bank of Kansas City Symposium, *Restructuring the Financial System.* Kansas City, MO: Federal Reserve Bank of Kansas City, pp. 167–205.

Vickers, J. (2013) *Banking Reform Five Years On.* Speech to the Regulatory Policy Institute, 9 September. Available at: http://www.rpieurope.org/Events2013/Vickers_RPI.pdf (last accessed 28 July 2015).

Wolf, M. (2014) *The Shifts and the Shocks. What We Have Learned – and Have Still to Learn – from the Financial Crisis.* New York: Penguin Press.

6 Lender of last resort and banking union

Rosa M. Lastra

The advent of banking union in Europe – a remarkable achievement in the history of European integration – was made possible by the political consensus that surrounded the need to provide European supervision and crisis management of euro area credit institutions lest the euro area disintegrate. The urgency with which the plan was conceived and executed was rooted in the vicious link between bank debt and sovereign debt that engulfed several euro area member states in 2012. Banking union, as conceived by the European Commission and approved by the Council, is based upon three pillars: single supervision, single resolution and single deposit insurance. This chapter suggests that a fourth pillar is missing, namely lender of last resort (LOLR) or emergency liquidity assistance (ELA), and examines the theoretical foundations of such a function and the law that applies to it in the European context.

The chapter has two main parts. The first part explores the nature of lender of last resort and the second part analyses such a function in the context of banking union.

A revisionist account of LOLR[1]

The decision to serve as LOLR can be taken either to support a single bank suffering from a liquidity crisis (individual bank liquidity) or to preserve the stability of the banking system as a whole, by supplying extra reserves to all banks suffering from large cash withdrawals (market liquidity). An individual bank problem can, however, quickly convert into a system problem if a sudden collapse of confidence in one bank spreads by contagion to other banks.

LOLR therefore comes in two forms. The first form is the traditional Thornton-Bagehot[2] 'LOLR model' of collateralised lines of credit to individual illiquid, but solvent[3] banks;[4] the second form is the provision of 'market liquidity assistance' via ordinary open market operations and via extraordinary or unconventional measures.

Under the Thornton-Bagehot model, the following principles apply: (1) the central bank should prevent temporarily illiquid, but solvent banks from failing – this type of lending is by nature short term; (2) the central bank should be able to lend as much as is necessary (only the ultimate supplier of high-powered money has this ability), but charge a high rate of interest (a penalty rate as interpreted by some commentators[5]); (3) the central bank should accommodate anyone with good collateral, valued at pre-panic prices;[6] and (4) the central bank should make its readiness to lend clear in advance.

The central bank's LOLR role is discretionary, not mandatory. The central bank assesses not only whether the situation is one of illiquidity or insolvency but also whether the failure of an institution can trigger by contagion the failure of other institutions. It is difficult to calculate *ex ante* how far a crisis can extend. Market sentiment is often hard to predict and, sometimes, irrational, which renders any rational prediction meaningless. The dynamic of a panic is typically self-fulfilling. Indeed, it is the consideration of market sentiment that prompted Thornton back in 1802 to suggest that providing liquidity to the market (lending on security) was the best way of containing a panic. Bagehot and Thornton contend that the LOLR responsibility is to the market, to the entire financial system and not to specific institutions.

Why LOLR links monetary policy, macro prudential policy and micro prudential supervision

The nature of the LOLR role involves different aspects.

1   The discount rate at which the central bank lends, acting in its capacity as LOLR, is an instrument of monetary policy. Only the ultimate supplier of high-powered money can provide the necessary stabilising function in a nationwide scramble for liquidity.[7] The central bank can and does provide market liquidity via open market operations and via other non-conventional instruments.

2   The LOLR is an instrument of banking supervision in a 'crisis situation' stage. As part of its micro prudential functions, the central bank, via the LOLR, provides assistance to a bank (or banks) suffering from a liquidity crisis. The immediacy of the availability of central bank assistance (the central bank being the ultimate supplier of high-powered money) makes the LOLR a particularly suitable first line of defence in a crisis. This 'immediacy' contrasts with the 'time framework' of other crisis management instruments. Neither deposit insurance nor resolution and bank insolvency proceedings can achieve this. By their very nature they are lengthy and complicated processes, which take into account the interests of many stakeholders and are subject to greater legal constraints. The second important feature of this LOLR assistance is the unlimited capacity of the central bank to provide liquidity, either to the market in general or to individual banks as needed. Central banks provide liquidity, not capital.

3   The LOLR is a service provided by the central bank in its capacity as bankers' bank.

As I wrote in an article with Luis Garicano in 2010[8]:

> The lender of last resort function can only be undertaken by a central bank. The involvement of central banks in financial stability originates in their role as monopolist suppliers of fiat money and in their role as bankers' bank. Only the ultimate supplier of money can provide the necessary stabilising function in a nationwide scramble for liquidity, as the financial crisis has amply evidenced, with conventional and non-conventional monetary policy operations (quantitative easing (QE) and others). This is a clear lesson of the crisis in the UK, where the problems of Northern Rock caught the Bank of England by surprise: having timely information is particularly crucial during financial crises and the best way to ensure access is to have daily supervision by the central bank, as the literature has noted.[9]

While the Bank of England (with its 'one bank' mission) and the US Federal Reserve System emphasise the complementarity between their supervisory and their monetary policy responsibilities, the European Central Bank (ECB) published a decision emphasising the separation between these two functions on 17 September 2014.[10] Some – including myself – contend that it is the complementarity between the different central banking tasks that helps the central bank achieve its objectives of monetary and financial stability. The LOLR (ELA) role links supervision (macro and micro) with monetary policy.

LOLR and the 2007–2009 financial crisis

Unprecedented emerging liquidity assistance has been a defining and evolving feature of the responses to the global financial crisis since 2007. Central banks around the world operated as LOLRs, market makers of last resort and, at times, as lender of primary resort or lenders of only resort.

Furthermore, since the extraordinary provision of liquidity assistance amply benefitted financial institutions that were not commercial banks, it is fitting to conclude that, today, central banks are the 'financiers' banks' and not simply the 'bankers' banks'. The financial crisis has changed our understanding of central banking, ELA and systemic risk.

The expansion of central bank liquidity operations during the crisis turned what ought to have been extraordinary into 'ordinary'; ordinary in the sense that with the crisis central banks often became the lender of primary or only resort, and at times market makers of last resort. Rather than discouraging its use, the central bank was keen to encourage various types of LOLR operations, whatever qualification one wishes to attribute to them: ordinary or extraordinary. Furthermore, the contours between the domain of monetary policy and the domain of ELA became increasingly blurred.

In the UK the Bank of England launched the Special Liquidity Scheme[11] in April 2008, to deal with the failure of the interbank markets to return to normality, by injecting liquidity into the banks in the UK on a temporary basis. Funding was offered on a longer-term basis in the euro area through the long-term refinancing operations[12] and in the US via the term auction facility.[13] The ECB in response to the sovereign debt crisis in some euro area member states purchased assets through its securities market programme(SMP)[14] (to restore the monetary transmission mechanism), which was later replaced by the outright monetary transactions (OMTs) programme[15] and provided ample liquidity to the banking system.

The Federal Reserve System embarked on a massive programme of ELA during the financial crisis.[16] A number of facilities and programmes were added to the traditional discount window lending (DWL) for depository institutions and open market operations. The expanding list of facilities was characterised by the widening range of acceptable collateral, the lengthening of the term of the loan and the ability to reach non-depository financial institutions (such as Bear Stearns, the investment bank, and AIG, the insurance company).

For example, in October 2008 the Federal Reserve System opened the commercial paper funding facility; in November 2008 the Federal Reserve System announced the term asset-backed securities lending facility, with a longer duration than any previous facility – at least one year and available to all US persons. Many of these facilities had broad eligibility and were often characterised by the widening range of acceptable collateral and the lengthening of the term of lending.

The legal basis invoked since March 2008 in the US to justify the establishment of new facilities and the extension of ELA to non-bank financial institutions was section 13.3 of the Federal Reserve Act (an authority which has been curtailed by the Dodd-Frank Act 2010). It is also worth recalling that in September 2008, following the collapse of Lehman Brothers, some US financial firms such as Goldman Sachs[17] and Morgan Stanley[18] became bank holding companies in order to benefit from the Federal Reserve System's liquidity facilities.

Mark Carney, Governor of the Bank of England, in his Mansion House speech on 12 June 2014, stated that non-banks should also have access to the Bank of England's facilities.[19]

The question of ambiguity

Can ambiguity ever be constructive? In my opinion, ambiguity is seldom (if ever) constructive. There is a need to be clear about the responsibility for the LOLR before any crisis arises. There is also a need to be clear about the procedures, about the way things will work out and about which institutions can apply for Emergency Liquidity Assistance (ELA). Then, of course, the very provision of assistance should remain at the discretion of the authorities. It is this discretionary element – this uncertainty about whether or not the ELA will be provided – that reduces the moral hazard incentives inherent in any support operation. But there should not be any doubt about who is in charge and how the assistance will be provided. The law ought to be clear about these issues. I quite like the term 'constructive certainty' coined by Tom Huertas in the context of resolution.[20]

What is true is that the existence of a public 'safety net' creates moral hazard, that is, a set of incentives for the protected to behave differently – irresponsibly, carelessly or less conservatively – simply because of the existence of protection. Lending to insolvent institutions increases the potential for moral hazard.[21]

Central bank laws tend to provide scarce guidance with regard to their LOLR operations. [22] One exception is the US legislation on this topic, which happens to be very detailed and rather extensive.[23] Access to the discount window is governed by Regulation A[24] (the first regulation adopted by the Federal Reserve Board at its creation), which refers to the extension of credit – through advances or discounts – in both ordinary and extraordinary circumstances and which has been periodically revised over time.[25] Most other countries do not have such detailed operational rules.

The Federal Deposit Insurance Corporation Improvement Act (FDICIA) of 1991[26] linked the intensity of supervision to the level of capitalisation, with severe treatment for critically undercapitalised depository institutions.[27] Under FDICIA Federal Reserve banks should lend only to *viable* institutions, with penalties imposed in the case of extended lending to undercapitalised institutions, thus shifting the financial burden from the Federal Deposit Insurance Corporation to the Federal Reserve System if the latter chose to lend via its DWL to insolvent or critically undercapitalised institutions.

The crisis substantially expanded the extraordinary liquidity assistance provided by the Federal Reserve System. The Emergency Economic Stabilization Act (EESA), enacted in 2008, highlighted some systemic risk situations where LOLR assistance could be justified.[28] The legislative authority invoked in many cases since March 2008 to lend not only to banks but to other financial market participants was section 13.3 of the Federal Reserve Act, which allowed the Federal Reserve System to lend to financial institutions other than a regulated depository institution because of 'unusual and exigent circumstances'.[29] This was the first time since the 1930s that this provision was used. Section 13.3 ('Discounts for individuals, partnerships, and corporations') read as follows (before the Dodd-Frank Act amendment):

> In unusual and exigent circumstances, the Board of Governors of the Federal Reserve System, by the affirmative vote of not less than five members, may authorize any Federal Reserve bank, during such periods as the said board may determine, at rates established in accordance with the provisions of section 14, subdivision (d), of this Act, to discount for any individual, partnership, or corporation, notes, drafts, and bills of exchange when such notes, drafts, and bills of exchange are indorsed or otherwise secured to the satisfaction of the Federal Reserve bank: Provided, That before discounting any such note, draft, or bill of exchange for an individual, partnership, or corporation the Federal Reserve bank shall obtain evidence that such individual, partnership, or corporation is unable to secure adequate credit accommodations from other banking institutions. All such discounts for individuals, partnerships, or corporations shall be subject to such limitations, restrictions, and regulations as the Board of Governors of the Federal Reserve System may prescribe.[30]

Interestingly, some would say alarmingly or unwisely, the authority to provide LOLR assistance under section 13(3) of the Federal Reserve Act has been curtailed significantly by the Dodd-Frank Wall Street Reform and Consumer Protection Act.[31] The Dodd-Frank Act 2010 requires that any emergency lending programmes and facilities authorised by the Federal Reserve under section 13(3) of the Federal Reserve Act must have 'broad-based eligibility' and must be approved by the Secretary of the Treasury.[32] Thus, the Federal Reserve System cannot engage in rescues of individual firms (i.e. cannot use this authority for the 'purpose' of assisting a 'single and specific company'). This represents a significant restriction on the prior authority that the Federal Reserve System used in 2008 in the cases of AIG and Bear Stearns.

LOLR in the context of banking union[33]

The central bank provides liquidity. Then it is up to the government to provide capital (recapitalisation of troubled entities – bail-out programmes). The problem in Europe is that while we do have the ECB, which can provide such liquidity, we do not have a sufficiently credible fiscal backstop since fiscal policy remains decentralised and the member states are competent (albeit subject to increasing coordination, conditionality and stringent rules).

A limited fiscal backstop in Europe is provided via the European Stability Mechanism (ESM),[34] modelled upon the IMF (but with more limited funding, since it has a lending capacity of €500 billion, backed up by an authorised capital of €700 billion[35]). The Pringle ruling confirmed the legality of the ESM in 2012.[36] On 10 June 2014 euro area member states reached a political understanding on the operational framework of the ESM direct recapitalisation instrument.[37]

In the US, while the Federal Reserve System provided ample liquidity assistance (both market liquidity and individual liquidity assistance), the Treasury provided the necessary capital with the troubled asset relief programme.

The pillars of banking union

Banking union is based upon three pillars.[38] The first pillar is 'single supervision', with the establishment of the Single Supervisory Mechanism (SSM). Single supervision in the context of banking union means European supervision (conferred upon the ECB) for credit institutions of euro area member states and of non-euro area EU member states that choose to become part of the SSM. The second pillar is 'single resolution', with a Single Resolution Mechanism (SRM), which should be aligned with the EU Bank Recovery and Resolution Directive (BRRD),[39] and a Single Resolution Fund. The third pillar is 'common deposit protection'.[40] This third pillar has been discussed in terms of principles and 'high-level politics', though there are political and legal discussions going on as to the feasibility of different options, with the planned adoption of a proposal by end of November 2015.

The missing pillar of banking union: LOLR

Though LOLR is not included as a pillar of the current banking union plan, in my opinion it is clearly the fourth 'missing pillar'. LOLR is the first line of defence in a crisis. Central banks provide liquidity when no other sources of liquidity are readily available (or at least are not available at 'reasonable market prices').

LOLR comes – as discussed above – in two forms: market liquidity assistance and individual liquidity assistance. The ECB has clear competence when it comes to the first form, a competence which it has exercised widely, while due to its own restrictive interpretation of Article 14.4 of the European System of Central Banks (ESCB) Statute, so far it does not have competence with regard to the latter. The risks and costs arising from such a provision are incurred by the relevant National Central Bank (NCB), though a number of procedures – reiterated in a resolution of the Governing Council of 17 October 2013 – ought to be followed. This subject, however, has always triggered much controversy.[41]

Granting the ECB a clear LOLR does not require a treaty change. The ECB is already competent to provide liquidity assistance to 'financially sound' banks. ELA/LOLR links monetary policy and supervision. All that is needed is a

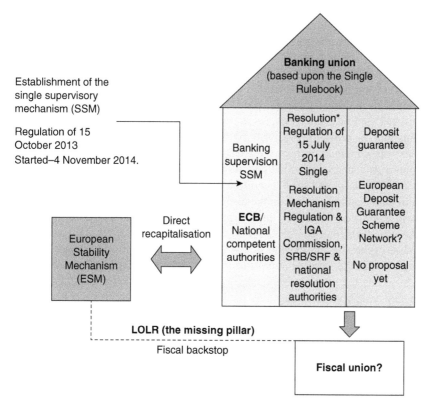

Figure 6.1 Banking union.

reinterpretation of Article 14.4 in the light of new circumstances (banking union) and in accordance with Article 18 and the principle of subsidiarity. At the very least, such an interpretation is required for significant institutions (Figure 6.1).

Since the SSM became operational on 4 November 2014, it is clear, in my opinion, that the ECB should formally be the ultimate provider of liquidity in the euro area, both in cases of market liquidity and in cases of individual liquidity assistance, and is a necessary consequence of the transfer of supervisory powers from the national to the European level.[42] The national competent authority (NCA) is neither the monetary policy authority nor the supervisor. The only advantage of continuing with the current interpretation is that any eventual loss is not shared (but yet it would have an impact on the whole euro area).

The ECB has always been competent to act as LOLR if the crisis originates in the payments system, according to Article 127(2) of the Treaty on the Functioning of the European Union (TFEU), which states that the ESCB is entrusted with the 'smooth operation of payment systems'. The ECB is also competent in the case of a general liquidity dry up to provide market liquidity according to Article 18 of the ESCB Statute, and the ECB has amply used this competence during the crisis, even leading to legal questioning of whether it has exceeded its mandate.

But it is the 'traditional' understanding of LOLR assistance à la Bagehot/ Thornton, in other words, collateralised lines of credit to an individual financial institution which becomes illiquid, but not necessarily insolvent, and whose illiquidity threatens to spread to other institutions and to other markets (the problem of contagion). Though the ECB is competent to provide liquidity assistance to 'financially sound' banks,[43] the provision of collateralised loans to troubled, illiquid, but solvent banks is understood to remain a national competence, because it has not been specifically transferred.[44]

In 1998 the ESCB adopted a restrictive reading of the ECB competences, concluding that the provision of LOLR assistance to specific illiquid individual institutions was a national task of the NCBs in line with Article 14.4 of the ESCB Statute (a provision which allows NCBs to perform non-ESCB tasks on their own responsibility and liability).[45] Therefore, the classic collateralised lines of credit to individual institutions remain the responsibility of the NCBs, at their own cost, but with the fiat of the ECB. This interpretation is somewhat awkward, though it has been reaffirmed in 2013.[46]

When prudential supervision was at the national level, it was perhaps logical to assume that the national authorities had the adequate expertise and information to assess the problems of banks within their jurisdictions (assistance on a rainy day – supervision on a sunny day). But now that supervision is European, the ECB should be to all intents and purposes the LOLR for all those institutions it now supervises. ELA in all forms should be an ECB competence, in accordance with Article 18 of the ESCB Statute, Article 127 TFEU and the principle of subsidiarity.

Indeed, even before banking union, Article 18 (ESCB) provided a perfectly valid legal basis for the ECB to provide the two forms of ELA/LOLR. Furthermore, according to Article 5.3 TFEU (principle of subsidiarity):

In areas which do not fall within its exclusive competence, the Union shall act only if and insofar as the objectives of the proposed action cannot be sufficiently achieved by the member states, either at central level or at regional and local level, but can rather, by reason of the scale or effects of the proposed action, be better achieved at Union level.

In a crisis, action by the ECB is more effective than action by an NCB or national authority. National supervisory authorities do not have the ability, authority or inclination to deal effectively with externalities with cross-border effects. The ECB is able to better judge the risk of contagion.

Fiscal assistance and state aid rules

The problem with having the ECB as LOLR is, of course, the 'fiscal backstop', when the institution receiving the assistance is no longer illiquid, but insolvent.

Goodhart points out: 'a central bank can create liquidity, but it cannot provide for new injections of equity capital. Only the fiscal authority can do that'.[47] The central bank should not lend over an extended period of time, committing taxpayers' money, without the explicit approval of the fiscal authority.[48] Any extended lending becomes the responsibility of the fiscal authority.

In practice, the central bank and the Treasury/Ministry of Finance need to work together in the case of a support operation. This can be arranged at the national level relatively easily. The problem at the EU level – as the recent financial crisis amply demonstrated – is that the relevant fiscal authorities are, by definition, national. Indeed, while the Bank of England is ultimately backed by the fiscal resources of the UK Treasury (though it must comply with the EU rules on state aid and the prohibition of monetary financing) and the Federal Reserve System is ultimately backed by the fiscal resources of the US Treasury, the ECB does not yet have a European fiscal counterpart.[49]

The ECB is therefore *sui generis* because of the 'fiscal constraint' and the EU treaty provisions (in particular Article 123 and Article 125).[50] The ECB did indeed provide hugely expanded liquidity operations during the crisis[51] and made ample use of the considerable set of operational tools at its disposal to handle a liquidity crisis.[52] The problem is that what constitutes 'ordinary' liquidity assistance as opposed to 'emergency'/LOLR liquidity assistance becomes blurred during a crisis, since the drying of the interbank market gives the central bank a primary role in the provision of liquidity.

A further twist is provided by the need to comply with the EU rules on state aid. Because an inherent subsidy exists whenever the central bank lends to an insolvent institution, under the EU rules on state aid, the granting of emergency aid to banking institutions can be considered illegal in some cases. The Luxembourg Court of Justice recognised in a ground-breaking decision, the *Züchner* case, that EC competition rules are also applicable to the banking sector.[53]

On 5 December 2007 the EU Commission in its approval of the rescue aid package for Northern Rock concluded: 'that the emergency liquidity assistance provided by the Bank of England on 14th September 2007, which was secured by sufficient collateral and was interest-bearing, did not constitute state aid'.[54] The Commission Communication of 13 October 2008 further reiterated this point.[55] In establishing a single market in financial services, it is important that the treaty's state aid rules are applied consistently and equally to the banking sector, though with a regard to the peculiarities and sensitivities of the financial markets.[56]

In August 2013 the Commission published another communication extending the 'crisis rules' for banks.[57] According to paragraph 53 of this August 2013 communication: 'Liquidity support and guarantees on liabilities temporarily stabilise the liability side of a bank's balance sheet. Therefore, unlike recapitalisation or impaired asset measures which in principle must be preceded by the notification of a restructuring plan by the member state concerned and approval by the Commission before they can be granted, the Commission can accept that member states notify guarantees and liquidity support to be granted after approval on a temporary basis as rescue aid before a restructuring plan is approved'.

Paragraph 62 further clarifies: 'The ordinary activities of central banks related to monetary policy, such as open market operations and standing facilities, do not fall within the scope of the State aid rules. Dedicated support to a specific credit institution (commonly referred to as "emergency liquidity assistance") may constitute aid unless the following cumulative conditions are met:

a   the credit institution is temporarily illiquid but solvent at the moment of the liquidity provision and is not part of a larger aid package;
b   the facility is fully secured by collateral to which appropriate haircuts are applied, in function of its quality and market value;
c   the central bank charges a penal interest rate to the beneficiary;
d   the measure is taken at the central bank's own initiative, and in particular is not backed by any counter-guarantee of the State'.

It is rather interesting that the Thornton-Bagehot doctrinal principles find their way into a legal text. Paragraph 63 of this 2013 communication further specifies that: 'interventions by deposit guarantee funds to reimburse depositors in accordance with member states' obligations under Directive 94/19/EC on deposit guarantee schemes do not constitute state aid'.

SMP, OMT, QE and LOLR

Some of the most controversial ECB non-conventional measures to combat the crisis remind us of the multipolar nature of LOLR. LOLR is the central banking function that links monetary policy and supervision (macro and micro).

The ECB decided to help keep down borrowing costs of crisis-hit countries through the SMP (a bond-purchasing programme) in 2010 in order to 'restore an appropriate transmission mechanism of monetary policy'[58] and then, in August 2012, announced the OMT programme.[59] Mario Draghi, the ECB president, publicly proclaimed that the central bank would do 'whatever it takes' to ensure the future stability of the euro.[60] The legality of the OMT programme was challenged in the German Constitutional Court (GCC). The GCC referred the case to the European Court of Justice (ECJ) for a preliminary ruling.[61]

In January 2015 Advocate General, Cruz Villalón, issued his opinion in the reference for a preliminary ruling on Gauweiler *et al.* vs Deutscher Bundestag on the ECB's OMT programme.[62] The GCC (Bundesverfassungsgericht, (BVerfG)) had asked the ECJ to clarify whether the OMT programme was an economic rather than a monetary measure and whether the ECB had therefore exceeded its powers by establishing it. The BVerfG had also raised the question of whether the OMT programme was in contravention of the prohibition of monetary financing (Article 123 TFEU). According to Advocate General, Cruz Villalón, the ECB's OMT programme is compatible in principle with TFEU, but if the programme is implemented, its compatibility will depend on certain conditions being met. Interestingly, the Advocate General pointed out (paragraph 6), addressing the question of admissibility, that 'a simple press release' (following the meeting of the ECB Governing Council on 5 and 6 September 2012) was fundamental, given the 'special role played by public communication in central bank activity'. The complainants had raised the substantial issue of whether the ECB is 'a lender of last resort for the States of the euro area' (paragraph 7).[63]

The ECB entered into uncharted territory with the approval by the ECB Governing Council of a large QE programme on 22 January 2015, with effective QE operations commencing on 9 March 2015.[64] The ECB started to buy government and private sector bonds (€60 billion a month until September 2016; total of €1 trillion)[65] in order to revitalise the euro area economies and to counter deflation. NCBs will assume most of the responsibility for losses on any default or restructuring of their national debt (80 per cent), while there will be risk sharing of the assets (20 per cent) issued by European institutions (such as the European Investment Bank).

In the absence of a true capital markets union, and considering the rise in asset prices QE may lead to, the question arises: will it benefit the real economy? The jury is out.

One immediate effect of the ECB's QE announcement was a weaker euro.

Non-conventional measures of monetary policy – the latest being negative interest rates – have become the new norm.

Concluding observations

Much has been written during the crisis about the treaty constraints within which the ECB operates. The Greek drama,[66] however, reminds us that there are limits as to how much central banks can do with the tools at their disposal – monetary policy and ELA – to deal with the causes and effects of a crisis in the absence of fiscal and structural reforms. This chapter considers the missing pillar of banking union, namely the LOLR.

As regards market liquidity, the ECB has provided ample support beyond normal operations, partly because the politicians could not agree on anyone else doing it (eventually the ESM was established – limited fiscal backstop – following a number of temporary facilities), and partly because the ECB committed to do everything it could within the limits of its mandate (often stretching such mandate via creative interpretation albeit in conformity with the law/treaty requirements) to avoid the collapse of the euro.

In terms of individual liquidity assistance, the ECB's own restrictive interpretation of Article 14.4 of the ESCB Statute (a provision which allows NCBs to perform non-ESCB tasks on their own responsibility and liability) is a stumbling block on the way to the fourth pillar of banking union. Such interpretation of Article 14.4 is somewhat awkward and clouded with uncertainty, since the ECB can provide some forms of ELA (open market operations and discount policies, for example), but not others (classic collateralised lines to individual institutions, which remain the responsibility of the NCBs, at their own cost, but with the fiat of the ECB). Article 18 of the ESCB Statute, in combination with Article 127 TFEU, provided a perfectly valid legal basis for the ECB to provide the two forms of ELA/LOLR. The case for a more expansive interpretation of Article 14.4 has been reinforced with banking union: assistance on a rainy day, supervision on a sunny day.

In the US federalisation of liquidity assistance and supervision took place in 1913 with the establishment of the Federal Reserve System.[67] With the advent of banking union, the ECB should be the ultimate provider of liquidity in the euro area, both in cases of market liquidity and in cases of individual liquidity assistance. This is a necessary consequence of the transfer of supervisory powers to the ECB.

Notes

1 This section of the chapter draws heavily on chapters 2 and 4 of Lastra (2015) *International Financial and Monetary Law*, 2nd ed., Oxford University Press, Oxford.
2 The theoretical foundations of the LOLR doctrine were first set by Thornton in 1802 and then by Bagehot in 1873, who further elaborated and refined them. See Henry Thornton (1802) *An Enquiry into the Nature and Effects of the Paper Credit of Great Britain* (Fairfield, NJ: AM Kelley, 1991, originally published in 1802); Walter Bagehot (1873) *Lombard Street. A Description of the Money Market* (New York: Wiley, 1999, originally published in 1873). Recent studies of the work of Thornton and Bagehot on the LOLR are found in Thomas M. Humphrey (1975) The classical concept of the lender of last resort, *Federal Reserve Bank of Richmond Economic Review* 61(1): 2; Michael D. Bordo (1990) Alternative views and historical experience, *Federal Reserve Bank of Richmond Economic Review* 76(1): 18.
3 Though the issue of solvency is often inserted here, Geoffrey Wood reminded me in private correspondence that Hawtrey (*The Art of Central Banking*, Frank Cass & Co. 1932, 1st ed.) had pointed out it is not easy to determine solvency quickly and not necessary either, so long as acceptable collateral is offered. See also Geoffrey Wood (2000) The lender of last resort reconsidered, *Journal of Financial Services Research* 18(2/3): 203–227 (Kluwer Academic Publishers).
4 See Rosa Lastra (1999) Lender of last resort, an international perspective, *International and Comparative Law Quarterly* 48(2): 340–361; and Lastra and Andrew Campbell (2009) Revisiting the lender of last resort, *Banking and Finance Law Review* 24(3): 453–497.

5 Charles Goodhard contends that Bagehot's proposal that LOLR lending be at 'high' rates is incorrectly translated into 'penalty' rates. See Charles Goodhart (1999) Myths about the lender of last resort, *International Finance* 2(3): 339–360. Several authors have suggested a rate lower than the market rate. Goodhart argues that the cost of the initial (borrowing) tranche should be kept very low to avoid the stigma problem associated with borrowing from the central bank. See Charles Goodhart (2009) *The Regulatory Response to the Financial Crisis*, Cheltenham, UK: Edward Elgar, p. 71. Also see R. Repullo (2000) Who should act as a lender of last resort? An incomplete contracts model, *Journal of Money, Credit and Banking* 32(3): 580–605 and ftp://ftp. cemfi.es/pdf/papers/repullo/Liquidity%202005.pdf and J. C. Rochet (2008) *Why are There so Many Banking Crises?* Princeton, NJ: Princeton University Press, p. 89.
6 The traditional lender of last resort practice, that the institution receiving assistance should provide 'good' collateral, has been the subject of much debate and criticism during the global financial crisis due to the widening range of acceptable collateral.
7 It can be argued that a nationwide demand for basic money can be satisfied by borrowing it abroad, in the case of a nation on an international monetary standard (such as gold).
8 Luis Garicano and Rosa Lastra (2010) Towards a new architecture for financial stability: Seven principles, *Journal of International Economic Law* 13(3): 597–621.
9 See Charles Goodhart and Dirk Schoenmaker (1993) Institutional separation between supervisory and monetary agencies and Charles Goodhart (1993) Price stability and financial fragility, both in Charles Goodhart (1993) (ed.) *The Central Bank and the Financial System*, Basingstoke, UK: Macmillan Press. See also Joseph G. Haubrich (1996) Combining bank supervision and monetary policy, *Federal Reserve Bank of Cleveland Economic Commentary*, November; Clive B. Briault (1999) *The Rationale for a Single National Financial Services Regulator*, UK FSA Occasional Paper 2; Richard K. Abrams and Michael W. Taylor (2001) *Assessing the Case for Unified Sector Supervision*, London School of Economics Financial Markets Group Special Papers 134; Joe Peek, Eric S. Rosengren, and Geoffrey M. B. Tootell (1999) Is bank supervision central to central banking? *Quarterly Journal of Economics* 114(2): 629–653.
10 https://www.ecb.europa.eu/ecb/legal/pdf/en_ecb_2014_39_f_sign.pdf
11 Bank of England news release 21 April 2008.
12 http://www.ecb.europa.eu/press/pr/date/2011/html/pr111208_1.en.html

For an analysis of these measures see Rosa Lastra (2012) The evolution of the European Central Bank, *Fordham International Law Journal* 35(Special Issue, Spring, From Maastricht to Lisbon: the Evolution of European Union Institutions and Law): 1260–1281.

13 http://www.federalreserve.gov/newsevents/reform_taf.htm
14 Decision of the ECB (ECB/2010/5) on 14 May 2010 establishing a Securities Markets Programme, published in OJ L 124/8 on 20 May 2010.
15 They were announced on 2 August 2012 and the technical details were published on 6 September 2012 at http://www.ecb.int/press/pr/date/2012/html/pr120906_1.en.html
16 See http://www.newyorkfed.org/markets/Forms_of_Fed_Lending.pdf
17 http://www.goldmansachs.com/media-relations/press-releases/archived/2008/bank-holding-co.html
18 https://www.morganstanley.com/about/press/articles/6933.html
19 See speech by Mark Carney (p. 10), available at: http://www.bankofengland.co.uk/publications/Documents/speeches/2014/speech736.pdf

20 See Thomas Huertas (2014) *A Resolvable Bank*, paper presented at a conference on Managing and Financing European Bank Resolution, held at the LSE on 24 March 2014. On constructive ambiguity see *inter alia*, Xavier Freixas (1999) *Optimal Bail Out Policy, Conditionality and Constructive Ambiguity*, working paper No. 400, available at SSRN http://ssrn.com/abstract=199054; Vinogradov Dmitri (2010) *Deconstructive Effects of Constructive Ambiguity in Risky Times*, available at www.ecb.int; and Sylvester Eijffinger and Rob Nijskens (2012) *A Dynamic Analysis of Bail Outs and Constructive Ambiguity*, CEPR working paper, available at http://papers.ssrn.com/sol3/papers.cfm?abstract_id=2118439

21 The operational aspects of the LOLR functions are affected by problems of asymmetric information, namely moral hazard and adverse selection. See George Akerlof (1970) The market for lemons: Quality uncertainty and the market mechanism, *Quarterly Journal of Economics* 84(3): 488–500.

22 The ambiguity in some treaty provisions is the result of a calculated obfuscation for political purposes, which expresses the labour pains that accompanied the drafting of some of these provisions. Padoa-Schioppa, in the first public statement by an ECB official on this controversial subject dismissed the concerns about the lack of a clearly defined LOLR for the ESCB on three counts: it reflected an outdated notion of LOLR, it underestimates the Eurosystem's capacity to act and it represented too mechanistic a view of how a crisis is actually managed.

23 12 USC 221 *et seq*. Congress has assigned to the Federal Reserve Board responsibility for implementing certain laws pertaining to a wide range of banking and financial activities. The Board implements those laws in part through its regulations, which are codified in title 12, chapter II, of the Code of Federal Regulations (CFR). See http://www.federalreserve.gov/bankinforeg/reglisting.htm

24 In the US the DWL operates according to rules set up in sections 10a and 10b of the Federal Reserve Act and in the implementing Regulation A. See 12 CFR Chapter II, Part 201 *Extension of Credit by Federal Reserve Banks* (Regulation A), available at http://www.gpo.gov/fdsys/pkg/CFR-2011-title12-vol2/pdf/CFR-2011-title12-vol2-part201.pdf. There are rules that specify the short-term nature of the lending (60 days, 120 days, etc.) as well as the penalty rate applicable and the type of instruments that can be used as collateral.

25 The central bank can also agree to supply emergency liquidity to foreign institutions operating in the country. Section 13.14 of the Federal Reserve Act allows the Federal Reserve banks to lend to a branch or agency of a foreign bank; it reads as follows:

> Subject to such restrictions, limitations, and regulations as may be imposed by the Board of Governors of the Federal Reserve System, each Federal Reserve bank may receive deposits from, discount paper endorsed by, and make advances to any branch or agency of a foreign bank in the same manner and to the same extent that it may exercise such powers with respect to a member bank if such branch or agency is maintaining reserves with such Reserve bank pursuant to section 7 of the International Banking Act of 1978. In exercising any such powers with respect to any such branch or agency, each Federal Reserve bank shall give due regard to account balances being maintained by such branch or agency with such Reserve bank and the proportion of the assets of such branch or agency being held as reserves under section 7 of the International Banking Act of 1978. For the purposes of this paragraph, the terms "branch", "agency", and "foreign bank" shall have the same meanings assigned to them in section 1 of the International Banking Act of 1978.

26 FDICIA was enacted on 19 December 1991, Public Law 102–242 (105 Stat 2236–2393).
27 An institution is critically undercapitalised, according to section 38 of the Federal Deposit Insurance Act as amended by FDICIA, when: 'it fails to meet any level specified under subsection c(3)(a)' (i.e. when the leverage ratio of tangible equity is less than two per cent of total assets).
28 Emergency Economic Stabilization Act of 2008, Pub L No 110–343 (2008).
29 http://www.newyorkfed.org/markets/Forms_of_Fed_Lending.pdf
30 Christian Johnson has conducted an analysis of the extensive use of this provision during the crisis in a paper entitled *Exigent and Unusual Circumstances* presented at the Hart Conference in London (2009), submitted to *European Business Organization Law Review*, available at http://papers.ssrn.com/sol3/papers.cfm?abstract_id=1584731
31 Dodd-Frank Wall Street Reform and Consumer Protection Act, Pub L No 111–203 (2010), commonly referred to as the Dodd-Frank Act 2010 or simply Dodd-Frank.
32 See http://www.federalreserve.gov/aboutthefed/section13.htm. A programme or facility that is structured to remove assets from the balance sheet of a single/specific company or that is established to assist a single/specific company to avoid bankruptcy, resolution or insolvency proceedings will not be considered a programme or facility with broad-based eligibility. The Dodd-Frank Act 2010 requests the Federal Reserve to give immediate notice and periodic reports to Congress regarding any Section 13(3) facility and also to disclose information concerning the participants and the amount of individual transactions in all credit facilities under Section 13(3) and borrowers or counterparties in discount window and open market transactions. See Bank for International Settlements, 'Central Bank Governance and Financial Stability' (Report by a Study Group, May 2011) available at http://www.bis.org/publ/othp14.pdf. See also http://www.federalreserve.gov/monetarypolicy/clbs-appendix-c-201203.htm and http://www.sec.gov/about/laws/wallstreetreform-cpa.pdf
33 This section of the chapter draws heavily on chapter 10 of Lastra (2015) *International Financial and Monetary Law*, 2nd ed., Oxford, UK: Oxford University Press. See also chapter 7 for the non-conventional responses by the ECB to the crisis and Lastra (2013) Banking union and single market: Conflict or companionship? *Fordham International Law Journal* 36(5): 1189–1223, for a consideration of how banking union fits within the single market in financial services. For a short account of banking union see Rosa Lastra, Bernd Krauskopf, Christos Gortsos and René Smits (2014) *European Banking Union*, MOCOMILA report to the ILA meeting in Washington DC, April 2014, available at http://www.ila-hq.org/en/committees/index.cfm/cid/22
34 The ESM treaty, concluded in Brussels on 2 February 2012, entered into force on 27 September 2012. The ESM was inaugurated on 8 October 2012 following the ratification by all euro area members.
35 The ESM raises funds by issuing money market instruments and medium- and long-term debt with maturities of up to 30 years, which are backed by a paid-in capital of €80 billion and the irrevocable and unconditional obligation of ESM member states to provide their contribution to ESM's authorised capital stock.
36 Case C-370/12, REFERENCE for a preliminary ruling under Article 267 TFEU from the Supreme Court (Ireland), made by decision of 31 July 2012, received at the Court on 3 August 2012, in the proceedings Thomas Pringle v Government of Ireland. http://curia.europa.eu/juris/document/document.jsf?text=&docid=130381&pageIndex=0&doclang=EN&mode=lst&dir=&occ=first&part=1&cid=37623 Pringle v. Ir., [2012] IESC 47, para. 5 (S.C.) (Ir.), available at http://www.courts.ie/__80256F2B00356A6B.nsf/0/E750 4392B159245080257A4C00517D6A?Open&Highlight=0,pringle,~language_en~

37 Following the relevant national procedures and the formal adoption by the ESM Board of Governors, the instrument is expected to be added to the toolkit of the ESM. Once operational, it is expected that the instrument may be activated in case a bank fails to attract sufficient capital from private sources and if the ESM member concerned is unable to recapitalise it, including through the instrument of indirect recapitalisation of the ESM. For a transitional period until 31 December 2015, a bail-in of 8 per cent of all liabilities will be a precondition for using the instrument, as well as the use of the resources available in the ESM member's national resolution fund. From 1 January 2016 bail-in in line with the rules of the Bank Recovery and Resolution Directive will be required. The financial assistance will be provided in accordance with EU state aid rules and the ESM member will be asked to invest alongside the ESM. Available at http://www.eurozone.europa.eu/media/533095/20140610-eurogroup-president-direct-recapitalisation.pdf

38 Underpinning these three pillars is the concept of a common supervisory rule book, laying down uniform terms for the authorisation and withdrawal of credit institutions, for the conduct of micro-prudential supervision over credit institutions, for the resolution of non-viable credit institutions and for the operation of deposit guarantee schemes.

39 The BRRD was published in the OJ in June 2014. See Directive 2014/59/EU of the European Parliament and of the Council of 15 May 2014 establishing a framework for the recovery and resolution of credit institutions and investment firms and amending Council Directive 82/891/EEC, and Directives 2001/24/EC, 2002/47/EC, 2004/25/EC, 2005/56/EC, 2007/36/EC, 2011/35/EU, 2012/30/EU and 2013/36/EU, and Regulations (EU) No 1093/2010 and (EU) No 648/2012, of the European Parliament and of the Council, OJ L 173, 12/06/2014, p. 190–348. Available at http://eur-lex.europa.eu/legal-content/EN/TXT/?uri=uriserv:OJ.L_.2014.173.01.0190.01.ENG

40 The rationale for a common deposit insurance scheme is clear: with perfect capital mobility, in order to prevent a flight of deposits from troubled countries to countries perceived to be 'safe', one needs to convince ordinary citizens that a euro in a bank account in one euro area member state is worth the same and is as secure as a euro in a bank account in another euro area member state. This is a real challenge, as the experience in Cyprus evidenced.

41 See, *inter alia*, Charles Goodhart (ed.) (2000) *Which Lender of Last Resort for Europe*, London, UK: Central Banking Publications; Jeroen Kremers, Dirk Schoenmaker and Peter J Wierts (eds) (2001) *Financial Supervision in Europe* (Cheltenham, UK: Edward Elgar Publishing; Tommasso Padoa-Schioppa (2004) *Regulating Finance*, Oxford, UK: Oxford University Press, chapters 4 and 5; and Crisis management in Europe, in Jeroen Kremers, Dirk Schoenmaker and Peter Wierts (eds) (2003) *Financial Supervision in Europe* (Cheltenham, UK: Edward Elgar, chapters 7 and 8, and Xavier Freixas). For a critique of the ECB's interpretation of its powers in respect of ELA see René Smits (2010) European supervisors in the credit crisis: Issues of competence and competition, in Mario Giovanoli and Diego Devos (eds) (2010) *International Monetary and Financial Law – The Global Crisis*, Oxford, UK: Oxford University Press, chapter 15, pp. 310–311.

42 Notwithstanding the ECB decision of 18 October 2013 on ELA, available at http://www.ecb.europa.eu/pub/pdf/other/201402_elaprocedures.en.pdf which assigns 'responsibility for the provision of ELA' to the 'NCB(s) concerned', further specifying that 'This means that any cost of, and the risks arising from, the provision of ELA are incurred by the relevant NCB'.

43 See ECB http://www.ecb.europa.eu/pub/pdf/other/gendoc2008en.pdf p. 11.
44 René Smits has always held a different opinion, regarding this LOLR responsibility as an exclusive EU competence. See René Smits (2005) The role of the ESCB in banking supervision, *Legal Aspects of the European System of Central Banks, Liber Amicorum, Paolo Zamboni Garavelli*, Frankfurt, Germany: European Central Bank, no. 32.
45 Article 14.4 reads as follows:

> National central banks may perform functions other than those specified in this Statute unless the Governing Council finds, by a majority of two thirds of the votes cast, that these interfere with the objectives and tasks of the ESCB. Such functions shall be performed on the responsibility and liability of national central banks and shall not be regarded as being part of the functions of the ESCB.

The ECB can assess whether a given LOLR operation by an NCB interferes with monetary policy and, if so, either prohibit it or subject it to conditions. To this effect, the ECB has some internal rules (MoU) requiring ex ante notification to the Governing Council of such LOLR operation (Article 14.4). I thank Antonio Sainz de Vicuña for observations on this point. The following is an excerpt from the ECB Annual Report 1999 (p. 98):

> The institutional framework for financial stability in the EU and in the euro area is based on national competence and international cooperation . . . Co-ordination mechanisms are primarily called for within the Eurosystem. This is the case for emergency liquidity assistance (ELA), which embraces the support given by central banks in exceptional circumstances and on a case-by-case basis to temporarily illiquid institutions and markets . . . If and when appropriate, the necessary mechanisms to tackle a financial crisis are in place. The main guiding principle is that the competent NCB takes the decision concerning the provision of ELA to an institution operating in its jurisdiction. This would take place under the responsibility and at the cost of the NCB in question. (. . .) The agreement on ELA is internal to the Eurosystem and does not affect the existing arrangements between central banks and supervisors at the national level or bilateral or multilateral co-operation among supervisors and between the latter and the Eurosystem.

46 See ELA decision by the ECB of 18 October 2013, available at http://www.ecb.europa.eu/pub/pdf/other/201402_elaprocedures.en.pdf
ELA means the provision by a Eurosystem NCB of (a) central bank money and/or (b) any other assistance that may lead to an increase in central bank money to a solvent financial institution, or group of solvent financial institutions, that is facing temporary liquidity problems, without such operation being part of the single monetary policy. Responsibility for the provision of ELA lies with the NCB(s) concerned. This means that any costs of, and the risks arising from, the provision of ELA are incurred by the relevant NCB.
NCBs must inform the ECB within two days of an ELA operation, with details of the counterparties involved, the value of the operation, the haircuts and collateral applied and the rate of interest paid on the funds. A limit of €500 million in ELA assistance can be provided to a given financial institution or group of institutions before the NCB(s) involved must inform the ECB as early as possible prior to the extension of

the intended assistance. If the overall volume of ELA operations passes €2 billion for a given central bank, the Governing Council considers whether there is a risk that the ELA involved may interfere with the objectives and tasks of the Eurosystem. Upon the request of the NCB(s) concerned, the Governing Council may then decide to set a threshold and not to object to intended ELA operations that are below that threshold and conducted within a pre-specified short period of time.

47 See Charles Goodhart (2004) Foreword, in Tommasso Padoa-Schioppa, *Regulating Finance*, Oxford, UK: Oxford University Press, xvii.

48 In the EU the prohibition of monetisation of government debt, also known as 'monetary financing' in accordance with the provisions of Article 123 TFEU applies.

49 Alexandre Lamfalussy remarked in an interview with *The Guardian* on 16 August 2003: 'The great weakness of EMU is the E. The M part is institutionally well organised. We have a solid framework. We don't have that for economic policy'.

50 This cast some legal doubts on the yet-to-be-activated OMT programme (for the referral by the German Constitutional Court to the ECJ of the legality of the OMT decision see http://www.bundesverfassungsgericht.de/pressemitteilungen/bvg14–009en.html, February 2014) and also raised concerns about QE programmes to stimulate the euro area economy. Article 123 TFEU only forbids the ESCB from giving credit to or purchasing sovereign debt directly from EU member states, but there is no ban on purchases of government bonds on the secondary markets, which the ECB has been doing since May 2010, when it began buying the government debt of Greece.

51 For a summary of significant liquidity provision measures adopted during the crisis see http://www.ecb.int/press/key/date/2009/html/sp090220.en.html. As regards the OMT see the press release on the technical features of the OMT available at http://www.ecb.europa.eu/press/pr/date/2012/html/pr120906_1.en.html. For unconventional ECB monetary policies see also https://www.ecb.europa.eu/pub/pdf/scpwps/ecbwp1528.pdf

52 ECB open market operations are described in chapter 3 of *The Implementation of Monetary Policy in the Euro Area*, European Central Bank, November 2008, available at http://www.ecb.europa.eu/pub/pdf/other/gendoc2008en.pdf

53 See Case 172/80 *Züchner v Bayerische Vereinsbank* [1981] ECR 2021.

54 http://europa.eu/rapid/pressReleasesAction.do?reference=IP/07/1859&format=HTML&aged=1&language=EN&guiLanguage=en. 'However, the guarantee on deposits granted by the Treasury on 17th September, as well as the measures granted on 9th October, which provided further liquidity and guarantees to Northern Rock and were secured by a Treasury indemnity, do constitute state aid'. On 17 March 2008, six months after the first state aid measures ('rescue aid') took place, the UK authorities submitted a restructuring plan to the Commission. The Commission then launched an in-depth investigation into this 'restructuring aid'. Available at http://europa.eu/rapid/pressReleasesAction.do?reference=IP/08/489

55 Official Journal C 270, 25.10.2008, paragraph 51:

> The Commission considers for instance that activities of central banks related to monetary policy, such as open market operations and standing facilities, are not caught by the State aid rules. Dedicated support to a specific financial institution may also be found not to constitute aid in specific circumstances. The Commission considers that the provision of central banks' funds to the financial institution in such a case may be found not to constitute aid when a number of conditions are

met, such as: the financial institution is solvent at the moment of the liquidity pro-vision and the latter is not part of a larger aid package; the facility is fully secured by collateral to which haircuts are applied, in function of its quality and market value; the central bank charges a penal interest rate to the beneficiary; the measure is taken at the central bank's own initiative, and in particular is not backed by any counter-guarantee of the State.

56 From the beginning of the global financial crisis in the autumn of 2008 to December 2010, the Commission issued four communications, which provided detailed guid-ance on the criteria for the compatibility of state support to financial institutions with the requirements of Article 107(3)(b) TFEU: (1) communication on the application of state aid rules to measures taken in relation to financial institutions in the context of the current global financial crisis (banking communication); (2) communication on the recapitalisation of financial institutions in the current financial crisis: limitation of aid to the minimum necessary and safeguards against undue distortions of competi-tion (recapitalisation communication); (3) communication from the commission on the treatment of impaired assets in the community banking sector (impaired assets communication) and (4) communication on the return to viability and the assessment of restructuring measures in the financial sector in the current crisis under the state aid rules (restructuring communication). Available at http://ec.europa.eu/competition/state_aid/legislation/temporary.html

57 Communication from the Commission on the application, from 1 August 2013, of state aid rules to support measures in favour of banks in the context of the financial crisis (banking communication), 2013/C 216/01, available at http://eur-lex.europa.eu/legal-content/EN/ALL/?uri=CELEX:52013XC0730(01)

58 https://www.ecb.europa.eu/ecb/legal/pdf/l_12420100520en00080009.pdf?e0e193dbae13419ec1d5208de7cc65b9

59 See European Central Bank (2012) *Technical Features of Outright Monetary Transactions*, 6 September, available at http://www.ecb.int/press/pr/date/2012/html/pr120906_1.en.html

60 'Within our mandate, the ECB is ready to do whatever it takes to preserve the euro. And believe me, it will be enough'. See Speech by Mario Draghi (26 July 2012), avail-able at http://www.ecb.europa.eu/press/key/date/2012/html/sp120726.en.html

61 Referral for a preliminary ruling to the Court of Justice of the European Union by the German Constitutional Court (Bundesverfassungsgericht) regarding the decision of the Governing Council of the European Central Bank of 6 September 2012 on Technical Features of Outright Monetary Transactions (OMT Decision) lodged on 10 February 2014 – Peter Gauweiler and Others (Case C-62/14) [2014] OJ C129/11. See press release, 18 March 2014, available at http://www.bundesverfassungsgericht.de/en/press/bvg14–009en.html

This case concerns the question of whether the ECB, announcing in a press release in the autumn of 2012 its intention to buy under certain conditions and in unlimited amounts bonds of the governments of euro area programme countries, overstepped its mandate and entered into the nation competency of economic/fiscal policy. The applicants, German citizens, German political parties and German MPs, repeated their arguments in court. The German government pleaded that the OMT is legal and within the ECB mandate, but asked the court to decide in a way that would allow the German Constitutional Court to be able to consider the programme also compatible with the German constitution (which, one judge remarked, is not an easy thing). The

ECB defended the OMT as compatible with the treaty and necessary under the circumstances. The European Commission, the European Parliament and the member states that intervened (9) all supported the ECB.

62   http://curia.europa.eu/juris/document/document.jsf?docid=161370&doclang=EN For the press release see http://curia.europa.eu/jcms/upload/docs/application/pdf/2015–01/cp150002en.pdf The decision by the court is normally 2–3 months after the opinion of the Advocate General is issued.

63   The Court of Justice of the European Union made its final ruling of the OMT case in June 2015, declaring the conditional OMT program to be legal, since it 'does not exceed the powers of the ECB in relation to monetary policy and does not contravene the prohibition of monetary financing of EU nations' (http://curia.europa.eu/jcms/upload/docs/application/pdf/2015-06/cp150070en.pdf).

64   http://www.ecb.europa.eu/press/pressconf/2015/html/is150305.en.html

> Following up on our decisions of 22 January 2015, we will, on 9 March 2015, start purchasing euro-denominated public sector securities in the secondary market. We will also continue purchasing asset-backed securities and covered bonds, which we started last year. As previously stated, the combined monthly purchases of public and private sector securities will amount to €60 billion. They are intended to be carried out until the end of September 2016 and will, in any case, be conducted until we see a sustained adjustment in the path of inflation which is consistent with our aim of achieving inflation rates below, but close to, 2 per cent over the medium term.

65   http://www.ecb.europa.eu/press/pressconf/2015/html/is150122.en.html

66   The 'extend and pretend policies' when it comes to sovereign debt 'management' (restructuring) cannot hide a few uncomfortable truths. The ECB may have to take losses. Memories of the 'less-developed-country' debt crisis in the 1980s and the lost decade in Latin America cast a long shadow on the current situation in some euro area member states – it took years for the Brady plan to replace the misguided Baker Plan. Where you draw the dividing line for loss-sharing arrangements and who provides what sort of support are key issues yet to be resolved.

67   In the US federalisation of bank insolvency (today resolution) and deposit insurance took place in 1933 with the establishment of FDIC. In the same way as in supervision we went from Lamfalussy to De Larosière to SSM, when it comes to resolution, the SRM is only a first step on the way towards the design of an adequate resolution framework.

7 Resolution planning and structural bank reform within the banking union

Jens-Hinrich Binder

Among the global regulatory responses to the global financial crisis, the development of harmonised concepts for the reorganisation and resolution for large, complex, internationally active banks and banking institutions clearly has been one of the most important aspects. Both in international fora[1] and at the national levels,[2] standard setters and legislators have come to agree on a harmonised set of resolution tools, partly innovative and partly based on precedents in national legislation prior to the crisis.[3] However, the residual problems associated with the resolution of large, complex, internationally active banks and banking groups will continue to create significant impediments to swift and effective insolvency management and the ability to contain its repercussions on the stability of national and international markets. The reasons range from the complexity and opacity of existing legal structures of firms and groups, including the statutory and contractual frameworks for intra-group funding arrangements, to organisational issues, such as intra-group arrangements for IT support, conflicting national legal frameworks (in particular outside the EU, where the recent harmonisation of the legal framework does not apply) and conflicting national powers and interests.[4]

Against this backdrop, reactive tools for the management of financial institutions' insolvency have been complemented and preceded by preventive steps to enhance resolvability ex ante, which has to include both the *identification* of possible impediments to swift resolution and, where possible, the *removal* of such impediments in 'good times', before a crisis hits. Efforts to that end have essentially been made in two different, but functionally related, forms. First, reflecting an international trend,[5] the recent EU Directive establishing a framework for the recovery and resolution of credit institutions and investment firms (the Bank Recovery and Resolution Directive (BRRD))[6] and the EU regulations that jointly establish the banking union authorities (the Single Supervisory Mechanism (SSM) regulation and Single Resolution Mechanism (SRM) regulation, respectively)[7] have established a broadly identical regime for preventive contingency planning by both the relevant institutions and groups ('recovery planning')[8] and relevant supervisory and resolution authorities ('resolution planning').[9] It is expected that both recovery plans, or 'living wills', of banks and resolution plans of resolution authorities will play an important role: as pre-commitments for both institutions and authorities to specific options for resolutions, which could help to identify and to mitigate impediments to swift resolution, as a means to reduce complexity in both banks and decision-making processes among authorities and as vehicles for reliable burden-sharing arrangements ex ante.[10]

Second, not just the United States[11] and the United Kingdom,[12] the forerunners in this regard, but also a number of jurisdictions in Continental Europe[13] have adopted legislative steps towards a comprehensive structural reform of banking, which essentially aim, in one form or another, to insulate at least some traditional commercial banking activities from the risks associated with investment banking. At the EU level, negotiations are underway over a Commission proposal for a regulation on structural bank reform,[14] which takes up recommendations by the High-Level Expert Group on Reforming the Structure of the EU Banking Sector, chaired by Bank of Finland Governor, Erkki Liikanen, which were published in 2012.[15]

Both developments are related from a functional perspective. Indeed, one of the motives for structural reforms, in addition to the preservation of certain systemically relevant business functions, has been to remove impediments to effective crisis resolution.[16] Furthermore, as a matter of course, policy choices made in the process of resolution planning will have a bearing on the legal and organisational structure of firms and groups, as will any measure aimed at redesigning existing business models. However, neither the academic debate nor the relevant political and legislative reform projects have fully recognised the interrelation between the two aspects so far. The legal framework for bank resolution and for resolution planning has been adopted ahead of structural reform projects, forcing authorities and the industry to draw up recovery and resolution plans that could be rendered meaningless if, and to the extent that, structural bank reforms were to enforce substantial changes to existing firm and group structures in the future. Only very recently initiatives have been taken to re-integrate both developments, but with little tangible results so far. In a report *Structural Banking Reforms*, addressed to the November 2014 G20 summit, the Financial Stability Board (FSB) for the first time expressly recognised the need for greater consistency in this respect and called for future work towards this objective.[17]

Against this backdrop, this chapter presents an analysis of how the requirements for resolution planning, on whose implementation work has already begun, could possibly be reconciled with existing proposals for structural reforms of banks and banking groups within Europe in future supervisory practice. In reality, the problems relating to resolution planning go much further than that. A significant part of the relevant policy decisions under the new resolution framework will have to be made at the planning stage rather than at the point when the relevant institution or group enters resolution. Resolution plans, therefore, will have to address some highly technical, fundamental questions, and they will do so on the basis of complex prognoses with regard to both the future financial condition of the relevant institutions or groups and future market conditions.[18] Given the dynamic nature of financial markets, recovery and resolution plans are unlikely to be of any use if seen as 'blueprints' for future action. The future inevitably will look different from the scenarios anticipated in the drafting process, and different conditions in real life will necessitate approaches that differ from those identified in good times.[19] Nonetheless, recovery and resolution plans certainly can help both banks and their supervisors in a number of ways. First and foremost, they are likely to enhance the mutual understanding of business structures, which in turn can be useful in that it could alert both sides of potential impediments to resolution. If, for example, the planning process reveals a group's dependence on a centralised IT infrastructure provided by a group member, resolution action with regard to other members of the group may encounter severe impediments if these services are not available. Such findings could then trigger preparatory action to help mitigate these problems in advance.

These benefits are likely to be particularly important in the context of groups, where complex intra-group arrangements significantly enhance the logistical problems caused by any insolvency of a major financial institution. Perhaps most importantly in this regard, resolution planning will have to define whether groups will be resolved under what has become known as a 'single point of entry' (SPOE) approach, i.e. with resolution action taken only with regard to the parent company, or under a 'multiple point of entry' (MPOE) approach, whereby individual group companies will be subjected to resolution.[20] Decisions made in this respect will, in turn, have to be reconciled with policies adopted in relation to regulatory minimum requirements for debt and capital instruments eligible for bail-in (known as 'minimum requirements on capital instruments and eligible liabilities' (MREL)),[21] or in the international standard setting discussion, as 'total loss absorbing capacity (TLAC)',[22] agreement on which is still pending. The focus of this chapter is related to these aspects, as existing business models and organisational and legal structures of firms and groups inevitably have to be taken into account as key determinants for the relevant policy decisions. As the relevant policy decisions are still unfolding, and as the empirical evidence on differences between different markets still appears to be extremely thin, the chapter does not present any view on these aspects, however. Accepting, as a working hypothesis, that differences exist and that they could prove detrimental to the definition of consistent resolution strategies in future practice, the focus is on how such differences could be mitigated or even removed under the powers available to the relevant authorities within Europe in general and the banking union in particular. In this sense, the chapter is about the interplay between the relevant legal regimes, the BRRD and the SSM and the SRM regulations, rather than on firm-specific substantive aspects of resolution planning.[23]

Unlike the requirements for resolution planning under Title I, § 165(d) of the US Dodd-Frank Act, which have already triggered a lively debate in the academic literature,[24] and unlike the various structural bank reform projects,[25] the harmonised regime for recovery and resolution planning within the banking union and the EU more generally has not attracted much attention in the academic literature yet. For this reason, the chapter starts with an analysis of the relevant parts of both the BRRD and the SSM and SRM regulations, respectively, in the next two sections. The chapter then explores the potential future practice, specifically with regard to the key questions that have motivated this chapter: How will the authorities use their powers to influence the choice of organisation, hitherto left exclusively to the boards of banking institutions and banking groups? Also, more specifically: Is a consistent approach to recovery and resolution planning at all conceivable without fundamental changes to existing, highly diverse, market structures, business models and corporate structures within Europe?

From the start, three caveats are appropriate in order to define the scope of the chapter further. First, it hardly makes sense to focus exclusively on resolution planning by resolution authorities and to exclude 'recovery planning' or 'living wills' on the part of the regulated industry. Both concepts are derived from similar considerations and, as is discussed in further detail below, the relevant provisions of both the BRRD and the SSM and SRM regulations are highly interconnected. In line with international discussion,[26] the term 'resolution planning' will be used throughout in a broad, non-technical sense, i.e. not restricted to the plans to be drawn up by resolution authorities within the new EU framework. Second, it is, as of late 2014, too early to predict what the future practice at both national and European Union levels will look like. In this light, only some tentative suggestions will be made as to which way the authorities could proceed on the basis of their powers under the new framework. Third, it will not be possible to explore, given both the limits of this chapter and the lack of reliable, cross-country empirical evidence in this respect,[27] the full range of complicated policy issues pertaining to the potential merits and unknowns of structural bank reform. While further research in this regard is certainly critical for the evaluation and refinement of the incoming regulatory reforms, the objective of this chapter is rather to identify some key questions that are likely to become relevant in the context of resolution planning before long and thus to help prepare the ground for further debate.

The legal framework for recovery and resolution planning under the BRRD

The framework in context

The BRRD's provisions on recovery and resolution planning, which have also been the blueprint for the corresponding regime under the SSM and SRM regulations,[28] reflect the FSB's *Key Attributes of Effective Resolution Regimes for Financial Institutions*, which were published in October 2011 and also informed the harmonised set of resolution tools under the BRRD.[29] Section 11 with Annex III of the Key Attributes set out in some detail requirements for the development and on-going reviews of recovery and resolution plans by institutions and resolution authorities, including for the cooperation of home and host country authorities. The responsibilities for recovery and resolution planning under the BRRD have been arranged in a rather complex way, reflecting the FSB's Key Attributes approach to recovery and resolution planning.[30] In this framework, as indicated above, supervisory and resolution authorities respectively are assigned a set of powers relating to the assessment of recovery plans (which are to be developed by the institutions)[31] and the development of resolution plans and the assessment of the resolvability of institutions and groups.[32] For both types of plans, simplified obligations apply to less complex and interconnected institutions with a low risk profile, which is not discussed any further in this chapter.[33]

Fully in line with international standards and a growing convergence of international best practice,[34] the concept underlying the relevant BRRD provisions in this respect is rather simple: to prepare for more effective recovery efforts by the banks themselves and for more effective administrative resolution action by identifying, and addressing, risks in advance. By requiring banks and relevant authorities to pre-commit to a range of specific options, the concept thus serves to reinforce the notion that, following the global crisis, *all* financial institutions, regardless of size, complexity and interconnectedness, should be resolvable.[35] In this regard, resolution planning is an essential part of a market-orientated incentive structure that is hoped to substitute taxpayer funded bail-outs of institutions deemed too big to fail, too complex to fail and/or too interconnected to fail in the future.

Recovery plans

Under the BRRD, individual recovery plans are to be developed by those regulated institutions that are not part of a group subject to consolidated supervision[36] (for which group resolution plans have to be developed[37]). With both individual and group recovery plans, the purpose is to identify possible 'measures to be taken by those institutions for the restoration of their financial position following a significant deterioration', including 'possible measures which could be taken by the management of the institution where the conditions for early intervention are met'.[38] These plans have to be updated at least annually, or after a change to the legal or organisational structure of the institution.[39] As part of the overall objective of protecting fiscal interests in bank resolution,[40] recovery plans shall not 'assume any access to or receipt of extraordinary public financial support',[41] but may provide for the use of 'central bank facilities', that is, central bank loans against collateral.[42]

Recovery plans are to be based on an in-depth analysis of each institution's or group's financial and organisational position. This is specified in further detail by section A of the annex to the directive, which lists the range of information to be included in recovery plans. These provisions have since been complemented by European Banking Authority (EBA) draft technical standards on the contents of recovery plans[43] and EBA guidelines on scenarios to be used in recovery plans.[44] In particular, the plan will have to identify possible impediments to the execution of the plan,[45] critical functions that will have to be preserved in the interest of financial stability,[46] as well as adequate contingency funding sources,[47] and it will have to set out how the institution seeks to restore its capital base, reduce risk and leverage, restructure liabilities and business lines, ensure the continuity of essential operational systems and facilitate the sale of assets or business lines.[48] For groups, recovery plans have to be drawn up by EU parent undertakings and provide the relevant information with regard to both the parent undertaking and each individual subsidiary.[49] In both individual institutions and groups the plans shall include a framework of indicators. 'which identifies the points at which appropriate actions referred to in the plan may be taken'.[50]

Importantly, recovery plans under the BRRD – and, in fact, globally[51] – will not remain in the sphere of the institution or group, but will be subjected to scrutiny by the relevant supervisory authority, or 'competent authority' in the terminology of the directive. For individual institutions, this will be the home supervisor as defined by article 2(21) of the BRRD and article 4(1)(40) of the Capital Requirements Regulation[52] in cooperation with the competent authorities of member states where significant branches are located.[53] Specifically, the authority, under article 6(2) of the directive, will be required to assess the plan's compliance with the requirements set out in article 5 (just discussed) and to analyse whether the plan is likely to accomplish the proposed objectives. In addition, article 2(3) of the BRRD requires that the competent authority: 'shall take into consideration the appropriateness of the institution's capital and funding structure to the level of complexity of the organisational structure and the risk profile of the institution'. These criteria will be complemented by regulatory technical standards, a draft of which was released by the EBA in July 2014.[54]

The plan shall also be communicated to the relevant resolution authority, which may conduct a further assessment: 'with a view to identifying any actions in the recovery plan which may adversely impact the resolvability of the institution, and make recommendations to the competent authority with regard to those matters'.[55] On this basis, the competent authority is empowered, in a graduated approach, (a) to notify the institution of 'material deficiencies' or 'material impediments' to the implementation of the plan and require the institution to submit a revised plan and, possibly, (b) to direct the institution to make specific changes to the plan.[56] If the institution fails to comply with such directions, even more intrusive measures may be imposed. Pursuant to article 6(6) of the directive, the competent authority may require the institution to identify adequate changes to its business and, as *ultima ratio*, even direct the institution 'to take any measures it considers to be necessary and proportionate, taking into account the seriousness of the deficiencies and impediments and the effect of the measures on the institution's business'. Possible changes are defined to include *inter alia* recapitalisation measures, reviews of the institution's strategy and structure, changes to the funding strategy and changes to the governance structure of the institution.[57]

As for group resolution plans, the requirements are broadly similar, but the framework is understandably more complex.[58] This will include both measures at the group level and measures at the level of the individual entities, including significant branches.[59] The group recovery plan will have to be submitted to the relevant consolidating supervisor and the college of supervisors established under article 116 of the Capital Requirements Directive IV,[60] the competent authorities of member states where significant branches are located, the group-level resolution authority and the resolution authority of subsidiaries.[61] They shall then assess the plan and endeavour to reach a joint decision. If this fails, it will be for the consolidating supervisor and for the competent authorities of subsidiaries to decide on the appropriate course of action on their turf,[62] with the EBA acting as arbiter between conflicting views among the relevant competent authorities.[63]

Resolution plans

Resolution plans under the BRRD are devised as an 'inhouse' exercise to be conducted by resolution authorities in consultation with the competent authorities and the resolution authorities of member states where significant branches are located.[64] The relevant institutions themselves have to play a role in their development only if, and to the extent that, the resolution authority decides to get them involved,[65] and can be subjected to extensive requests for information by resolution authorities.[66] Resolution plans shall explore possible responses, in the terminology of the directive: 'options for applying the resolution tools and resolution powers' defined in Title IV of the BRRD, for cases of idiosyncratic failure and of failure within 'broader financial instability or system wide events'.[67] Again, extraordinary financial support, defined rather broadly, is ruled out as an option in this context.[68]

Broadly similar to the dual system characteristic of individual and group recovery plans, group resolution plans will have to be developed by group-level resolution authorities in cooperation with the resolution authorities of subsidiaries and in consultation with resolution authorities in member states with significant branches.[69] These plans shall identify resolution options with regard to EU parent undertakings, subsidiaries that are located within the EU, financial holding companies and parent financial holding companies located within the EU, and – subject to Title VI of the directive – subsidiaries located in third countries (i.e. outside the EU). Detailed requirements apply with regard to the coordination of plans with the EBA and all relevant resolution authorities, with a framework for conflict resolution similar to the one for recovery plans.[70]

Both individual and group resolutions will have to be developed on the basis of a so-called 'assessment of resolvability', which is to be carried out by resolution authorities under articles 15 (for individual institutions) and 16 (for groups) of the directive, respectively. While authorities are required to take into account possible repercussions of their policy decisions for markets in other member states,[71] whether or not this will work out as intended remains to be seen, of course, and perhaps a natural bias towards protecting own markets, market players and depositors could prove persistent in practice.

The relevant criteria are then specified further in section C of the annex to the directive and include both organisational and financial aspects of resolution, as well as requirements with regard to the interconnectedness between the individual institution (or group) and counterparties and market infrastructure both within and outside the EU. If the resolution authority, in consultation with the competent authority, determines that there are 'substantive impediments to the resolvability' of an institution, the authority may notify the institution accordingly, which then has to propose measures to resolve these impediments.[72] If these proposals are found to be deficient, the authority may require the institution to take a broad range of alternative measures proposed by the authority,[73] including the reorganising of financing arrangements, changes to the business or organisational structure and changes in the group structure.[74] In the context of group resolution planning, the directive prescribes a regime of cooperation similar to the one just described with regard to group recovery plans.[75] In both cases, all measures are subject to a proportionality test.[76]

Recovery and resolution plans under the BRRD: some key findings

Looking back to the rather complex structure just described, it is important to note that the BRRD envisages recovery and resolution planning as a two-step procedure, which is to be carried out under the auspices of the competent supervisory authority in the first step and the resolution authority in the second. As a result, as mentioned before, *resolution* planning – in the technical, narrow sense – depends on the outcome of the interaction of institutions (or groups) and competent authorities with regard to *recovery* planning: policy choices made with regard to recovery planning, as the first step of interference with individual firms' and groups' existing organisation and legal structures, will inevitably come with implications for resolution planning, in particular in cases where the competent authority uses its powers to impose and enforce substantial changes to business models, funding arrangements, organisational or indeed legal structures. In this sense, the directive's requirements for the close cooperation between competent and resolution authorities are clearly necessary. Whether they are sufficient to remove practical problems is quite another story, however, and there are reasons for substantial doubts in this regard given the residual potential for disagreement among home and host authorities and its repercussions on the available resolution strategies.[77]

At any rate, the concept of recovery and resolution planning as developed under the BRRD clearly goes far beyond mere contingency planning. In fact, both the competent authorities' powers to require changes to the recovery plan and the resolution authorities' powers to enhance resolvability could be used in a way that drastically interferes with the institution's business portfolio and financial and organisational structure, including group structures. In terms of the powers available under the BRRD, both competent and resolution authorities have indeed been provided with tools to accomplish no less than fully fledged market reorganisation, in the sense of substantial changes in the way the industry has organised itself. Used wisely, this could indeed remove at least some of the problems preventing effective crisis resolution today, especially problems attributable to the complexity and opacity of business models and organisations. In other words, on the basis of their powers given under this part of the directive, authorities could go a long way towards implementing fully fledged structural reforms of banking in the relevant jurisdictions, even without a more specific formal mandate to do so.

Against this backdrop, however, the delineation of powers between supervisory and resolution authorities defined under the BRRD may well turn out to be a second best solution. From a functional perspective, the framework essentially splits up what ideally should be inseparable. Although from different perspectives, recovery and resolution planning both deal with options that could be used in the event of a failure, and both regimes, for the sake of effectiveness, should be as consistent as possible. Having (at least) two authorities in charge, consistency could fall victim to conflicting views between the authorities, which in turn may adversely affect the capacity of the regime to work effectively in the interests of enhanced resolvability. There may be reasons for separating resolution powers from supervisory functions, but separating recovery from resolution planning is a different story. This problem is even more acute in the case of recovery and resolution plans for groups, where the framework for coordination between a multitude of different authorities at the national and EU levels is even more complicated. All this may result in, at best, duplicative or indeed even contradictory requirements imposed on individual institutions and groups.

The situation within the banking union: recovery and resolution planning under the SSM and SRM regulations

Within the banking union, the European Central Bank (ECB), in its capacity as sole supervisor, will also assume the 'supervisory tasks in relation to recovery plans', including the power to impose 'structural changes', for credit institutions or groups in relation to which the ECB is the consolidating supervisor.[78] In addition, the ECB will replace national competent authorities for branches of credit institutions established in third countries.[79] The Single Resolution Board (SRB), by contrast, will be in charge of drafting resolution plans for:

1   credit institutions established in a participating member state;
2   parent undertakings established in a participating member state, if subject to consolidated supervision by the ECB;
3   investment firms and financial institutions established in a participating member state, if subject to consolidated supervision by the ECB; and
4   groups, if they are considered to be significant in accordance with article 6(4) of the SSM regulation, or if the ECB has decided to exercise directly the supervisory powers in accordance with article 6(6)(b) of the SSM regulation.[80]

National resolution authorities in participating member states will continue to be responsible for all other institutions or groups under the national laws transposing the BRRD.[81] The SRB retains some oversight powers, however, and may exercise the relevant powers directly, in particular where the national resolution authorities fail to comply with its warnings.[82] Participating member states have the right to transfer the relevant powers to the SRB pursuant to article 7(5) of the SRM regulation.

Where the Board is directly responsible, the relevant provisions are to be found in the SRM regulation, not the national laws transposing the BRRD. Article 8 of the regulation first sets out the procedure for the development of resolution plans for those individual entities and groups for which the SRB is responsible. Within this framework, the SRB shall draw up the plans after consulting the ECB or relevant national competent authorities, as well as the resolution authorities in participating member states where the relevant entities are established and resolution authorities in non-participating member states with significant branches. The SRB may require national resolution authorities to prepare drafts for individual and group resolution plans.[83] The board shall issue guidelines and address instructions to national resolution authorities for such drafts.[84] As for substantive requirements, the regulation then basically replicates the requirements set out for individual and group resolution plans in the BRRD.[85] Just as under the BRRD, the resolution plans developed by the SRB shall be based on an assessment of resolvability of the individual entities and groups. In this respect, article 10 of the SRM regulation essentially prescribes broadly the same procedure and substantive criteria as articles 15–18 of the BRRD for individual entities and groups, respectively.

Possible policy options: an assessment

Authorities' incentives to change the status quo

The centralisation of supervisory and resolution powers within the banking union is, of course, not an end in itself. It serves the fundamental objective to help remove the participating member state's abuse of their control over domestic banking systems and, in a much quoted formulation, to 'break the link between sovereign debt and bank debt and the vicious circle which has led to over €4.5 trillion of taxpayers' money being used to rescue banks in the EU'.[86] Within the context of this chapter, this translates into a rather simple question: Is the new regime on recovery and resolution planning likely to work more effectively within the banking union framework than under national legislation transposing the BRRD in non-participating EU member states? In other words, is it, as such, likely to mitigate the deficiencies of the BRRD in terms of overly complicated decision-making processes and the potential for contradictory decisions by supervisory and resolution authorities?

At first sight, the answer seems to be in the negative, since the need to reconcile a multitude of different views from actors at both the EU and national levels has not been removed. All in all, the framework for recovery and resolution planning under the SSM and SRM regulations does not deviate substantially from the relevant procedures and substantive requirements under the BRRD. The ECB and the SRB merely assume the functions otherwise allocated to national authorities under the BRRD. Just as the coordination between national competent authorities and national resolution authorities is not problem-free under the BRRD framework, nor is the coordination between the ECB in its capacity as supervisory authority and the SRB. These problems are likely to be complicated further by the need to consult with national authorities. Against this background, the advantages of having a single authority in place for groups and institutions established within the banking union have been watered down considerably. Finally, with regard to third country relations outside the EU, it may be advantageous to have the SRB as a 'one stop' counterpart for foreign authorities. But whether this really can improve the effectiveness of cross-border resolution will also depend on whether or not the SRB will be able to establish consistent strategies across the banking union, which is likely to be difficult in view of residual differences between national markets and banking systems.

On closer inspection, however, this assessment could prove too simplistic. As mentioned before, the dimension of the powers granted under the BRRD to design and enforce drastic changes to existing business models, funding arrangements and indeed corporate and group structures, should not be underestimated. For certain, the relevant regulatory policies will have to be developed on the basis of existing market structures and will have to respect that different markets have evolved differently over time.[87] This will, for the time being, preclude a 'one size fits all' approach. For example, within the German banking system, different resolution strategies will have to be developed for the three major subsectors, reflecting the differences in the legal structures of commercial banks in the form of partnerships or companies, cooperative banks and banks incorporated as public law bodies under public ownership. Nonetheless, clearly not all residual differences that have developed over time are invariably worth preserving, or simply have to be accepted as a fact of life. Given the obvious need to apply the new regime in a non-discriminatory way to all firms located in the EU,[88] it is likely that both the ECB and the SRB could eventually decide to enforce greater consistency of business models, funding arrangements and the legal structures of individual firms and groups, to the extent that residual differences in this respect stand in the way of a consistent application of the resolution tools across the banking union (as they certainly have to date). In other words, although subject to proportionality tests that may be relied upon by banks in defending the existing arrangements, both the ECB and, in particular, the SRB have incentives to use their powers analysed above to accomplish substantial changes to the different markets under their control. Furthermore, they are, perhaps, better placed than national authorities to use their powers free from national biases. In effect, a certain streamlining of business models and group structures could indeed be the consequence.[89] Even though resolution should be planned with a view to accommodating existing structures, effective responses to future crises – both individual and systemic – may, in the long run, be possible only with greater convergence in terms of funding models and group structures. In this sense, the problems highlighted above with regard to the effective implementation of recovery and resolution planning within the EU could well turn out to be resolvable only if the authorities use their powers with a view to forcing changes to existing market structures.

There are, in fact, signs that future regulatory policies could well be inspired by this sort of reasoning. In its recent report to the G20 summit in November 2014, the FSB emphasises the need for cross-border consistency in structural bank reforms and discusses possible effects and impediments to the 'supervisability' and 'resolvability' that could be triggered by differing reforms.[90] As mentioned before, this is a clear signal that the interplay between the legal and organisational structure of institutions and groups on the one hand and the 'resolvability' of institutions on the other hand are attracting increasing attention among regulators worldwide. Thus, there seems to be a growing awareness of possible impediments to resolvability originating from organisational diversity of banks, which might in turn provide incentives for regulators and supervisors to counter these effects by nudging, or forcing, the institutions and firms into substantial changes in this respect. If this assessment is correct, the responsible authorities may be expected to make wide use of their powers in order to address such impediments by 'optimising' business models and funding, organisational and legal structures of banks, and thus to enhance both the resolvability and the supervisability of the relevant entities and groups.

Instruments and strategies

The legal powers for accomplishing substantial changes to existing business models, funding arrangements, organisational and legal structures *ex ante*, that is before the state of insolvency has been reached, have been identified above. They are to be found in the powers to evaluate recovery plans and assess the resolvability of institutions and firms and in the corresponding powers to impose changes to existing structures and arrangements.[91] In this respect, the definition of potential strategies would not have to start from zero. Indeed, to a larger extent than with regard to the resolution tools, authorities could rely on past experience and make use of existing approaches to preventive structural measures that have been adopted in a number of jurisdictions with a view to containing the impact of bank failure.

Structural bank reforms in the form adopted by the United States and the United Kingdom outside the banking union, and by Belgium, France and Germany within,[92] are only one, albeit rather bold, example among others of a top-down re-engineering of existing organisational, financial and legal arrangements in cross-border banks and groups. Leaving all conceptual differences aside, all those recent examples of structural bank reforms clearly are what could be described as 'activities-orientated', in the sense that they are designed to separate certain business functions of banks and protect, in one way or the other, those functions that are deemed particularly relevant in macroeconomic terms.[93] While the focus is on the prevention of contagious effects in crisis by separating those functions *ex ante*, the expectation is that it will also be easier to resolve the reformed business formally once it has reached the proximity of insolvency after the structural reforms have drawn a clearer line between systemically important and less important functions before a crisis hits.[94]

In this regard, the separation of existing business functions can be classified as a functional alternative to strategies that have been employed for a long time by regulatory authorities in many jurisdictions specifically in relation to cross-border banks and banking groups, with a view to 'regionalising' the fallout of individual failures on domestic markets by splitting up the firm's or group's assets and liabilities along jurisdictional borders. Such strategies are commonly referred to as the 'ring fencing' of assets and liabilities. Applied by host authorities to domestic branches of foreign-registered banks, they can take two forms. In the first, in what is known as 'ex ante ring fencing', host authorities will require that domestic branches of foreign banks, at any given point in time, maintain sufficient domestic assets to be available to domestic creditors if the foreign bank were to enter insolvency. By contrast, 'ex post ring fencing' occurs once a foreign bank has entered into insolvency liquidation or resolution. In this case, similar to secondary insolvency proceedings under general international insolvency law, host authorities responsible for supervising branches will subject the branch to a liquidation procedure that is separate from the liquidation or resolution procedure initiated and administered by home country courts or authorities.[95] Where coordinated and enforced ex ante, both forms of ring fencing, to some extent, serve similar objectives as activities-orientated structural reforms.[96] From a functional perspective, the jurisdictional separation of business activities also aims at reducing complexity in the interests of enhanced resolvability, inasmuch as it reallocates the relevant bank's resources in a way that facilitates domestic crisis management without the need to rely on the home country authorities' willingness to cooperate and appropriately protect stakeholders in other jurisdictions.[97] As an even more aggressive strategy, host jurisdictions could force foreign banks active within their territory to reorganise their business by way of legal separation from the foreign bank, and to conduct domestic business exclusively through subsidiaries – or through an intermediate holding subject to supervision by host authorities – rather than through branches that would be supervised by the home authorities.[98] As a result, it would be even easier for host authorities to cut out the domestic part of a group in the event of insolvency, to determine exclusively the level of capital required for this business and to ensure that domestic assets will be available to local creditors. In this light, what has become known as the 'subsidiarisation' of foreign-owned banking business is very similar to the ring fencing of foreign-owned branches described above, but goes even further in terms of the legal and functional separation of home and host country activities.[99]

As mentioned before, it is impossible within the restrictions of this chapter to present a comprehensive assessment of the merits and shortcomings of these different concepts.[100] For present purposes, it is sufficient to note that *all* forms of forced changes to existing organisational, funding and legal structures will inevitably come with – possibly substantial – implications for the firm's or group's profitability, in terms of both short-term (adjusting) and long-term costs, e.g. because of reduced efficiency.[101] Moreover, the regionalisation of banking activities, which could follow from a forced separation of existing groups along jurisdictional borders, could eventually reduce market liquidity, which may be detrimental especially in distressed markets.[102] There clearly are trade-offs between the resilience of the relevant financial systems, which may be furthered by such reforms, and the profitability of firms and groups, as well as the macroeconomic benefits of integrated, deep markets, which may be compromised. This is not to suggest that the existence of such costs should preclude, or just deter, attempts to redesign existing business models, financial, organisational and legal structures *a limine*. In fact, similar trade-offs exist with regard to all aspects of the re-regulation of financial systems after the crisis and may have to be accepted as a price to be paid for avoiding future taxpayer exposure to 'too big to fail' bail-outs. As has been noted with regard to increases in bank capital requirements, the assessment of the merits should be done on a 'net-social-welfare' basis, taking into account not just the costs to banks but also the possible gains resulting from greater financial stability to the taxpayer.[103] To be sure, this is a rather complex task, as the assessment of such benefits, in turn, needs to consider possible social gains (in terms of greater growth potential) that may be realised only at the expense of greater market volatility.[104] Given the lack of reliable empirical evidence on the trade-offs between business models, financial, organisational and legal infrastructures, bank profitability and systemic resilience, it is certainly advisable for the relevant authorities to proceed with care and to improve the empirical basis before engaging in comprehensive structural measures that will substantially change the way banks and banking groups are organised today. However, a gradual convergence of regulatory policies in this respect – and, as a result, of the relevant market structures as a whole – may be simply unavoidable over time. This holds true particularly in the banking union, where the centralisation of responsibilities and powers comes with both a greater need for consistency and improved ways to accomplish it.

What could it look like? Four scenarios and some speculation

As mentioned before, the future practice with regard to resolution plans will involve a number of yet undecided policy choices, including both the fundamental choice between 'SPOE' and 'MPOE' scenarios and the structure of minimum requirements for bailinable debt.[105] Whichever solution is ultimately agreed upon, the feasibility will also depend on how the authorities will use their powers in order to force institutions and groups to reorganise themselves in a way that removes potential impediments to the preferred approach. Some preliminary observations can be made even pending future agreement in this respect. In order to explore how such efforts could evolve in future practice and to illustrate the scope and limitations for relevant policies, it is appropriate to differentiate between a number of highly stylised group scenarios, which will occur in various different combinations in future practice, but nonetheless highlight some important aspects:

a   a 'pure' banking union scenario, where all individual group companies and the group as a whole are supervised by the ECB;
b   a 'mixed' European scenario, where the ECB acts as consolidating supervisor for a group with branches and/or subsidiaries located within both participating and non-participating member states;
c   a 'mixed' European scenario, with the ECB as competent authority for a subsidiary of a group or a branch of an institution that is under (consolidated) supervision by home authorities in another EU member state; and
d   a 'third country' scenario, where the ECB is the supervisor for a subsidiary of a foreign group.

'Pure' banking union groups

Consider, first, a group of credit institutions located in different member states participating in the banking union, with both the parent located within the banking union and the ECB in charge as consolidating supervisor for the group and competent supervisor for the individual credit institutions and branches. In this scenario, the SRB would also be fully responsible for all tasks related to resolution planning at both the individual firm and group levels.[106] Consequently, both the ECB, in its capacity as competent authority for the assessment for individual and group recovery plans,[107] and the SRB[108] would be in a position to determine and enforce policies in a rather autonomous way, with only limited influence of national authorities in the respective national markets. In this scenario, the highest possible degree of consistency for the entire group can be expected.[109]

Assuming that the group is organised in a highly integrated way, with a wide range of business functions carried out across the different legal entities and with capital allocated on a consolidated basis, potential impediments to swift and effective group-wide resolution could result from a variety of sources in such a setting. These could include *inter alia* a high regional concentration of risky business and exposure to specific market risks,[110] complicated intra-group funding arrangements,[111] a mismatch between the allocation of capital and liquidity within the group on the one hand and the sources of risks on the other hand,[112] and/or interdependencies between group companies in terms of the provision of essential operating services (e.g. IT services) across the group.

Taking these features as examples of a wider range of potential problems, it is clear that not all potential impediments to resolution that emanate from business models, funding, organisational and legal structures can be appropriately addressed by way of the different forms of structural changes discussed above. While a lack of risk diversification certainly is detrimental, not just in terms of long-term sustainability, but also in terms of resolvability, this and similar deficiencies in business models can hardly be corrected merely by top-down administrative intervention in the organisation of the relevant firms and groups. It would be for management and bank owners, not for the ECB or the SRB, to define possible remedies and change the business model in this respect. Intra-group funding arrangements, by contrast, will be much easier to deal with, as the relevant legal framework has been harmonised by the BRRD,[113] and a common approach is likely to emerge within the EU generally in the context of the forthcoming regime on minimum requirements on bailable liabilities under article 45 of the BRRD.[114] In effect, these problems will be, to some extent, addressed through general prudential requirements, not in the context of individual or group recovery and resolution plans.[115]

In the context of recovery and resolution planning, the relevant authorities could, however, try to address issues such as the remaining two problems mentioned above, e.g. by forcing groups to reallocate or consolidate their business and service functions within the existing group landscape. Alternatively, they could force the group to restructure and simplify itself, e.g. by reducing the number of group companies and realign business functions with the legal structure.[116] A fundamental policy choice to be made in this respect is whether firms and groups should also be required to increase the functional and/or geographical segregation of business activities within the group, e.g. by separating traditional commercial from investment banking services, or by reallocating local business to locally incorporated subsidiaries. Both strategies could yield benefits in terms of improved resolvability. However, the case for either would have to be carefully explored within a pure banking union scenario, where the centralised responsibility for resolution would mitigate some of the complexities in normal cross-border cases anyhow. Instead, the relevant authorities could opt for a reverse option, by concentrating all business into one legal entity, effectively consolidating existing subsidiaries into the parent. Under the former option, the execution of resolution action would be 'regionalised', while under the latter, 'centralised'.

Neither the BRRD nor the SSM and SRM regulations offer clear guidance in this respect. Essentially, the relevant provisions merely require that the implications for systemic stability in all member states be duly considered,[117] be proportionate[118] and must not discriminate on the grounds of nationality,[119] or prevent the exercise of the treaty freedoms of movement.[120] None of this would appear to preclude functional separation as a guiding principle for regulatory interference with the organisational choice of institutions and groups within the resolution planning framework. Much the same applies with regard to the choice between regionalisation and decentralisation of resolution by way of structural changes in the form discussed above. As long as the proposed changes can be justified against the benchmark of 'resolvability' on the one hand and the legal safeguards set out above on the other hand, they are permissible under both the BRRD and the SSM and SRM regulations, and the responsible authorities will enjoy a high degree of discretion in this regard.

That said, even if 'regionalised' groups may be easier to resolve even within the institutional framework of the banking union, the likelihood that the ECB or the SRB would actually opt for a strategy aimed at the regionalisation of banking operations within the euro area is probably low. Notwithstanding centralised supervisory powers, restructuring existing groups in a way that reallocates regional business to regional subsidiaries will probably be difficult to accomplish without increasing the fragmentation of banking markets within the banking union, which would be incompatible with the very rationale of the banking union.[121] It is highly likely, therefore, that the ECB will treat the entire euro area as a truly integrated market, which would, for example, rule out the ring-fencing of assets within branches in order to protect the relevant 'host' jurisdictions against the risk of insolvency of a bank that is licensed in another member state,[122] even if a reliable agreement between host and home countries on ring-fencing could possibly be mutually advantageous in theory.[123] In this respect, not just the banks but also the relevant authorities within the banking union are confronted with a dilemma between enhanced resolvability and systemic stability, which could be facilitated by regionalisation, and the need to strive for market integration, which would not.

'Mixed' European scenario with ECB as consolidating supervisor

Turning to the second scenario, where the ECB acts as consolidating supervisor for groups with subsidiaries and branches both within the banking union and the rest of the EU, the situation *prima facie* looks less different from 'pure' banking union scenarios that could be expected. In this scenario, the ECB, as consolidating supervisor, and the SRB would retain considerable power to influence the structure of firms within their supervision, and of the group as a whole, even though one or more subsidiaries would be supervised by home country authorities in a non-participating member state. Moreover, the key governing principles for 'pure' banking union scenarios, i.e. the need to maintain financial stability across the *entire* EU, proportionality, non-discrimination and respect for the treaty freedoms of movement,[124] equally apply to the relationship between the banking union authorities and subsidiaries located in other EU member states.

Both the ECB, when assessing group recovery plans under the national laws transposing article 7 of the BRRD, and the SRB, as the authority responsible for drawing up group resolution plans and for the assessment of resolvability under articles 8 and 10 of the SRM regulation, will nonetheless be in a position that is different from a 'pure' banking union environment. Arguably, the potential for conflicts with the home supervisors of group companies licensed in non-participating EU member states, i.e. foreign authorities that are not part of the institutional hierarchy established within the banking union, will be higher vis-à-vis national supervisory and resolution authorities in participating member states, which occupy a lower rank than the ECB and the SRB, respectively. The same applies with regard to non-participating member states with significant branches of institutions licensed within the banking union. Although bound to the principle of non-discrimination and the treaty freedoms of movement, the ECB and the SRB could find themselves in considerable tension with the corresponding authorities in non-participating member states, especially with respect to the allocation of risks (and, correspondingly, the division of powers and responsibilities for resolution action) between jurisdictions within 'mixed' cross-border groups. Conflicting interests to support specific market places (e.g. Frankfurt versus London) could add to that.

While starting from the same set of substantive principles laid down in the BRRD for the treatment of banks across the entire EU, it is therefore conceivable that the ECB and the SRB might follow a different approach in dealing with subsidiaries or branches located in non-participating member states. In order to enhance the supervisability and resolvability of such groups from the perspective of the banking union authorities, they could, for example, use their powers with a view to concentrating all group business conducted within the euro area into legal entities directly under their control. Although in conflict with the treaty freedoms of movement,[125] in that it would lead to enhanced disintegration between markets in participating and non-participating member states and could benefit financial centres within the banking union at the expense of others outside, this could be justified on the public policy grounds of systemic stability gains and, indeed, would be an almost logical consequence of the institutional division between the banking union and the rest of Europe.

With regard to branches of banking union-licensed institutions that are located in non-participating EU member states and operate under the European Passport, the relevant strategic choices would be even more complex. Whether or not the banking union authorities would prefer to maintain the existing branch structure, or force the relevant firms or groups to restructure branches into subsidiaries, would probably depend on a case-by-case analysis of the respective costs and benefits. From the banking union authorities' (home country) perspective, allowing existing extra-territorial branches to continue trading would secure more effective control over business conducted outside the euro area both on a going concern and gone concern basis, which could be attractive in cases where the ECB or the SRB are uncomfortable with the strategies employed by the relevant host countries.[126] On the other hand, this would mean full responsibility for the coordination of resolution action beyond the euro area, which could be risky for operational and logistic reasons as well as because of potential turf wars with the relevant home authorities.[127] Moreover, the full cost of resolution, in this scenario, would be ultimately borne by the Single Resolution Fund, with no direct access to funding mechanisms in the relevant non-participating member states. Forcing the relevant institutions to restructure their business outside the euro area into subsidiaries would avoid these problems, albeit at the price of reduced control over resolution proceedings on the part of the banking union authorities and, correspondingly, an increased dependence on cooperation with the relevant host authorities.[128]

It is not difficult to see that in any of these different scenarios, the result could be enhanced 'regionalisation' along the jurisdictional border between the banking union and the rest of the EU in terms of supervisory and resolution powers, but also in the way groups are organised. Although expressly required to adopt a truly European perspective – and respect the interests of non-participating member states[129] – under the relevant legal frameworks, both the ECB and SRB may be expected to demonstrate an almost natural, and justifiable, bias towards restructuring existing cross-border groups to the disadvantage of markets outside the banking union. This could give market centres within the banking union (not least, Frankfurt) a competitive edge over their competitors outside their jurisdiction (in particular, London). In summary, the recovery and resolution planning regime could thus prove to be a powerful driver of an increasing division between the two realms, although much will depend on how specifically the banking union authorities will use their powers in future practice. In fact, despite the need to comply with the treaty framework for a level playing field across the entire internal market, firms outside the direct control of the banking union authorities could find themselves in a position that is closer to that of third country institutions than it is to the position of institutions located within the banking union.

'Mixed' European scenario with ECB as host country supervisor
over subsidiaries licensed within the banking union or branches
of institutions in non-participating EU member states

For obvious reasons, the picture would look entirely different in a setting where the ECB, not being the consolidating supervisor, merely assumes the role of the home supervisor for a subsidiary of a firm that is supervised, on a consolidated basis, by the authorities of a non-participating member state, or indeed a (significant) branch of such a firm. In the case of a subsidiary, although the banking union authorities would retain the responsibility for recovery and resolution planning for the individual firm, they would not have control over the structure of the entire group. They could be drawn, therefore, into a conflict with their counterparts in non-participating member states that would amount to a reversed image of the one just described for a scenario for groups under the consolidated supervision by the banking union authorities. However, given the relevance of the euro area as a market even to institutions licensed in non-participating member states, chances are that the relative influence of banking union authorities on the development of group resolution strategies could well be higher than in the reverse scenario. Even without the powers available to the consolidating supervisor, the ECB and SRB could thus effectively use their powers under the recovery and resolution planning regime in a way that ultimately forces the relevant groups to concentrate all business conducted within the euro area in a subsidiary under direct ECB supervision, which could, in the event of an insolvency, be operated on a stand-alone basis.[130]

With regard to the treatment of euro area branches of institutions licensed in a non-participating member state, the situation, once again, would be different. Just as in the opposite case discussed above, the policy choice would probably be made on a case-by-case basis, taking into account the trade-off between the advantages of autonomous control of resolution strategies on the one hand and the potential costs on the other hand. Where the banking union authorities feel comfortable with the supervisory and resolution practices adopted by the relevant non-banking union home authorities, they will probably leave the existing branch structure untouched, which would relieve them of the burden of pursuing independent resolution action in addition to action taken by the responsible home authorities. In such circumstances, the banking union authorities could even try to have existing subsidiaries, which are operating under a banking union licence, restructured into branches of foreign institutions, thus removing the need to act as host resolution authority should the euro area business run into problems. Where these conditions are not satisfied, by contrast, just the opposite could happen, and the banking union authorities could use their powers to nudge foreign groups into turning their euro area branches into subsidiaries.

In summary, even where the responsibility for consolidated supervision is not within the banking union, the recovery and resolution planning regime could turn out to be a source of increased disintegration between markets in participating and those in non-participating member states, regardless of whether existing cross-border business is pursued by branches or by subsidiaries on foreign, non-euro area banks.

'Third country' scenario

In scenarios where the ECB is acting as supervisor for a subsidiary whose parent company is located in a third country outside the EU, the banking union's position will look (perhaps surprisingly) similar to the 'mixed' scenario just described. In this regard, the specific contents of the relevant contingency plans and the underlying strategies will depend, to a large extent, on the degree of trust between the banking union authorities and the relevant third country authorities, which will operate under the framework for cooperation established by the BRRD and the SSM and SRM regulations.[131] As a rule, however, just as in relation to groups supervised on a consolidated basis by authorities in a non-participating member state, the banking union authorities, in a third country scenario, will have both powers and incentives to force the subsidiaries under their supervision to reinforce their legal, financial and operational independence from the remainder of the group, so as to facilitate recovery and, ultimately, resolution with minimum impact on the stability of the financial system within the euro area. In this respect, the banking union authorities would not be restricted by the treaty freedoms of movement, which – as discussed above – could play a (limited) role as safeguards for the protection of non-euro area banks in 'mixed' European settings with the ECB as consolidating supervisor. In cases where the foreign group operates a multitude of subsidiaries or branches within the euro area, this could even include a restructuring of all banking union, or indeed European, business into a holding structure with a holding in a participating member state, which is expressly envisaged as a possible course of action in both the BRRD and the SRM regulation.[132]

Conclusions

Even with a reformed toolbox of instruments for the resolution and reorganisation of banks and banking groups, complex and opaque organisational, financial and legal structures within banks and banking groups will continue to stand in the way of effective resolution. In order to remove such impediments, supervisory and resolution authorities in Europe, both within and outside the banking union, have been provided with a wide range of powers to force the relevant institutions and groups to make appropriate changes. This chapter analyses these powers and their background in international standard setting and explores how strategies for the future use of these instruments could evolve within the banking union. Specifically, where the banking union authorities (ECB and SRB) are, qua consolidated supervision, in control over the organisational and legal structure of an entire group, they could use their powers in a way that could enhance further integration of the banking systems within the banking union, while driving disintegration between participating and non-participating member states. This would be different where the consolidated supervision is exercised by authorities in non-participating EU member states, but even in such scenarios, the banking union authorities could seek to protect the interests of participating jurisdictions by measures that would increase disintegration, possibly placing strong market places in non-participating member states into a competitive disadvantage. Judging from a purely technical perspective, such policies could perhaps be justified against the benchmark of resolvability of institutions and groups within the banking union, on the grounds of increased systemic resilience. However, for the relevant authorities to be able to make the relevant policy choices, which may or may not include the measures discussed above, and to calibrate the relevant instruments in scope and content, further research into the relevant trade-offs between business models, funding arrangements, organisational and legal structures on the one hand and resolvability and systemic stability on the other hand, is certainly essential. The available evidence that exists to date is hardly a sufficient basis for a drastic reorganisation of present firm and group structures in this respect.

Acknowledgement

This chapter was prepared for the conference 'European banking union: Prospects and Challenges' on 21–22 November 2014 at the University of Buckingham. Parts of it build on research presented at conferences at the Universities of Munich and Bad Homburg in July and October 2014, respectively. The author thanks participants in all three events for numerous insightful comments.

Notes

1 See, in particular, Basel Committee on Banking Supervision *Report and Recommendations of the Cross-Border Bank Resolution Group* (2010), available at www.bis.org/publ/bcbs169.pdf; FSB *Key Attributes of Effective Resolution Regimes for Financial Institutions* (October 2011), available at www.financialstabilityboard.org/publications/r_111104cc.pdf.

2 See, e.g. for the United States, Dodd-Frank Wall Street Reform and Consumer Protection Act of 2010, Pub. L. No. 111–203, 124 Stat. 1376 (2010), Title II – 'Orderly Liquidation Authority'. Within the EU, a harmonised framework for the resolution of banks has been adopted with Directive 2014/59/EU of the European Parliament and of the Council of 15 May 2014 establishing a framework for the recovery and resolution of credit institutions and investment firms and amending Council Directive 82/891/EEC, and Directives 2001/24/EC, 2002/47/EC, 2004/25/EC, 2005/56/EC, 2007/36/EC, 2011/35/EU, 2012/30/EU and 2013/36/EU, and Regulations (EU) No 1093/2010 and (EU) No 648/2012, of the European Parliament and of the Council, OJ L 173 of 12 June 2014, p. 190, Title IV – 'Resolution'. For the banking union, broadly identical instruments have since been adopted by the provisions of Part II, Chapter 3, of Regulation (EU) No 806/2014 of the European Parliament and of the Council of 15 July 2014 establishing uniform rules and a uniform procedure for the resolution of credit institutions and certain investment firms in the framework of a Single Resolution Mechanism and a Single Resolution Fund and amending Regulation (EU) No 1093/2010, OJ L 225 of 30 July 2014, p. 1.

3 For further discussion of the historical roots, focusing on the BRRD see, e.g. Jens-Hinrich Binder *Resolution: Concepts, Requirements and Tools*, conference paper (September 2014), available at http://ssrn.com/abstract=2499613, at pp. 13–14.

4 See, for further discussion of these aspects with regard to the BRRD, Binder, supra no. 3, pp. 11–13 and pp. 29–38. See also generally John Armour 'Making bank resolution credible' (11 February 2014), in E. Ferran, N. Moloney and J. Payne (eds) *Oxford Handbook of Financial Regulation* (Oxford, UK: Oxford University Press, 2014) (preprint available at SSRN: http://ssrn.com/abstract=2393998).

5 See, in particular, Basel Committee, supra n. 1, at paras. 94–97, and FSB, supra no. 1, pp. 15–18, and see later in the chapter. Also see, for general discussion and analysis, Emilios Avgouleas, Charles Goodhart and Dirk Schoenmaker (2013) 'Bank resolution plans as a catalyst for global financial reform' *Journal of Financial Stability* 9: 210–218. On the international background, see also Eva Hüpkes (2013) '"Living wills" – An international perspective', in: A. Dombret and P. Kenadjian (eds) *The Bank Recovery and Resolution Directive – Europe's Solution for 'Too Big To Fail'* Berlin, Germany: De Gruyter Recht, p. 71; Nizan Geslevich Packin (2012) 'The case against the Dodd-Frank Act's living wills: Contingency planning following the financial crisis' *9 Berkeley Business Law Journal* 29: 37–38.

6 Supra, no. 2.

7 Council Regulation (EU) 1024/2013 of 15 October 2013 conferring specific tasks on the European Central Bank concerning policies relating to the prudential supervision of credit institution, OJ L 287 of 29 October 2013, p. 63 (hereafter: the 'SSM Regulation'). For the SRM Regulation, see supra, no. 2.

8 See BRRD, articles 5–9; SSM regulation, article 4(1)(i) and, for further discussion, see later in the chapter .

9 See BRRD, articles 10–14; SRM regulation, articles 8 and 9 and, for further discussion, see later in the chapter .

10 See, e.g. Avgouleas *et al.*, supra no. 5, at pp. 212–213; and see (with focus on the US approach) Adam Feibelman (2012) 'Living Wills and Pre-commitment', 1 *American University Business Law Brief* 95; Packin (2012) *9 Berkeley Business Law Journal* 29: 37–38.

11 With §619 of Dodd-Frank Wall Street Reform and Consumer Protection Act of 2010, Pub. L. No. 111–203, 124 Stat. 1376 (2010).

12 With the Financial Services (Banking Reform) Act 2013 (chapter 33).

13 For *Belgium*, see Loi relative au statut et au contrôle des établissements de crédit, 25 April 2014, Moniteur Belge Ed. 2, 7 June 2014, p. 36794, articles 117–133. For *France*, see Loi no. 2013–672 du 26 juillet 2013 de séparation et de régulation des activités bancaires, *Journal Officiel de la République Française* no. 0173 du 27 juillet 2013, p. 12530. For *Germany*, see Gesetz zur Abschirmung von Risiken und zur Planung der Sanierung und Abwicklung von Kreditinstituten und Finanzgruppen, 7 August 2013, Bundesgesetzblatt Part I, p. 3090. Also see, for a comparative discussion of these reforms, Jens-Hinrich Binder (2014) *To Ring-Fence or Not, and How? Key Questions for Structural Bank Reform in Europe*, available at SSRN: http://ssrn.com/abstract=2543860.

14 EU Commission *Proposal for a Regulation of the European Parliament and the Council on Structural Measures Improving the Resilience of EU Credit Institutions*, COM(2014) 43 final.

15 High-Level Expert Group on Reforming the Structure of the EU Banking Sector *Final Report* (2012), available at http://ec.europa.eu/internal_market/bank/docs/high-level_expert_group/report_en.pdf ('Liikanen Report').

16 See, e.g. Liikanen *et al.*, supra no. 15, at pp. 95–97 (stressing the need to enhance resolvability).

17 FSB *Structural Banking Reforms. Cross-Border Consistencies and Global Financial Stability Implications. Report to G20 Leaders for the November 2014 Summit*, 27 October 2014, available at www.financialstabilityboard.org/publications/r_141027.pdf.

18 For a detailed discussion of the relevant aspects and problems in this respect (focusing on the legal framework under the US Dodd-Frank Act, but in principle

nonetheless applicable to European institutions), see Packin (2012) 9 *Berkeley Business Law Journal* 29: 39–72.

19 Cf. ibid., pp. 75–77.

20 See, e.g. FSB *Recovery and Resolution Planning for Systemically Important Financial Institutions: Guidance on Developing Effective Resolution Strategies* (16 July 2013), available at www.financialstabilityboard.org/publications/r_130716b.pdf, pp. 14–19. For a useful discussion of these approaches see, e.g. Jeffrey N. Gordon and Wolf-Georg Ringe (2014) 'Bank resolution in the European banking union: A Transatlantic perspective on what it would take' *Columbia Law Review*, available at SSRN: http://ssrn.com/abstract=2361347.

21 See BRRD, article 45 (requiring member states to ensure minimum levels). The EBA released draft *Technical Standards on Minimum Requirements on Own Funds and Eligible Liabilities (MREL)* for consultation on 28 November 2014 (EBA/CP/2014/41, available at www.eba.europa.eu/regulation-and-policy/recovery-and-resolution). Unlike the FSB's proposals for standards on total loss absorbing capacity (see note 22), this proposal does not specifically address the compatibility with SPOE and MPOE solutions, however.

22 FSB *Adequacy of Loss-Absorbing Capacity of Global Systemically Important Banks in Resolution. Consultative Document*, 10 November 2014, available at www.financial stabilityboard.org/wp-content/uploads/TLAC-Condoc-6-Nov-2014-FINAL.pdf; see also FSB, supra no. 17, pp. 7–8.

23 For a detailed discussion of which, see, Packin (2012) 9 *Berkeley Business Law Journal* 29: 39–72.

24 E.g. Clay R. Costner (2012) 'Living wills: Can a flexible approach to rulemaking address key concerns surrounding Dodd-Frank's resolution plans?' 16 *North Carolina Banking Institute Journal* 134; Feibelman, supra no. 10; Joseph Karl Grant (2012) 'Planning for the death of a systemically important financial institution under title I §165(d) of the Dodd-Frank Act: The practical implications of resolution plans or living wills in planning a bank's funeral', 6 *Virginia Law & Business Review* 467; Randall D. Guynn 'Resolution planning in the United States', in: A. Dombret and P. Kenadjian (eds) *The Bank Recovery and Resolution Directive – Europe's Solution for 'Too Big To Fail'* (2013), p. 109; Packin (2012) 9 *Berkeley Business Law Journal* 29: 39–72.

25 For detailed discussion and review of the literature, see Binder, supra no. 13.

26 See, again, Avgouleas *et al.*, supra no. 5; Hüpkes, supra no. 5.

27 For a more detailed analysis of the available evidence and of the need for further research, see Binder, supra no. 13.

28 See infra, III.

29 Supra no. 1.

30 See FSB, supra no. 1, pp. 15–18.

31 BRRD, articles 6 and 8.

32 BRRD, articles 10, 12 and 13 (development of resolution plans) and 15–18 (assessment of resolvability).

33 BRRD, article 4; SRM regulation, article 11.

34 See, again, Avgouleas *et al.*, supra no. 5; Hüpkes, supra no. 5.

35 See also BRRD, preamble, recitals 1, 5, 25.

36 BRRD, article 5.

37 BRRD, article 7.

38 BRRD, preamble, recitals 21 and 22, respectively, and article 5(6).

39 BRRD, article 5(2).
40 See also BRRD, preamble, recitals 5 and 31.
41 BRRD, article 5(3).
42 BRRD, article 5(4).
43 EBA, Final draft Regulatory Technical Standards on the content of recovery plans under Article 5(10) of Directive 2014/59/EU establishing a framework for the recovery and resolution of credit institutions and investment firms, EBA/RTS/2014/11 (18 July 2014), available at www.eba.europa.eu/regulation-and-policy.
44 EBA, *Guidelines on the Range of Scenarios To Be Used in Recovery Plans*, EBA/ GL/2014/06 (18 July 2014), available at www.eba.europa.eu/regulation-and-policy.
45 BRRD, annex, section A, point 6; see also Draft Regulatory Technical Standards, supra no. 43, article 6(5)(d) ('feasibility assessment').
46 BRRD, annex, section A, point 7; see also Draft Regulatory Technical Standards, supra no. 43, article 6(3)(b).
47 BRRD, annex, section A, point 11; see also Draft Regulatory Technical Standards, supra no. 43, article 6(3)(c), 5(b).
48 BRRD, annex, section A, points 10, 12–14, 16 and 17, respectively; see also Draft Regulatory Technical Standards, supra no. 43, article 6(4).
49 BRRD, article 7(1).
50 BRRD, article 9.
51 On the role of relevant resolution authorities generally, see Hüpkes, supra no. 5, p. 81.
52 Regulation (EU) No 575/2013 of the European Parliament and of the Council of 26 June 2013 on prudential requirements for credit institutions and investment firms and amending Regulation (EU) No 648/2012, OJ L 176 of 27 June 2013, p. 1.
53 BRRD, article 6(2).
54 EBA, Final draft Regulatory Technical Standards on the assessment of recovery plans under Article 6(8) of Directive 2014/59/EU (Bank Recovery and Resolution Directive – BRRD), EBA EBA/RTS/2014/12 (18 July 2014), available at www.eba. europa.eu/regulation-and-policy.
55 BRRD, article 6(4).
56 BRRD, article 6(5).
57 BRRD, article 6(6)(3).
58 Cf. BRRD, article 7(4).
59 BRRD, article 7(1).
60 Directive 2013/36/EU of the European Parliament and of the Council of 26 June 2013 on access to the activity of credit institutions and the prudential supervision of credit institutions and investment firms, amending Directive 2002/87/EC and repealing Directives 2006/48/EC and 2006/49/EC, OJ L 176 of 27 June 2013, p. 338.
61 BRRD, article 7(3).
62 BRRD, article 8(3).
63 BRRD, article 8(4)).
64 BRRD, article 10(1).
65 BRRD, article 10(5).
66 BRRD, article 11.
67 BRRD, articles 10(3) and (7).
68 BRRD, article 10(4).
69 BRRD, article 12(1).
70 BRRD, article 13.

71 For the relevant criteria, see BRRD, article 15(1)(2).

72 BRRD, article 17(3).

73 BRRD, article 17(4).

74 BRRD, article 17(5).

75 BRRD, article 18.

76 BRRD, article 17(4).

77 Cf. e.g. Valia S. G. Babis *European Bank Recovery and Resolution Directive: Recovery Proceedings for Cross-Border Banking Groups*, [2014] *EBLR* 459, 462 and 473–477.

78 SSM regulation, article 4(1)(i).

79 SSM regulation, article 4(2).

80 SRM regulation, article 7(2).

81 SRM regulation, article 7(3).

82 SSM regulation, article 7(4).

83 SRM regulation, article 8(1).

84 SRM regulation, article 8(3).

85 Contrast SRM regulation, article 8(6)-(12) with BRRD, article 10(3)–(4) and (7) and article 12(1)–(5).

86 EU Commission, Communication from the Commission to the European Parliament and the Council *A Roadmap towards a Banking Union*, 12 September 2012, COM(2012) 510 final, p. 3. See generally, Eilis Ferran and Valia S. G. Babis (2013) 'The European Single Supervisory Mechanism' 13 *Journal of Corporate Law Studies* 255; Tobias H. Tröger (2014) 'The Single Supervisory Mechanism – Panacea or Quack Banking Regulation? 15 *EBOR* 449; Guido Ferrarini and Luigi Chiarella *Common Banking Supervision in the Eurozone: Strengths and Weaknesses*, ECGI – Law Working Paper No. 223/2013 (1 August 2013), available at SSRN: http://ssrn.com/abstract=2309897; Eddy Wymeersch *The European Banking Union, A First Analysis*, Financial Law Institute Working Paper Series WP 2012–07 (23 October 2012), available at SSRN: http://ssrn.com/abstract=2171785; for a detailed review of the economic rationale and legal and institutional implications (in German), see also Jens-Hinrich Binder (2013) 'Auf dem Weg zu einer europäischen Bankenunion? Erreichtes, Unerreichtes, offene Fragen', in: *Zeitschrift für Bankrecht und Bankwirtschaft* 297.

87 See also BRRD, preamble, recitals 14, 21; SRM regulation, preamble, recital 44 (all requiring that the structure of the institutions and firms be duly taken into account).

88 This is expressly recognised both by the BRRD and the SRM regulation, see BRRD, preamble, recital 29; SRM regulation, preamble, recitals 12 and 29.

89 For a similar conclusion, see Babis, [2014] *EBLR*, 459, 470–477.

90 FSB, supra no. 17, pp. 12–17.

91 See, again, BRRD, articles 6 and 8 (assessment of recovery plans) and articles 15–18 (assessment of resolvability and corresponding powers), and see earlier in the chapter.

92 See, again, supra, nos. 11–13 and accompanying text.

93 For further discussion, see Binder, supra no. 13.

94 See also supra, text accompanying no. 16. This is now expressly recognised in FSB, supra no. 17, pp. 12–17.

95 See, for a seminal discussion of ring-fencing in this sense, Steven L. Schwarcz (2013) 'Ring-Fencing', 87 *Southern California Law Review* 69: 74–81; and see Binder, supra

no. 13, for a detailed discussion of the merits and shortcomings in the present context. See also FSB, supra no. 17, p. 13.

96 See also, noting the similarities between structural reforms and the 'subsidiarisation' of cross-border banking activities (discussed below), FSB, supra no. 17, p. 14.

97 Binder, supra no. 13.

98 Witness the introduction of mandatory intermediate bank holding companies for the domestic banking operations of foreign-owned financial institutions in the United States, see Federal Reserve System, Enhanced Prudential Standards for Bank Holding Companies and Foreign Banking Organizations (amending 12 CFR 252) ('Regulation YY') 79 F.R. 17240 (27 March 2014).

99 See, for further discussion, Binder, supra no. 13; and see, discussing the implications for the resolvability of the group as a whole, FSB, supra no. 17, pp. 13–14.

100 For further discussion, see Binder, supra no. 13.

101 Binder, supra no. 13; FSB, supra no. 17, pp. 14–15.

102 FSB, supra no. 17, p. 15.

103 See Adam J. Levitin (2014) 'The politics of financial regulation and the regulation of financial politics: A review essay', 127 *Harvard Law Rev*iew 1991: 2033–2034.

104 Ibid., p. 2034 (critiquing Anad Admati and Martin Hellwig (2013) *The Bankers' New Clothes. What's Wrong with Banking and What to Do about It* Princeton, NJ: Princeton University Press, pp. 145–147, 161–166).

105 See supra nos. 18 and 19 and text.

106 SRM regulation, articles 8(1) and 7(2)(a); also see earlier in the chapter.

107 Under articles 6 and 8 of the BRRD and article 4(1)(i) of the SSM regulation. See, again, earlier in the chapter.

108 Under articles 8 and 10 of the SRM regulation.

109 Cf., again, Babis, [2014] *EBLR* 459, 477 supra no. 89.

110 Which could, if the relevant regional market enters into significant problems, stand in the way of a swift recovery or resolution, for example, because it may be difficult to restructure or indeed sell off the group's operations under such circumstances.

111 Which may be difficult to disentangle, where necessary in order to accomplish effective group-wide resolution.

112 For example, a legal entity operating in a particularly risky type of business may be insufficiently capitalised on a solo basis, which would be problematic upon resolution even if the total assets available in the group are appropriate.

113 BRRD, articles 19–26. EBA is presently engaged in a number of consultations over additional standards and guidelines in this respect: see www.eba.europa.eu/regulation-and-policy/recovery-and-resolution.

114 See supra, no. 21 and accompanying text.

115 But note, again, the power for the SRB to require institutions and groups to make substantial changes to financial arrangements pursuant to article 10(11) of the SRM regulation.

116 Which is presently anticipated by regulators as a potential trend for future structural reforms, see, again, FSB, supra no. 17, pp. 13–14.

117 BRRD, preamble, recitals 14, 23, 34 and articles 12(3) and 16(1); SRM regulation, preamble, recital 46, articles 10(3), (5), (10) and 11(11).

118 BRRD, preamble, recital 29 and articles 6(6), (7), 10(5), 17(4) and 18(2); SRM regulation, preamble, recital 46 and articles 8(6) and 10(7).

119 BRRD, preamble, recital 29; SRM regulation, preamble, recital 46.

120 BRRD, preamble, recital 30.

121 Cf. e.g. SSM regulation, preamble, recital 2:

> The present financial and economic crisis has shown that the integrity of the single currency and the internal market may be threatened by the fragmentation of the financial sector. It is therefore essential to intensify the integration of banking supervision in order to bolster the Union, restore financial stability and lay the basis for economic recovery.

122 E.g. speech by Mario Draghi, President of the European Central Bank, at the conference for the 20th anniversary of the establishment of the European Monetary Institute, Brussels, 12 February 2014, available at http://www.bis.org/review/r140213a.htm.

123 This is at least debatable, but far from settled. See, for further discussion, Binder, supra no. 13; FSB, supra no. 17, pp. 13–14.

124 Supra no. 127.

125 The forced 'subsidiarisation' in this form would essentially cut back on the relevant institutions' right to conduct banking business across the EU under their home country licence as a 'European Passport', as set out by the CRD IV.

126 Cf. analysing home and host authorities' incentives with regard to the organisational choice between branches and subsidiaries, Jonathan Fiechter *et al. Subsidiaries or Branches: Does One Size Fit All?'*, IM Staff Discussion Note (7 March 2011), available at https://www.imf.org/external/pubs/ft/sdn/2011/sdn1104.pdf, pp. 16–18; see also Tobias H. Tröger (2013) 'Organizational choices of banks and the effective supervision of transnational financial institutions', 48 *Texas International Law Journal* 177: 194–195 and 197–199. For an in-depth discussion of potential sources of conflict, cf. Richard J. Herring, 'Conflicts between home and host country prudential supervisors, in Douglas D. Evanoff, George G. Kaufman and John R. LaBrosse (2007) (eds) *International Financial Instability: Global Banking and National Regulation*, Singapore: World Scientific, pp. 201–219; Dirk Schoenmaker (2013) *Governance of International Banking – The Financial Trilemma*, New York: Oxford University Press, pp. 69–71.

127 See, again, Babis, [2014] *EBLR* 459, 474–477, supra no. 89.

128 See, again, Fiechter *et al.*, supra no. 126.

129 This is most clearly captured by article 17(3) of the SSM regulation, which requires the ECB, in fulfilling its tasks under the regulation, to 'respect a fair balance between all participating Member States . . . and . . . , in its relationship with non-participating Member States, [to] respect the balance between home and host Member States established in relevant Union Law'.

130 Alternatively, the banking union authorities could make arrangements to ring fence assets located within branches in the banking union.

131 See, in particular, BRRD, Title V, SSM regulation, article 8, and SRM regulation, articles 11(d) and 32.

132 See BRRD, article 17(5)(h), and the identical provision in SRM regulation, article 10(11)(h).

8 Shadows and mirrors

The role of debt in the developing resolution strategies in the US, UK and European Union

Michael Krimminger

The 2007–2009 financial crisis was a watershed event that shook the confidence of people around the globe in the stability of the international financial system. Many public and private investigations, analyses and articles have been written describing a variety of causes and pointing to a number of culprits. Whatever the causes, the period before the crisis led to a massive mispricing of risk and distortion of fundamental credit and pricing analyses by many, with the result that when housing prices in the US declined, the mortgage markets and the credits built upon them collapsed, leading to a destabilising repricing of risk and illiquidity in some markets.[1] Governments across the globe intervened to varying degrees in order to prevent an even greater destabilisation of financial markets and financial functions. The crisis demonstrated a failure of market discipline and the government responses only exacerbated this problem by confirming the long-standing expectation that some firms – particularly globally active financial companies – were too big or interconnected to fail.

Many of the steps taken by governments to stem the crisis deviated substantially from those outlined in the then-existing insolvency frameworks. Many countries acted to stabilise the situation by providing taxpayer funds to buttress illiquid financial companies and, as in the US, to provide capital injections and liquidity across the financial system. In some cases, regulators did take action to resolve financial institutions using existing insolvency frameworks, but the reliance on insolvency frameworks typically was limited to less systemically significant financial companies, such as smaller banks in the US. Even in cases where the banks were relatively small and domestically orientated, regulators often took action outside normal insolvency frameworks, such as in the UK, because of the fear that using the liquidation-orientated insolvency frameworks available might create additional systemic instability by causing creditors at other firms to 'run' and deprive those companies of liquidity.[2]

In some countries authorities acted quickly to adopt emergency legislation to enable the necessary resolution actions. The UK adopted emergency legislation to permit bank nationalisation, the transfer of deposits and assets to third parties and the establishment of bridge banks. This authority expired and it was subsequently replaced with a new statutory special resolution regime. In the US the Troubled Asset Relief Program (TARP) was initially proposed as a strategy to purchase troubled assets off the balance sheets of financial institutions, but was ultimately implemented principally to allow capital injections into those companies as well as certain so-called 'ring fence' transactions to back-stop the losses possible from more troubled assets. Germany recapitalised banks with state funds and restructured them, including by transferring bad assets to asset management companies through a newly established agency that provided the necessary funding and acted as umbrella for the separate asset management companies. In Switzerland the regulators supported the capital position of one of their two systemically important banks by subscribing to mandatory convertible notes and financing the transfer of some of the bank's illiquid assets to a special purpose vehicle. France similarly adopted legislation that permitted extensive state financial aid to banks. The Netherlands and Belgium adopted legislation to provide for the recapitalisation or restructuring of assets and liabilities of Fortis into separate national components. The Netherlands also used its authority to transfer assets and liabilities from some other banks or insurers to another financial or bridge institution and to intervene in a parent or holding company. Other countries, as well, adopted new legislation in an effort to stem the crisis.

In all of these cases, the funding for the resolution and restructuring of failing financial companies came from public sources – generally national governments and central banks – with very few losses or funding provided by the private creditors or other private sector sources. European countries such as Belgium, France, The Netherlands and the UK relied solely on taxpayer financing. Some countries, including France, Germany and Spain, established special public entities to provide funding and expertise. In the US the government's actions relied on Federal Reserve funding, Treasury funding through the TARP and Federal Deposit Insurance Corporation (FDIC) funding from the Deposit Insurance Fund.[3]

While these actions may have protected creditors from the full consequences of an unassisted failure of the debtor institution, many governments often required punitive steps and highly politicised responses that created significant losses and uncertainty about market pricing and market functions. Equally important, these bail-outs created an intense public and political backlash in many countries, particularly in the US, which has affected the policy and political discourse ever since.

In response, international standard setters and national authorities have sought to create a more resilient financial system while fashioning statutory frameworks and strategies to make the resolution of so-called systemically important financial institutions (SIFIs) possible. The effort to create more resilient SIFIs has included significantly higher capital and liquidity requirements, as well as restrictions in some countries on the activities in which banks can engage. The initiatives designed to make SIFIs resolvable have focused on adopting common resolution tools – such as the authority to place companies into insolvency proceedings, impose losses on equity and debt-holders, restructure their operations and maintain critical functions – and on identifying viable strategies to resolve globally active SIFIs. Those strategies have begun to coalesce around approaches that focus on restructuring and recapitalising the failing SIFI through the bail-in or conversion of debt into a new capital base. This chapter examines some of the differences in the approaches taken in the US, UK and EU member states and the possible implications for the industry and the financial system.

International responses

In response to these challenges, the international community has pursued changes to the domestic and cross-border resolution frameworks. While these changes have only partially been implemented to date, their evolution and the resulting changes to national insolvency frameworks will be critical to understanding the environment in which creditor and stakeholder claims will be determined in the future. While the policy debates may appear somewhat disconnected from the specific creditor rights and procedural issues discussed in the other sections of this chapter, these debates will continue to shape and modify those rights and processes for the foreseeable future.

The financial crisis demonstrated the importance of reform of the legal infrastructure for dealing with failing financial companies. Whether or not the pre-existing insolvency frameworks were theoretically adequate, the crisis proved that regulators were not prepared to wager the financial system on their effectiveness, and this fact alone established that market confidence that the insolvency rules would be applied in a future crisis depended on significant legal reform. Implicit reliance on public support was shown to be a policy that penalised taxpayers, contributed to moral hazard and distorted market mechanisms. The political repercussions continue to be felt in many countries, including the US. Many countries recognised the need to enhance resolution powers, undertake more formal recovery and resolution planning, strengthen arrangements for domestic and cross-border cooperation in dealing with failing financial companies and develop mechanisms to recoup any public funds used in resolution. Quite a few countries decided that major reforms were necessary to the pre-crisis legal frameworks. These reforms include measures to introduce new resolution tools and to expand resolution authority to non-bank financial institutions. Several other countries, as well as the EU, are implementing or considering reforms to their frameworks.

At the 2009 Pittsburgh Summit, the G20 leaders called on the Financial Stability Board (FSB) to develop 'internationally-consistent firm-specific contingency and resolution plans' by the end of 2010 and a framework for recommended legal changes. In response, the FSB developed the 'Key Attributes of Effective Resolution Regimes for Financial Institutions' (Key Attributes). The Key Attributes is a set of recommendations approved by the FSB following a public consultation and endorsed by the G20 in 2011.

The Key Attributes seek to address the too big to fail problem by providing that countries should have in place a resolution framework to resolve SIFIs, so-called global systemically important banks (G-SIBs), in an orderly manner and without exposing the taxpayer to the risk of loss, while protecting vital financial functions. The importance of the Key Attributes lies both in establishing an internationally recognised set of resolution tools and principles and, perhaps most importantly, in its endorsement by the G20 and the extensive efforts made to codify the Key Attributes into national or, in the case of the EU, into a multilateral legal framework.

Among the critical elements of the Key Attributes are the following:

- ensure they have designated resolution authorities with a broad range of powers to intervene and resolve a financial institution that is no longer viable, including through the establishment of bridge entities, the transfers of business and creditor-financed recapitalisation (so-called bail-in resolution) that allocate losses to shareholders and unsecured and uninsured creditors in their order of seniority;
- remove impediments to cross-border cooperation and provide resolution authorities with incentives, statutory mandates and powers to share information across borders and achieve a coordinated solution;
- ensure that recovery and resolution plans are put in place for all G-SIBs, which are regularly reviewed and updated, under the control of top officials and informed by rigorous annual resolvability assessments that assess the feasibility and credibility of resolution strategies for each G-SIB;
- maintain crisis management groups for all G-SIBs, bringing together home and key host authorities, underpinned by institution-specific cross-border cooperation agreements.

The FSB continues to conduct peer reviews and analyses of progress by member countries.[4] It is also pursuing further work to develop the international standards for contingency and resolution plans and to evaluate how to improve the capacity of national authorities to implement orderly resolutions of large and interconnected financial firms.

The FSB's programme has built on work undertaken by the Basel Committee on Banking Supervision's Cross-Border Bank Resolution Group (CBRG), co-chaired by the author. In its final *Report and Recommendations of the Cross-Border Bank Resolution Group*, issued on 18 March 2010, the Basel Committee emphasised the importance of pre-planning and the development of practical and credible plans to promote resiliency in periods of severe financial distress and to facilitate a rapid resolution should that be necessary. In its review of the financial crisis, the report found that one of the main lessons was that the complexity and interconnectedness of large financial conglomerates' corporate structures made crisis management and resolutions extremely difficult.

The US response

In the wake of the financial crisis, the US created a special insolvency regime for a failing SIFI under the Orderly Liquidation Authority (OLA) provisions of Title II of the Dodd-Frank Wall Street Reform and Consumer Protection Act (the Dodd-Frank Act). OLA is designed exclusively to address the failure of SIFIs in cases where such an insolvency would have serious adverse effects on the US economy.[5]

It is important to note that OLA supplements, rather than replaces, existing insolvency regimes. All companies eligible for orderly liquidation remain subject to otherwise applicable insolvency law (generally, the Code) unless Federal regulators determine, at the time of the financial company's failure, that the company should be liquidated under OLA.[6] Of course, FDIC-insured banks remain subject exclusively to resolution under the Federal Deposit Insurance Act.

Under OLA, the principal reason for appointment of the FDIC is to resolve the company in a way that avoids systemic consequences for the US, while complying with standards designed to avoid moral hazard – defined as bailing out shareholders, management or creditors of the failing financial company. This policy goal of OLA is succinctly summarised in section 204(a) as the liquidation of: 'failing financial companies that pose a significant risk to the financial stability of the United States in a manner that mitigates such risk and minimises moral hazard'. Creditors and shareholders are to 'bear the losses of the financial company' and the FDIC is instructed to liquidate the covered financial company in a manner that maximises the value of the company's assets, minimises losses, mitigates risk and minimises moral hazard.[7]

As receiver, the FDIC has the power to transfer assets and liabilities of the company to either a third-party acquirer or one or more specially chartered bridge financial companies. Special provisions, similar to those under the Federal Deposit Insurance Act controlling US bank receiverships, govern the treatment of certain financial market contracts commonly referred to as qualified financial contracts. OLA can be helpfully viewed as combining four key powers in the resolution of systemically important companies – that follow the guidance provided in the CBRG Report as well as in the FSB's Key Attributes. Those four powers are:

1   the ability to conduct advance resolution planning for SIFIs through a variety of mechanisms similar to those used for problem banks (these mechanisms will be enhanced by the supervisory authority and the resolution plans, or living wills, required under section 165(d) of Title I of the Dodd-Frank Act);
2   an immediate source of liquidity for an orderly liquidation, which allows continuation of essential functions and maintains asset values;
3   the ability to continue key, systemically important operations, including through the formation of one or more bridge financial companies; and
4   the ability to temporarily stay (for one business day) and then transfer all qualified financial contracts[8] with a given counterparty to another entity (such as a bridge financial company) and avoid their immediate termination and liquidation to preserve value and promote stability.[9]

The UK and broader EU response

The UK's response

The UK's initial response to the financial crisis was focused on putting in place emergency measures in response to the failure of a number of financial institutions.

The Banking (Special Provisions) Act 2008 (BSPA) was passed in February 2008, in order to permit the government to take the collapsed bank, Northern Rock, into public ownership and perform a number of other interventions against failing lenders. The BSPA was replaced by the Banking Act 2009 in February 2009, which introduced a special resolution regime (SRR) that allows failing or collapsed banks to be transferred into public ownership or into the hands of other market participants under exigent circumstances.

The Banking Act 2009 was followed by the Financial Services Act 2012, which restructured the UK's financial services regulatory framework. The Financial Services Act became effective on 1 April 2013. It gave the Bank of England (BoE) responsibility for macro-prudential oversight for the financial system, supervisory authority for systemically important financial services companies and authority for implementation of the SRR.

The UK adopted a further reform through the Banking Reform Act 2013 to provide for a bail-in tool. The bail-in power was introduced into the legislation in October 2013, late in its passage, and was accompanied by a briefing paper. The bail-in tool gives the BoE the power to impose losses on shareholders and creditors of certain banks and other SIFIs *before* initiation of insolvency proceedings, in order to prevent them becoming insolvent. The aim is to ensure that critical banking services continue to be provided, while imposing recapitalisation costs on shareholders and creditors rather than meeting this cost out of UK Government funds.

Bail-in constitutes an additional tool within the BoE's toolkit, to be deployed as an additional pre-insolvency stabilisation power within the SRR contained in Part 1 of the Banking Act 2009. The BoE is the lead resolution authority for banks. It will also become the lead resolution authority for systemically important investment firms (SIIFs) and certain companies within the same group as a bank or SIIF (banking group companies (BGCs)), where such entities are incorporated in (or formed under the law of) any part of the UK, after the relevant provisions extending the SRR to SIIFs and BGCs are brought into force.

The conditions that must be met for the use of the bail-in power are the same as for the other stabilisation powers. Broadly, the conditions require a determination:

1   by the Prudential Regulation Authority (PRA) that:

   a   the bank is failing or is likely to fail; and
   b   that in the circumstances, it is not reasonably likely that any other action can be taken to avert the failure; and

2   by the BoE that it is in the public interest to use the bail-in tool.

The bail-in tool provisions give the BoE broad powers to make resolution instruments (similar to its powers under the SRR to make share transfer instruments and property transfer instruments pursuant to the existing pre-insolvency stabilisation options). In addition, provisions in the BRB make clear that resolution instruments will take effect notwithstanding any contractual or legislative provision to the contrary. A resolution instrument can include a number of types of provision set out in the Banking Reform Act 2013. Among the types of provision that can be made is a special bail-in provision, the aim of which is to stabilise the financial position of a bank. In particular, special bail-in provision in a resolution instrument can:

- cancel, reduce or defer liabilities owed by the bank;
- specify that a contract takes effect as if a specific right was exercised (for example, a close out right); or
- convert the form of a liability (for example, it can convert debt into equity securities).

In a paper released by the BoE on 23 October 2014, the BoE described at a high level how it anticipates using its authority under UK law in a resolution of a systemically important financial company in the future.[10] Of particular interest is how the BoE describes its authorities as modified by the new Bank Recovery and Resolution Directive (BRRD) issued by the European Commission in 2014.

The broader European response

At the time of the financial crisis there was no harmonisation of the insolvency regimes for resolving banks or other financial institutions in the EU, and the crisis underscored a lack of adequate tools both at the EU level and in the member states to deal effectively with unsound or failing banks.[11] The BRRD, which was published in the Official Journal of the EU on 12 June 2014, is designed to fill this gap by laying out a harmonised toolbox of resolution powers that will be available to national authorities in each member state.[12]

The BRRD should be considered in the larger context of the proposed banking union. It is one of its building blocks and it is important to understand how it fits into the overall framework. The other blocks of the banking union include:

- the single supervisory mechanism composed of national authorities and the European Central Bank (ECB) and mandated with direct supervision of any banks or groups of banks whose failure may pose systemic risk;
- the single resolution mechanism (SRM), which builds on the measures and tools laid down in the BRRD and provides a framework for prompt and coordinated resolution action of the institutions participating in the SRM; and
- the single resolution fund, which will replace and mutualise national resolution funds.

The BRRD will provide national authorities with four resolution tools: the sale of business tool, the bridge institution tool, the bail-in tool and the asset separation tool. In common with other directives, the BRRD sets out a 'floor' and member states are free to introduce or maintain stricter or additional rules in their resolution schemes as long as they are consistent with the BRRD. The implementation process will inevitably introduce some variations in how certain principles and rules laid out in the BRRD will be addressed by national law. While this chapter provides an outline of the new legal process, I cannot define precisely either the details of the final creditor protections or fully assess the potential impact of final laws on creditors and other stakeholders. Moreover, many of the requirements in the BRRD provide resolution tools and safeguards, but do not address the many details that will be required to apply those tools and safeguards in an actual resolution. The technical standards and guidance are left for the European Banking Authority (EBA), the European Commission and national authorities to develop in the months and years following the BRRD's adoption. As a result, the meaning of many of the BRRD's provisions and the value of its safeguards will not become apparent until such standards and guidance are adopted.

The role of bail-in under the resolution authorities

Although it may not be suitable for some financial companies, the international debate about the best resolution strategies to apply to complex, global financial companies has been dominated since 2011 by the single point of entry strategy (SPOE). While SPOE was developed to implement OLA under the Dodd-Frank Act, it has come to be viewed as the most promising approach for the resolution of SIFIs from other jurisdictions as well.

Summary of the FDIC SPOE strategy

On 10 December 2013 the FDIC released a notice and request for comment entitled *The Resolution of Systemically Important Financial Institutions: The 'Single Point of Entry Strategy'* (the SPOE notice). The stated purpose of the SPOE notice was to provide additional details on SPOE strategy for the resolution of failing SIFIs, highlight issues identified in its development and seek public comment on certain key components. While the SPOE notice did not include as many details about how the FDIC would implement an SPOE strategy as had been hoped, it did reaffirm that the SPOE strategy is the FDIC's preferred option. The SPOE notice also provided additional details in some areas, such as the FDIC's funding approach and authority to guarantee obligations, while raising key issues that remain to be addressed. Finally, the SPOE notice posed a number of complex implementation issues and questions, and hopefully the FDIC will continue to refine the SPOE strategy and provide more information about its approach to addressing the many remaining implementation issues. While the comment period has expired, there are currently no indications that the FDIC plans to issue a revised analysis or provide additional guidance on OLA in the near future. However, there is no doubt that work on OLA, and particularly on the cross-border implications of SPOE and other resolution strategies, continues.

The Dodd-Frank Act defines specific policy goals for a FDIC receivership under OLA, such as holding culpable directors and management accountable, imposing losses on the SIFI's creditors and shareholders in accordance with statutory priorities and protecting taxpayers from loss, while giving the FDIC considerable flexibility to design specific resolution strategies. To implement its authority under OLA, the FDIC has developed the SPOE strategy. While the SPOE notice provides additional details, the SPOE resolution strategy has been discussed previously by the FDIC in a variety of communications including speeches, the joint paper issued by the BoE and the FDIC in December 2012[13] and in prior presentations to the FDIC's Systemic Resolution Advisory Council.

Under the SPOE strategy, only the top-level holding company of a failed SIFI would be placed into FDIC receivership. The operating subsidiaries, in which the systemically important financial businesses are conducted, would remain open and operating and would not be placed into insolvency proceedings.

The SPOE strategy would be implemented immediately after appointment of the FDIC as receiver by the transfer of all of the SIFI's assets, including ownership of its subsidiaries, to a newly chartered bridge financial company ('bridge'). The transfer would also include secured creditor claims, obligations to critical vendors and guarantees related to subsidiaries. Claims by equity, subordinated debt and senior unsecured creditors would be left behind in a FDIC receivership, resulting in a bridge that is extremely well capitalised. Following the transfer, the bridge would become the new top-tier holding company of all of the operating subsidiaries of the failed SIFI.

The SPOE strategy builds on several interrelated factors. First, US financial holding companies are not operating companies, but provide funding for their subsidiaries by issuing equity and debt. As a result, the receivership of the holding company would not be likely to affect continuity in the systemically important financial operations that could spread instability, including the settlement of payment transactions. Second, the potential systemic consequences of a failure of a SIFI derive principally from the operations of the holding company's subsidiaries. If those continue to operate unimpaired, the systemic effects on financial stability are likely to be mitigated. Third, since the parent holding company serves principally as a source of capital and liquidity, if it can continue to fulfil those functions in resolution, it can provide liquidity and sources for the recapitalisation of its subsidiaries and continue to facilitate their continued operations.

The SPOE strategy has a number of key advantages including:

- potentially greatly reducing the likelihood of systemically destabilising disruptions to subsidiary operations;
- imposing losses on the equity holders and creditors of the holding company, which are structurally subordinated to the trading and other creditors of operating subsidiaries;
- mitigating potential cross-border coordination issues by keeping foreign subsidiaries open and operating; and
- preserving the going concern value of the SIFI, which should minimise losses for creditors and lessen the impact of the failure on the broader economy.

Once the bridge has been established, it would be managed by private sector directors and officers appointed by the FDIC to replace those accountable for the SIFI's failure. However, the SPOE notice makes it clear that control over decision-making on several key issues will be retained by the FDIC during the period of bridge operations, including any merger, consolidation or reorganisation, changes in directors and the payment of dividends, among others.

Funding for the bridge operations would be available from private sector sources or through the Orderly Liquidation Fund (OLF), as described in more detail below. The SPOE notice states a strong FDIC preference for private sector funding when available.

A central component of the SPOE strategy is the exit strategy designed around an eventual swap of creditor claims for equity in a new company that will emerge from the bridge. This exit strategy would help mitigate systemic risks by preserving operational continuity and reducing the potential increased industry concentration that would occur if the bridge or its assets were acquired by other SIFIs. As described in greater detail below, the capitalisation of the bridge and the subsequent emergence of a new, privately owned and operated holding company is one area in which the FDIC provided significant new details about its planned approach. As described by the SPOE notice, the exit strategy would be implemented in approximately six to nine months through the exchange of creditor claims for equity or debt of the restructured bridge (or one or more successors to the bridge) in satisfaction of the claims of creditors left behind in the receivership. As described in some detail, this timeframe is driven by the time needed to complete a reliable valuation, achieve systemic stabilisation and comply with the Securities and Exchange Commission standards for the issuance and trading of the new equity and debt. Ownership and control of the newly capitalised bridge would thereby be transferred to its former holding company creditors. This result would be similar in effect to a restructuring under Chapter 11 of the Bankruptcy Code. Similarly, the SPOE notice states that the FDIC plans to use the 'fresh start' accounting model commonly used for companies emerging from bankruptcy.

There are a number of vital implementation issues that must be addressed to ensure that an SPOE strategy could actually be implemented for a failing SIFI. Those issues include efficiently transferring operations and maintaining continuity in interactions with critical financial market utilities, vendors and customers; funding for bridge operations; providing timely and accurate financial information to reassure all stakeholders; preserving business as usual operations for subsidiaries; and recapitalising the potentially insolvent subsidiaries among others.

Progress on a number of these issues continues to be made – although inevitably much of this progress occurs during inter-agency discussions that are not public. Two particularly notable recent steps forward were the announcement on 11 October 2014 of an international industry and regulator agreement on a new protocol for stays in termination of derivatives contracts and the continuing work on key elements necessary to improve resolveability, including development of a framework for 'total loss absorbing capacity' and further cross-border coordination and consultation by national authorities.

The stay protocol involved complex negotiations between major global banks, the International Swaps and Derivatives Association (ISDA) and regulators. The protocol will allow imposition of a stay on cross-default and early termination rights within standard ISDA derivatives contracts with the 18 largest global financial companies in the event one of them is subject to resolution action in its jurisdiction. The stay is intended to give resolution authorities time to facilitate an orderly resolution of a troubled bank. Under the stay protocol counterparties will opt into certain overseas resolution regimes by modifying the default provisions of their derivatives contracts. This is particularly important, because the existing statutory stays may only apply to domestic counterparties trading under domestic law agreements. As a result, the ability to stay contracts involving cross-border parties could be challenged. In addition to the agreed contractual changes, regulators have committed to develop new regulations during 2015 that will promote broader adoption of the stay provisions beyond the 18 largest global financial institutions. In turn, the banks have also committed to expand coverage of the stay protocol once regulations are enacted to include a stay that could be used when a US financial holding company becomes subject to proceedings under the US Bankruptcy Code. The scope of the stay protocol is very significant. First, the protocol will help prevent the unwinding of a financial group if a global SIFI's holding company is closed, by barring the termination of contracts with its subsidiaries under the commonly used 'cross-default' provisions. Second, once regulations are adopted in the US, the extension to the US Bankruptcy Code will help prevent direct defaults and the termination of contracts otherwise permitted under the current US Bankruptcy Code. This will significantly improve the effectiveness of the US Bankruptcy Code in resolving financial companies.

While there has been relatively little information made available about the 13 October 2014 meeting between senior officials from the US and the UK, the fact that heads of all of the key agencies and executive departments of the US and UK governments met is significant. According to the released information, the heads of the US Treasury, FDIC, Federal Reserve, Federal Reserve Bank of NY, Commodities Futures Trading Commission and the Securities and Exchange Commission met the Chancellor of the Exchequer and the heads of the BoE, PRA and the Financial Conduct Authority to discuss resolution strategies, areas requiring coordination and future challenges that must be addressed. A meeting at this senior level cannot be held without months of detailed work by senior staff to identify the issues, progress that must be made and steps that should be taken in the short and longer term. This does, at the least, indicate that the US and UK authorities have continued their on-going dialogue about coordination issues and have deepened the work streams that are essential to better understanding. Whether that will translate into more coordinated actions in a future crisis, in a world that appears to be moving towards greater separation between home and host country operations of financial companies compelled by the Federal Reserve's foreign banking rules and the policies of other regulators, including the PRA and BoE, must remain an open question.[14]

However, in this chapter I focus on the essential restructuring and recapitalisation of the failing SIFI that the FDIC, as well as other regulators, plan to accomplish through a bail-in of pre-existing debt-holders. As we move from the FDIC's description of its SPOE resolution strategy, it is important to note that the focus for the FDIC remains on a transfer of operations to a temporary bridge followed by restructuring and an exit through a recapitalisation using a bail-in of debt-holders of the failed SIFI. The approach to the SPOE strategy preferred by the UK and other European regulators is significantly different.

Summary of the UK and broader EU approach to SPOE

The BoE's approach to SPOE

In its 23 October 2014 paper entitled *The Bank of England's Approach to Resolution* ('BoE resolution paper'), the BoE provided further insights into its approach to using the SPOE strategy. While the BoE resolution paper does not discuss SPOE by name, it is clear from the BoE's prior public pronouncements as well as through its citation to its 2012 joint paper with the FDIC that its preference is to use SPOE to resolve most, if not all, UK global SIFIs.[15]

Since the 2008 financial crisis, the FDIC and BoE have been engaged in an active dialogue about managing future crises and developing the tools and strategies necessary to successfully resolve a G-SIB without imposing losses on taxpayers. In January 2010 the FDIC and BoE signed a memorandum of understanding recognising the need for the FDIC and BoE, alongside other US and UK authorities, to work closely to maintain confidence and systemic stability. While building on pre-existing memoranda of understanding on supervisory issues, this new memorandum provided a framework for expanded cooperation and sharing of information specifically on resolution contingency planning and, should the need arise, resolution implementation. The FDIC's focus on cooperation and coordination with UK authorities was an obvious choice since the UK hosts 88 per cent or more of the international assets and operations of top US banks. UK financial companies similarly have substantial majorities of their cross-border operations in the US.

On 10 December 2012 the FDIC and the BoE released a joint paper entitled *Resolving Globally Active, Systemically Important, Financial Institutions* (the 'joint paper') outlining a resolution strategy for global SIFIs. The joint paper describes the way US and UK resolution powers could be used to execute the preferred approach of an SPOE resolution. OLA provides the essential statutory powers for the strategy, but the joint paper noted that the UK's Banking Act 2009 and related laws lacked several key powers needed to successfully execute an SPOE resolution. Most of these missing elements were included in the final BRRD, and the BoE resolution paper repeatedly references the role the BRRD powers play in its resolution approach.

The joint paper identified the desired 'exit strategy' as a recapitalisation accomplished by converting certain creditor claims against the failed financial company into equity in a newly restructured financial company. This would have the effect of imposing losses on existing equity, subordinated and senior unsecured debt, and converting part of the remaining debt into the new equity according to the order of creditor priority. As a result, ownership of the restructured group would shift to the former creditors of the parent entity. This debt for equity conversion process is likely to be accompanied by other restructuring actions to address the causes of failure, such as winding down troubled assets or unprofitable lines of business, and may include splitting the group into smaller, less systemically significant groups of companies.

The BoE resolution paper builds on the SPOE descriptions in the joint paper, as well as the new authority provided in the BRRD, to give us additional details about how the BoE anticipates implementing a resolution. First, the BoE resolution paper describes bail-in as a preferred resolution strategy for global SIFIs compared to use of its transfer powers, which include the power to transfer operations of the failing SIFI to a bridge. The reason lies in the BoE's concern that it will be exceedingly difficult to separate the critical economic functions of the SIFI from those that are less critical in making the transfer.[16] In contrast, the FDIC plainly considers that a transfer to a bridge will involve all (other than equity, litigation and matters under investigation) of the operations of the failed SIFI, while noting that one advantage of applying the SPOE at the holding company level is that there are few, if any, critical operations actually conducted by the holding company.

Second, the bail-in strategy is perceived as having the advantage of better facilitating continuity in critical operations. To the extent it is effective at recapitalising the SIFI and achieving renewed market confidence, this could prove an advantage. However, as noted above, if the transfer to the bridge involves all key operations of the SIFI or if the 'point of entry' is at a holding company level where there are few, if any, operating facilities, the bail-in strategy may not achieve any significant benefits over the US approach.

Third, the bail-in strategy is viewed as presenting an advantage, because it can potentially operate before insolvency as well as after initiation of resolution actions.[17] However, as is clear from the discussion in the BoE resolution paper, the decision to impose any official action is likely to be only at the moment just before insolvency, if at all, given the issues that must be addressed regarding safeguards for equity holders under the European Convention of Human Rights.[18] If bail-in occurs at that time, the need for central bank or governmental liquidity will be clear as the SIFI most likely will be on the doorstep of failure due to its inability to obtain sufficient market liquidity.

Fourth, the BoE resolution paper discusses a further issue that continues to create challenges in implementing a bail-in approach before resolution as well as after resolution under some proposals. This question revolves around the reliability of valuations of the assets of the failing SIFI in order to determine the extent of necessary writedowns for creditor claims and the resulting terms of the bail-in.[19] If the bail-in occurs before resolution, this issue becomes more difficult since obtaining accurate valuations in the midst of a near-failure scenario will prove complex, at best. The BoE and the FDIC have noted that this issue may be addressed by issuing new equity based on an estimated valuation, while providing 'warrants' or 'certificates of entitlement' to creditors, so that a true-up of the value of their claims can be completed when more complete market valuations are available.

Both the BoE and the FDIC have focused considerable attention on design-ing the strategy for the exit from resolution for the 'reformed' SIFI. The FDIC's SPOE notice emphasised the importance of the bridge developing a clear strat-egy to restructure and potentially dispose of certain businesses and operations so that it would emerge from resolution as a company that could be resolved under the non-OLA insolvency frameworks available under US law. FDIC Chairman Gruenberg has emphasized that this is a principal purpose of the resolution strat-egy. The BoE's discussions of SPOE do not include such strictures.

Somewhat separately from the principal purpose of this chapter, the FDIC's SPOE notice and its discussion of a requirement for a restructuring plan before the new entity would be allowed to exit from resolution, raises a number of questions. For example, what is the relationship between the required restructuring plan and the statutory goals to mitigate potential systemic risks from the immediate failure of the SIFI and to maximise the value achievable in the resolution of the SIFI? Will the restructuring plan be public or implemented as part of a supervisory or subsequent resolution plan process? Will the six- to nine-month period allotted in the SPOE notice for the termination of the bridge and the emergence of the new holding com-pany provide sufficient time to define the necessary restructuring strategy, address implementation and set up the specific steps to accomplish it? What role will credi-tors and the new equity holders after the creditor claim-to-equity swap play in the restructuring plan? How does this requirement dovetail with the regulatory living will requirements? Consideration of these and other issues will be important to pro-vide needed certainty for stakeholders about the proposed restructuring requirement.

The BoE and the FDIC clearly agree that the exit strategy is likely to involve a bail-in of creditors of the failed SIFI to recapitalise the SIFI (or more properly in a bridge scenario, to capitalise this newly chartered entity for the first time). This inherently demands that the SIFI holds sufficient loss-absorbing capacity to provide sufficient bailinable creditor claims to provide a strong base of capital for future operations that, at the least, fully complies with Basel capital standards and, perhaps more importantly, meets market expectations for sufficient capital.[20] Before addressing these issues in greater detail, I should describe the framework for bail-in under the BRRD.

The EU's approach to SPOE

Under the BRRD, the EU has also expressed support for SPOE as one option for resolution though, given the diversity of institutional structures within the EU, it has recognised the necessity for openness to a diversity of resolution approaches, including a multiple point of entry (MPOE) strategy.[21] This remains a much debated issue and one that may benefit from allowing some diversity given the nascent stage of development of any global resolution strategy.

The BRRD provides bail-in as one of the four principal tools for resolution. The bail-in tool gives resolution authorities the power to write down all equity and subordinated debt and to write down or convert senior liabilities to equity.[22] Specifically, resolution authorities will have the power to:

- reduce to zero the nominal amount of shares or other instruments of ownership and cancel them;
- reduce to zero the outstanding principal amount of eligible liabilities;
- convert eligible liabilities into ordinary shares or other instruments of
  ownership;
- cancel debt instruments (except for secured liabilities);
- require an institution under resolution or a relevant parent company to issue
  new equity or other capital instruments, including preferred shares and contingent convertible instruments;
- amend or alter the maturity of debt instruments and other eligible liabilities
  or amend the amount of interest payable thereunder or the date on which the
  interest becomes payable, including by suspending payment for a temporary
  period (except for secured liabilities); and
- close out and terminate financial or derivatives contracts and haircut amounts
  owing by the debtor for the purposes of applying the bail-in tool to liabilities
  arising from derivatives.[23]

The goal of the bail-in tool is to ensure that direct stakeholders of the failing institution (i.e. its shareholders and unsecured creditors) bear the costs of resolution
instead of taxpayers, while minimising disruption to the markets.

It is important to note that, unlike the US OLA approach, the BRRD authorises
the use of bail-in before the financial company has been placed into an insolvency
proceeding. The tool may be used when a covered institution is still a going concern, but meets the conditions for resolution specified under Articles 32 and 33
of the BRRD. In this case, the purpose of the bail-in tool is to restore its ability to
comply with the conditions for authorisation, to carry on its authorised activities
and to sustain sufficient market confidence in the institution.[24] Implementing the
bail-in tool under these circumstances is only permitted if there is a reasonable
prospect that it will restore the institution to financial soundness and long-term
viability.[25]

The bail-in tool may also be used in a wind-down scenario in order to convert
debt to equity or reduce the principal amount of claims or debt instruments that
are transferred either to a bridge institution to provide it with capital or under the
sale of business or the asset separation tools.[26]

The scope of the bail-in tool is very broad: it may be applied to all liabilities
except those that are specifically excluded.[27] The following liabilities cannot be
bailed in:

- deposits covered under the EU's deposit guarantee scheme;
- secured liabilities (including 'covered bonds');
- liabilities arising by virtue of holding client assets or client money or a fidu-
  ciary relationship, but only if such client or beneficiary is protected under
  applicable insolvency law;
- liabilities to institutions (excluding intragroup liabilities) with an original
  maturity of less than seven days;

- liabilities with a remaining maturity of less than seven days owed to payment, clearing or other systems arising from the participation in such system; and
- liabilities to:

  a   employees in relation to accrued salary, pension benefits or other fixed remuneration except for the variable component of remuneration that is not regulated by a collective bargaining agreement;

  b   commercial or trade creditors arising from the provision of goods or services that are critical to the daily functioning of its operations (such as IT services, utilities, rent, servicing and upkeep of premises); and

  c   tax and social security authorities, but only to the extent such liabilities are preferred under applicable national insolvency law.

In exceptional circumstances, the resolution authority may request the exclusion of certain other liabilities, including liabilities arising from derivatives, from the application of the writedown or conversion powers if certain conditions are met. The circumstances under which such exclusion could be allowed include:

- it is impossible to bail in those liabilities within a reasonable time despite good faith efforts;
- the exclusion is strictly necessary to achieve the continuity of critical functions or core business lines;
- the exclusion is strictly necessary to avoid giving rise to widespread contagion and disruption of the financial markets; or
- the bailing in of such liabilities would cause a destruction in value such that the losses borne by other creditors would be higher than if these liabilities were excluded from bail-in.[28]

The resolution authority must notify the European Commission if it wants to exercise the discretion to exclude a liability that is otherwise eligible for bail-in. The European Commission will have the right to prohibit or require amendments to the proposed exclusion to protect the integrity of the EU's internal market.[29]

Where exclusions are applied and as a result the losses that would have been borne by these creditors have not been passed on fully to other creditors of the failing institution, the resolution authority may seek funding from the national resolution funds established in accordance with the BRRD either to cover any losses which have not been absorbed by eligible liabilities and restore the net asset value of the institution to zero, or to recapitalise it.[30] Such funding will be permitted only if shareholders or holders of other eligible liabilities have absorbed losses equal to an amount of not less than 8 per cent of the total liabilities including own funds of the institution under resolution, measured at the time of resolution action. Once the 8 per cent threshold is reached, the contribution from the national resolution funds cannot exceed 5 per cent of the total liabilities.[31] In extraordinary circumstances, the resolution authority may seek further funding from alternative financing sources after the 5 per cent limit has been reached and all unsecured, non-preferred liabilities, other than eligible deposits, have been written down or converted in full.[32]

The BRRD also allows an exception to the 8 per cent test. A contribution may be made from the national resolution fund to the failing institution even if the 8 per cent threshold has not been reached if all of the following conditions are met:

1   the contribution to loss absorption and recapitalisation by the holders of eligible liabilities is equal to an amount of not less than 20 per cent of the risk weighted assets of the institution;
2   the national resolution fund of the member state concerned has at its disposal, by way of ex ante contributions, an amount equal to at least 3 per cent of covered deposits of all the credit institutions authorised in that member state; and
3   the institution has assets below €900 billion on a consolidated basis.[33]

MINIMUM REQUIREMENTS FOR OWN FUNDS AND ELIGIBLE LIABILITIES

Article 45 of the BRRD creates a requirement to maintain at all times a minimum amount of own funds and eligible liabilities (i.e. liabilities that may be written down or converted under the bail-in tool). The minimum requirement is to be calculated as the amount of own funds and eligible liabilities (including subordinated debt and senior unsecured debt with a remaining maturity of at least 12 months that are subject to the bail-in power) expressed as a percentage of the total liabilities and own funds of the institution.[34]

If a liability is governed by foreign laws, in order for that liability to count towards the required minimum, the resolution authority has to be satisfied that any decision to write down or convert such liability under the bail-in tool will be effected under the relevant laws.[35]

Resolution authorities, after consultation with the supervising authorities, are tasked with determining the minimum requirement on an individual basis for each institution based on a number of criteria, taking into account the size, the business model, the funding model and the risk profile of each institution as well as the potential effect of the institution's failure on the financial markets.[36] While this additional capital will provide a greater cushion to shield trade creditors from loss, the amount of additional debt that must be issued will have an effect on the strength and credit quality of the financial institution and therefore will directly or indirectly affect all of its existing creditors.

Generally, the levels at which the minimums are to be set should be proportionate and adopted for each category of institution on the basis of their risk or the composition of their funding sources. Covered institutions may also be required to meet their minimum through a certain number of contractual bail-in instruments. For a liability to qualify as a contractual bail-in instrument, it has to contain a contractual term allowing for its writedown or conversion before other eligible liabilities are written down or converted, and it is subject to a binding subordination agreement under which, in the event of normal insolvency proceedings, it ranks below other eligible liabilities and cannot be repaid until other eligible liabilities outstanding at the time have been settled.[37]

In addition to the required minimum of own funds and eligible liabilities at the institution level, EU parent companies must comply with the minimum requirements on a consolidated basis, which is to be determined by the group-level resolution authority.[38] The group-level resolution authority and the resolution authorities responsible for the subsidiaries on an individual basis will strive to reach a joint decision within four months, but as with the application of early intervention measures and the recovery and resolution planning, each authority will retain ultimate power to set the minimum requirements for any entity under its jurisdiction.

Further legislative proposals are contemplated by the end of 2016 on the harmonised application of the minimum requirement of own funds and eligible liabilities (including proposals to introduce a certain number of minimum levels, taking into account different business models of institutions and groups, appropriate adjustments to the parameters and, if necessary, amendments to the application of the minimum requirement to groups).

IMPLEMENTATION

EU resolution authorities will determine the amount by which eligible liabilities are to be written down or converted by assessing the aggregate amount that needs to be written down to ensure that the net asset value of the institution under resolution is zero and the aggregate amount that needs to be converted into shares or other types of capital instruments in order to restore the common equity Tier 1 capital ratio of either the institution under resolution or the bridge institution.[39] The assessment will take into account any contribution of capital by the national resolution fund. The goal of the bail-in is to sustain sufficient market confidence in the institution under resolution or the bridge institution and enable it to operate over a period of at least one year.[40] Eligible liabilities are to be bailed in in the following order:

- Tier 1 common equity should be cancelled first;
- additional Tier 1 instruments next,
- Tier 2 instruments should be bailed in third;
- then subordinated debt that is not additional Tier 1 or Tier 2 capital (in accordance with the hierarchy of claims in normal insolvency proceedings); and
- the rest of eligible liabilities should be bailed in last, again in accordance with the hierarchy of claims in normal insolvency proceedings.[41]

Tier 1 common equity is to be reduced in proportion to the losses and to the extent of its capacity and the principal amount of additional Tier 1 instruments and, if necessary, Tier 2 instruments are to be written down or converted into common equity Tier 1 instruments to the extent required to achieve the resolution objectives or to the extent of their capacity, whichever is lower.[42]

The losses must be allocated equally between shares or other eligible liabilities of the same priority by reducing their principal amount pro rata to their value, except where a different allocation of losses among liabilities of the same rank results from the exclusion of certain liabilities from the application of the bail-in by the resolution authorities.[43] Liabilities that have been excluded from bail-in may receive more favourable treatment than other eligible liabilities of the same priority.[44]

Upon entry into resolution, resolution authorities have the power to terminate and close out any derivative contract in order to exercise writedown and conversion powers in relation to a liability arising from a derivative.[45]

Resolution authorities may apply a different conversion rate to different classes of capital instruments and liabilities, but to the extent senior liabilities are bailed in in accordance with the sequence of conversion set out in Article 48, the conversion rate applicable to liabilities that are considered senior under applicable insolvency law must be higher than the conversion rate applicable to subordinated liabilities.[46]

After application of the bail-in tool, a business reorganisation plan must be prepared laying out a detailed diagnosis of the factors and problems that caused the institution to fail, a description of the measures aimed at restoring long-term viability that should be adopted and a timetable for implementing these measures, which should be no longer than two years.[47]

Total loss-absorbing capacity and bail-in

The success of the SPOE strategy depends on there being sufficient equity and/or debt at the holding company to absorb the losses of, and recapitalise, the consolidated group. As the FDIC noted in its SPOE notice, the equity and debt of the holding company fulfils two related, but somewhat separate, functions in implementing an SPOE strategy. First, the shareholders and debt-holders in the SIFI would absorb losses, and their claims would be converted into equity in a new holding company after it exits from the bridge. Second, the equity and debt of the holding company would absorb the cost of providing liquidity and, perhaps, capital to subsidiaries to enable the subsidiaries to continue operating. This is true whether direct holding company claims against the subsidiaries – either as deposits or debt holdings – are converted to the use of the subsidiaries as funding or capital, or whether funds drawn from the OLF are downstreamed to the subsidiaries. In many ways, the distinction is merely one of how the subsidiaries are supported. The holding company shareholders and debt-holders bear the losses in either process.

These latter considerations illustrate the integrated analysis that must be advanced regarding the relationship between external and internal loss-absorbing capacity. The requisite amount of equity and debt that global SIFIs will be required to maintain has been the subject of much speculation and numerous unofficial leaks. After several years of discussions around global loss-absorbing capacity (GLAC), the consensus appears to have settled on total loss-absorbing capacity (TLAC) as the appropriate moniker.

Mark Carney, Governor of the BoE, recently noted publicly that the final term sheet:

> [d]etails a range for the minimum pillar 1 requirement for the total amount of loss-absorbing capacity a G-SIB must hold at all times; criteria that liabilities must meet in order to be considered loss-absorbing without disrupting the provision of critical functions or being subject to legal and compensation risk; and the distribution of loss-absorbing capacity within banking groups across home and hosted entities and the allocation of responsibilities between home and host authorities'.[48]

The FSB's consultative document entitled *Adequacy of Loss-Absorbing Capacity of Global Systemically Important Banks in Resolution* (the 'TLAC framework') was published on 10 November 2014.[49] The final TLAC principles include the same elements. At the time of writing, and in broad outline, the TLAC includes the following key elements:

- *Applicability*: The requirements apply to the 30 G-SIBs framework identified by the FSB, with the exception of G-SIBs in developing countries, including China. How to phase out this 'special treatment' has remained a very controversial issue.
- *External TLAC issuer*: Each entity (referred to as a 'resolution entity') identified by the G-SIB's crisis management group of regulators as being a 'point of entry' during resolution is subject to the external TLAC requirement:

  a   In an SPOE G-SIB, only the single entity that would enter resolution would be subject to the external TLAC requirement.

  b   In an MPOE G-SIB, each point of entry entity would be subject to the external TLAC requirement.

- *Amount of external TLAC*: The minimum TLAC requirement will be set by reference to the consolidated balance sheet of each resolution group. A resolution group is the resolution entity and any direct or indirect subsidiaries that are not themselves resolution entities.

  a   The Pillar 1 common minimum TLAC requirement will be a defined per cent of the resolution group's risk weighted assets (RWAs), calibrated at approximately double the relevant capital requirements but without considering required buffers.

  b   Regulators would be able to establish firm-specific, 'Pillar 2' enhancements to these requirements based on the risk profile of the bank.

- *Interaction with regulatory capital*: Regulatory capital instruments could be applied towards the external TLAC requirement, but debt instruments would need to constitute 33 per cent of external TLAC.

  a   Instruments satisfying capital buffer requirements, including the capital conservation buffer, countercyclical buffer and G-SIB surcharge buffer, may not be included in meeting the external TLAC requirement.

b   Accordingly, depending on the applicable G-SIB surcharge, G-SIBs would be required to maintain a combination of TLAC-eligible instruments and regulatory capital instruments equal to between 19.5 and 27 per cent of RWAs (16 – 20 per cent TLAC, plus a G-SIB surcharge of between 1 per cent and 4.5 per cent, plus the 2.5 per cent capital conservation buffer), assuming no countercyclical buffer.

- *Instruments eligible for external TLAC*: Eligible instruments would need to be unsecured, issued by the resolution entity, have a remaining maturity of more than one year and be subordinated (structurally, contractually or statutorily) to 'excluded liabilities'.

a   Eligible instruments would also need to be subject to the law of the issuing entity's incorporation or, if subject to another law, include legally enforceable contractual provisions recognising the application of the resolution tools of the issuing entity's jurisdiction of incorporation, unless there is an equivalent binding statutory provision for cross-border resolution.

b   Credible ex ante commitments to recapitalise a G-SIB in resolution from the authorities may also count towards minimum external TLAC. The TLAC proposal requires that these commitments be pre-funded by industry contributions and cannot fulfil the entire TLAC requirement.

- *Excluded liabilities*: The following instruments would be considered 'excluded liabilities' to which eligible instruments would need to be subordinated:

a   insured deposits;
b   liabilities callable on demand without supervisory approval;
c   liabilities funded directly by the issuer or a related party of the issuer (except where the Crisis Management Group agrees that liabilities issued to a resolution entity's parent may be counted);
d   liabilities arising from derivatives or debt instruments with derivative-linked features (e.g. structured notes);
e   liabilities arising other than through a contract (e.g. tax liabilities);
f   liabilities that are preferred to normal senior unsecured obligations under the applicable insolvency regime;
g   any other liabilities that, under the law governing the issuing entity, cannot be written down or converted into equity by the applicable resolution authority.

- *Internal TLAC*: Each material foreign subsidiary of a G-SIB would be required to have internal TLAC equal to 75 – 90 per cent of the external TLAC that would be required of the subsidiary on a stand-alone basis. Internal TLAC instrument requirements are similar to those for external TLAC, but may be held by the resolution entity parent.
- *Conformance period*: The conformance period will be determined following a quantitative impact statement by the FSB, but will not be before 1 January 2019.

In seeking comments on the policy proposal, the FSB set out 17 questions, with additional subparts, focused on many of the key issues that surround TLAC and bail-in. Among the issues addressed in the published questions are the calibration of the amount of TLAC, how to ensure TLAC will be available at the right entities to facilitate the resolution of cross-border groups, which instruments will count towards TLAC requirements and how breaches of the TLAC requirements will be addressed. These are key issues, but the issues implicated in the TLAC framework are much broader and deeper than the specific elements that will be applied. It is also virtually without question that the US will apply certain stricter standards than those to be announced by the FSB.

Implications of TLAC and the future of finance

The framework for the final TLAC framework from the FSB and, more importantly, how it is implemented by national regulators has significant implications for resolvability and for the future role, business models and structure of global financial institutions. While major reforms to the financial system were clearly necessary following the financial crisis – and the crisis's demonstration of fundamental challenges to the structural, financial and economic models for financial companies as well as for regulation – it is imperative that we begin to envisage the future contours of the financial system that is emerging from the crisis and the responses by legislators, regulators, investors and financial companies themselves. I do not presume to answer these crucial questions. I only wish to raise some of the pertinent questions and suggest a few implications for consideration and discussion.

Certainty of the goal

The TLAC requirement – and particularly its development with a focus on TLAC being issued from the top-tier parent or holding company level (or potentially the descriptively termed 'resolution entity') – presumes an SPOE approach rather than answers the question of the best resolution approach. While I participated in the original discussions leading to the suggestion of the SPOE approach, I have never believed that all eggs should be laid in a single basket.

The TLAC framework has clear implications for which entities will be issuers of debt. While the TLAC framework accommodates MPOE strategies by allowing for multiple resolution entities that must hold TLAC and can issue external TLAC, the original discussions around TLAC were driven primarily by the need for a resource of debt that could be written down to recapitalise a parent entity under an SPOE strategy. As a result, the logic of the TLAC framework implies that all external TLAC debt will be issued preferably by one resolution entity, or at least by a very limited number of resolution entities.

The TLAC framework does fortunately recognise that the preferred resolution strategy for the particular financial company should determine which entity will issue the TLAC. For some firms, SPOE seems quite the obvious choice. This includes US holding companies. For other firms, the answer likely should be quite different. The TLAC framework sensibly notes that a 'G-SIB may consist of one or more resolution groups' and accordingly that TLAC could be issued out of the top-tier entity for each of those groups. The 'attachment point' for TLAC is an important issue, because it has major implications for which entity should issue long-term debt, the relative quantum of debt to be issued, the financial and managerial relationship between parent and subsidiaries, the function of equity and debt within the financial company and many other issues.

However, since the TLAC framework was developed in the context of an SPOE strategy designed to maintain systemically important operations in subsidiaries, it favours holding companies with no or very limited operations. While this is the structure used by the US G-SIBs and some others, there are a considerable number of G-SIBs, particularly in Europe and Asia, which have operating banks as the topmost parent. Similarly, while US G-SIB holding companies tend to issue both equity and significant amounts of long-term unsecured debt, the same is not true for many of the other G-SIBs with holding company structures who tend to issue such debt out of their operating subsidiaries. The potential implications of the TLAC framework for corporate structure as well as the financing of operations for G-SIBs raises significant issues. In combination with requirements for recovery and resolution planning in many countries, the TLAC requirement could potentially contribute to greater homogenisation in G-SIB corporate structures and financing. While the SPOE strategy offers some significant advantages when applied to G-SIBs built around holding companies with operations conducted through subsidiaries, other G-SIBs built around top-level operating companies or relatively independent subsidiaries may be better suited to the MPOE strategy. If the TLAC requirement is interpreted by regulators as implying a need for the reorientation of G-SIB organisations towards a US-style holding company model, it would have significant consequences on the diversity of available business models and the flexibility previously allowed in financing business operations.

Relationship between external and internal TLAC

In some cases, a mandatory proportional relationship between external and internal TLAC (such as the proposed 75 to 90 per cent of internal to external) could lead to a multiplier effect that creates a much higher requirement for certain global SIFIs. While this may be comforting to those who have concluded that only much higher capital can ever address the 'rent' that some believe such global SIFIs impose on the financial system, we should consider the implications that this 'tax' may have on the resiliency of global companies. If increasing amounts of their economic capital are trapped in internal TLAC, this is equivalent to trapping that capital in the host jurisdictions of particular subsidiaries. This could achieve superficially improved resolvability at the price of more fragile and brittle companies that cannot redeploy economic capital to address challenging local or regional problems and, as a consequence, run a greater risk of failure.

Setting the standard

The underlying analytics for setting the standard for TLAC at a defined per cent of the resolution group's RWA and perhaps twice the Tier 1 leverage ratio (effectively twice the Basel 3 standards) are neither transparent nor apparent. While the history of all capital and similar regulatory standards is replete with examples of standards based solely on some multiplier applied to the prior standard – either directly or in effect – we should be careful in calibrating an international TLAC standard without identifying and analysing why and how the standard is determined. Given the significant effects that these standards could create, we should at a minimum clearly explain the rationale and calibration processes. Similarly, we should consider whether some differentiation between different businesses – beyond those inherent in different risk weights – is appropriate. Different global SIFIs fund their operations in different ways and invest in different assets. While that is obvious, it should also be considered in setting standards. There is always the danger of gamesmanship, but that should not eliminate appropriate gradation for the standards. At the time of writing, the results of the QIS are available to the regulators, but not to the public. These results may provide support for a specific range for required TLAC. Even if so, there should also be consideration of different business models and comparative elements that should underlie a sound TLAC framework.

The role of TLAC

An overarching question for the TLAC process is whether TLAC is designed effectively to set an additional capital requirement that must be met and enforced in the same way as existing capital standards. If a global SIFI falls below the minimum during the economic cycle, will it be subjected to capital-style supervisory remediation actions, or will the temporary decline in TLAC be treated as a normal part of economic cycles that can be remedied as appropriate given then-existing conditions? This has significant implications for the on-going supervisory process and should be addressed up front.

Market appetite and eligible instruments

A TLAC requirement should not be set without some consideration for the market appetite for the quantum of long-term debt that will be necessary. The FSB helpfully notes that it will consider the micro and macro-economic consequences of the TLAC requirements. This is not only an issue relating to whether or not global SIFIs today meet the requirements but also for the on-going marketability for the debt. Similarly, the market for the requisite debt will be affected by the instruments that are eligible to meet the TLAC requirements. Clearly, such instruments must be able to absorb losses *in extremis*, but consideration should be given to the current debt and equity structure of the global SIFIs in setting the conformance process, as well as in the final schedule and structure of debt issuance that final implementation will require.

Triggers

The event that will trigger the bail-in process remains a critical issue – as it has throughout discussions around contingent capital. The FSB TLAC framework simply says TLAC must: 'contain a contractual trigger or be subject to a statutory mechanism' that allows the resolution authority: 'to expose TLAC to loss or convert to equity in resolution'. For global SIFIs, as well as investors, it is essential that they be able to analyse the triggering event that is likely to lead to a determination by the regulators that the global SIFI is failing or likely to fail – often referred to as the 'point of non-viability' determination. Both global SIFIs and investors must have greater certainty about the standards that will be applied in order to assess their issuing costs on the one hand and their risks on the other. Naturally, this assessment is affected by the ultimate resolution strategy and approach as the creditor protections in the resolution framework will affect investors' evaluation of their risks.[50]

Cost-benefit analysis

This is, in some ways, the ultimate question that is inherent within the preceding issues. What are the costs and benefits to economic development and financial resiliency of a defined level of TLAC for global SIFIs? The FSB directly confronted this issue in its proposal. The FSB noted that: 'the added funding costs associated with a TLAC requirement will lead to a reduction of the implicit public subsidy for G-SIBs'. However, in assessing this effect, it presumptively adopted a relatively simple binary understanding of the potential relationships by concluding that: 'G-SIBs may pass on a share of their higher funding costs to their clients, prompting a shift of banking activities to other banks without necessarily reducing the amount of activity'. While this may be true for many activities, it appears to assume the answer and, at least, presents some questions about whether it is inevitably true about certain financial functions performed by G-SIBs, such as global capital formation, funding and certain more complex derivatives activities. These questions raise a great number of philosophical, economic, financial and legal quandaries that may be unresolvable given the on-going unresolved debates over the role of global SIFIs in the financial system. Nonetheless, it is an issue that must be considered. Effective regulation is essential to any efficient market economy. However, regulation has costs as well as benefits. More is not always better.

Final thoughts

The role of TLAC in the US, EU and UK resolution strategies and the effects TLAC requirements will have on the financing, operations and functions of global SIFIs, pose many other technical questions. With regard to internal TLAC, those questions include which subsidiaries will be required to issue internal TLAC and how to evaluate whether a company is a material subsidiary given the new importance this acquires, how should internal TLAC be calibrated based on the business and interconnections between the subsidiary and its affiliates as well as its parent, and many others.

As is evident, the answers to the foundational questions posed above are critical to answering the underlying and more technical questions for every level of the TLAC framework. We must assume that international and national regulators will be open to a transparent discussion about these issues. These issues are too important to resolve without bringing the best analytics together in an open dialogue.

Notes

1 See, e.g. Mark Jickling (2010) *Causes of the Financial Crisis*. Congressional Research Service, April (sources listed in summary).
2 See HM Treasury *The Nationalisation of Northern Rock* (March 2009), available at http://www.nao.org.uk/wp-content/uploads/2009/03/0809298.pdf.
3 The Federal Reserve's actions were principally based on a previously obscure section of the Federal Reserve Act, Section 13(3), 12 USC §343, which had been used only sparingly since the Great Depression. For a discussion of the background and the use of the authority, see Office of Inspector General (2010), Board of Governors of the Federal Reserve System *The Federal Reserve's Section 13(3) Lending Facilities to Support Overall Market Liquidity: Function, Status, and Risk Management* (November). The FDIC acted through a new interpretation of its systemic risk authority in 12 USC §1823(c)(4). This authority was subsequently curtailed in the Dodd-Frank Wall Street Reform and Consumer Protection Act.
4 FSB (2013) *Thematic Review on Resolution Regimes: Peer Review Report* (April).
5 Dodd-Frank Wall Street Reform and Consumer Protection Act of 2010, Title II— Orderly Liquidation Authority, codified at 12 USC §§5381–5397.
6 OLA §210(a)(11) makes eligible for resolution any company that:

A is incorporated or organized under any provision of Federal law or the laws of any State;
B is —

  i a bank holding company, as defined in section 2(a) of the Bank Holding Company Act of 1956 (12 USC §1841(a));
  ii a nonbank financial company supervised by the Board of Governors;
  iii any company that is predominantly engaged in activities that the Board of Governors has determined are financial in nature or incidental thereto for purposes of section 4(k) of the Bank Holding Company Act of 1956 (12 USC §1843(k)) other than a company described in clause (i) or (ii); or
  iv any subsidiary of any company described in any of clauses (i) to (iii) that is predominantly engaged in activities that the Board of Governors has determined are financial in nature or incidental thereto for the purposes of section 4(k) of the Bank Holding Company Act of 1956 (12 USC §1843(k)) (other than a subsidiary that is an insured depository institution or an insurance company); and

C is not a Farm Credit System institution chartered under and subject to the provisions of the Farm Credit Act of 1971, as amended (12 USC §2001 et seq.), a governmental entity, or a regulated entity, as defined under section 1303(20) of the Federal Housing Enterprises Financial Safety and Soundness Act of 1992 (12 USC §4502(20)).

7 While the term 'liquidation' is in the Dodd-Frank Act's OLA provisions, it does not require a value-destroying or destabilising sell-off of assets. The provisions defining OLA demonstrate that 'liquidation' as used in the Dodd-Frank Act means a resolution

that imposes losses on creditors, maximises recoveries and mitigates systemic risks. It is more akin to a US Bankruptcy Code Chapter 11 proceeding – with all of the similar powers to continue valuable businesses – with additional sources of liquidity and authority to respond to potential systemically problematic insolvencies. See sections 204(a)(1) and 210(a)(9)(E) of the Dodd-Frank Act, 12 USC §§5384(a)(1) and 5390(a)(9)(E).

8 Generally, qualified financial contracts are financial instruments such as securities contracts, commodities contracts, forwards contracts, swaps, repurchase agreements and any similar agreements. See section 210(c)(8)(D)(i) of the Dodd-Frank Act, 12 USC §5390(c)(8)(D)(i).

9 See generally section 165 of Title I of the Dodd-Frank Act, 12 USC §5365 and *The Orderly Resolution of Covered Financial Companies—Special Powers under Title II— Oversight and Advanced Planning*, infra.

10 BoE (2014) *The Bank of England's Approach to Resolution* (October), available at www.bankofengland.co.uk/financialstability/Documents/resolution/apr231014.pdf, which will be updated periodically. Another important recent paper released in the UK is the PRA's (2014) paper *Ensuring Operational Continuity in Resolution – DP1/14* published on 6 October, available at www.bankofengland.co.uk/pra/Documents/publications/cp/2014/dp114.pdf. This paper discusses, and seeks comment on, operational arrangements that may be necessary to facilitate operational continuity.

11 A directive dealing with reorganisation and winding up of credit institutions having branches in several member states was adopted in 2001(Directive 2001/24/EC), but its purpose was essentially to determine applicable laws and to provide for some coordination between member states.

12 As a practical matter, national authorities will be replaced by the single resolution board under the SRM in certain cases.

13 *Resolving Globally Active, Systemically Important, Financial Institutions: A Joint Paper by the Federal Deposit Insurance Corporation and the Bank of England*, available at http://www.fdic.gov/about/srac/2012/gsifi.pdf. For additional information on the joint paper, please see Cleary Gottlieb Steen and Hamilton's Alert Memo *FDIC and Bank of England Signal Significant Cooperation on Resolution Issues in Joint Paper Describing 'Single Point of Entry' Resolution of a Cross-border SIFI*, available at http://www.cgsh.com/files/News/14201174-9c48-43b4-9e59-83ae7b365cc1/Presentation/NewsAttachment/49cb8ec9-d7d8-4a53-af68-8462d68e7554/CGSH%20Alert%20-%20FDIC%20and%20BoE%20Signal%20Significant%20Cooperation%20on%20Resolution%20Issues.pdf.

14 See, e.g. 12 C.F.R. Part 252 *Enhanced Prudential Standards for Bank Holding Companies and Foreign Banking Organizations Final Rule*.

15 BoE Resolution Paper p. 12, footnote 2, in reference to holding company bail-in strategies. The 2012 Bank of England-FDIC paper is available at http://www.bankofengland.co.uk/publications/Documents/news/2012/nr156.pdf.

16 See BoE Resolution Paper p. 18.

17 See BoE Resolution Paper pp. 9–10.

18 See BoE Resolution Paper p. 8.

19 See BoE Resolution Paper pp. 18–19.

20 It is appropriate to note that there are many discussions around the issue of what liabilities should be eligible for bail-in. This is one of the reasons that regulators have sought to require a likely sufficient level of long-term debt so that shorter-term liabilities – more often used for liquidity rather than loss absorbance – are not bailed in.

21 See Michel Barnier, Commissioner for Internal Markets, European Commission, letter to Benjamin Bernanke, Chairman, Board of Governors of the Federal Reserve

System regarding Enhanced Prudential Supervision NPR (April 2013); Luis M. Linde, Governor of the Bank of Spain *Key Issues on Today's Banking Industry* at the 6th Santander International Banking Conference, Madrid (5 November 2013).

22 BRRD article 43.
23 BRRD article 43(1), 63(1).
24 BRRD article 43(2)(a).
25 BRRD article 43(3).
26 BRRD article 43(2)(b).
27 BRRD article 44.
28 BRRD article 44(3).
29 BRRD article 44(12).
30 BRRD article 44(4).
31 BRRD article 44(5).
32 BRRD article 44(7).
33 BRRD article 44(8). This provision created additional negotiations and questions in 2014, because of a concern by the UK that it could prevent certain extraordinary actions by UK authorities without requiring creditors to absorb losses even where doing so might create additional risks of contagion.
34 BRRD article 45(1). Derivatives are included in the total liabilities on the basis that full recognition is given to counterparty netting rights.
35 BRRD article 45(5).
36 BRRD article 45(6).
37 BRRD article 45(14).
38 BRRD article 45(8)–(10). For groups, under certain circumstances, these minimum capital requirements may be waived for the parent company and/or a subsidiary company on an individual basis where the authorities can rely on compliance with the capital requirements on a consolidated basis. BRRD article 45(11)–(12).
39 BRRD article 46(1)–(2).
40 Id.
41 BRRD article 48(1).
42 BRRD article 60.
43 BRRD article 48(2).
44 Id.
45 BRRD article 49. EBA is required to develop technical standards specifying methodologies used to determine the value of liabilities arising from derivatives. BRRD article 49(5).
46 BRRD article 50. EBA is required to develop guidelines on the setting of conversion rates. BRRD article 50(4).
47 BRRD article 52.
48 Mark Carney, Governor of the Bank of England and Chairman of the Financial Stability Board in 'Speech to the International Monetary and Financial Committee' (11 October 2014).
49 Available at: http://www.financialstabilityboard.org/wp-content/uploads/TLAC-Condoc-6-Nov-2014-FINAL.pdf
50 Unfortunately, there has been a tendency to characterise any liquidity support – whether or not secured – as a 'bail-out'. The danger is that normal central bank liquidity or access to funding resources under the new resolution frameworks will be mischaracterised as a 'bail-out' and that regulators will delay or limit access to this funding until it is too late.

9 Resolution of failing banks in the European banking union

Finishing the job or going back to the drawing board?[1]

Johan A. Lybeck

As a result of the recent financial crisis, a number of measures have been undertaken to make a repeat of the disaster of a similar magnitude less likely, but also to facilitate recovery and resolution of failing banks should a (systemic) financial crisis nevertheless occur again. Foremost among measures to increase the resistance of banks to financial stress are the Basel III rules for increasing the quality and quantity of capital, as well as the introduction of liquidity coverage ratios, implemented by the Dodd-Frank legislation in the US and by the CRD IV package in the EU. Whether the measures taken will be sufficient is hotly debated. Some see the failure to break up the too-big-to-fail (TBTF) banks as an indication that the next crisis may be similar to the last one. Others think that the curtailment of banks' activities will, instead, lead to a crisis beginning in the less-supervised so-called shadow banking system.

Be that as it may, measures have also been undertaken to change and hopefully improve the manner in which a banking crisis is resolved. In the US the Orderly Liquidation Authority (OLA) under Title II of the Dodd-Frank Act enhances the powers of the Federal Deposit Insurance Corporation (FDIC) to seize not only banks but also bank holding companies and other systemically important financial institutions (SIFIs), as well as granting it powers to impose losses on holders of unsecured debt on top of those of shareholders. Under the Single Resolution Mechanism (SRM), a euro area-wide single resolution authority has been created and a gradually communalised single bank resolution fund has been established for the euro area countries and other EU members that decide to join.

A trait common to OLA and the European Bank Recovery and Resolution Directive (BRRD) is to severely restrict – their respective authors would claim, making impossible – the possibility of bailing out banks using taxpayer money. To my mind, the restrictions imposed on the regulatory authorities' tool-kit may severely curtail their ability to resolve the next financial crisis, implying unnecessary costs not only to financial firms and the financial sector but unnecessary output losses and unemployment in the real economy. A study of the bank resolutions in financial crises shows that the use of taxpayer money is an inevitable feature of successful interventions. A credible resolution authority, irrespective of whether financing means are pre-funded or not, depends on having the treasury (i.e. the taxpayer) as a last resort.

The US, after Dodd-Frank, presents a consistent framework of resolution where some minor things need to be changed. Europe, on the other hand, is in a total mess. Whereas in the US the three 'legs' of a banking union (supervision, resolution and deposit insurance) are in place, the EU has introduced a Single Supervisory Mechanism (SSM) housed in the European Central Bank (ECB), but without communalising the other two 'legs'. A Single Resolution Board (SRB) has been created, but without its own powers of decision, without adequate (common) resources and without the vital taxpayer funded backstop. Common rules for deposit insurance have been enacted, but without the necessary common deposit insurance fund.

Either the EU should decide, within a very short period of time, to implement a true European banking union (as discussed in earlier chapters), or it would be preferable to reintroduce supervision, recovery and resolution at the national level. In that case, it would also be preferable to move from home country control to host country control, where cross-border banking would have to be undertaken by subsidiaries rather than by branches. This kind of 'international ring-fence' will not only increase average levels of capital in the banking system but also facilitate the resolution of cross-border banks. In demanding that large international banks operate as separately capitalised US subsidiary bank holding companies under the supervision of the Federal Reserve, the US may actually have shown a credible way forward also for the EU, a road that the UK also appears ready to take.

Regulatory actions in Europe and the US during the crisis contrasted

There are a number of features that distinguish and separate the handling of the financial crisis on the two sides of the Atlantic. By listing them, I may begin to find an answer to the questions as to why the American bail-out money under the Troubled Asset Relief Program (TARP) and the Capital Purchase Program (CPP) has, in the main, been repaid while the European has not and why US banks appear to be recovering from the crisis much faster than their European competitors:

1   American banks were better capitalised to begin with than their European counterparts thanks to the US focus on minimum leverage ratios (capital over total assets) rather than on capital in relation to risk-weighted assets. On entering the crisis, asset/capital ratios of the major European megabanks were, on average, double those of the major US banks, even correcting for the difference between IFRS and GAAP accounting principles. When the crisis struck in 2007, large North American banks had, on average, a ratio of Tier 1 capital to risk-weighted assets of 9.42 per cent, which may be contrasted with 4.74 per cent in Germany, 5.69 per cent in Italy and 6.29 per cent in Spain (but 11.68 per cent in Britain).[2] Obviously, adequate capital is only part of the story, albeit an important one.
2   Thanks not least to the opposition by the FDIC and its chairwoman, Sheila Bair, American (commercial) banks had avoided the disaster that Basel 2 brought to European banks from 2004 onwards by being forced to stay on Basel 1 with its fixed rather than bank-modelled risk weights – a blessing in disguise as it transpired.

3   The long built-up experience by the FDIC in the efficient resolution of failing banks had few similarities in Europe where virtually everything – legal as well as institutional frameworks – had to be learned and built from scratch. The FDIC had lived through the Latin American crises and the thrift crisis in the 1980s as well as the Asian and Russian crises in the 1990s, and the relevant pieces of legislation in the form of the FDIC Improvement Act of 1991 and the Federal Deposit Reform Act of 2005 were the happy results, as well as the changes brought to the bankruptcy legislation by the Bankruptcy Abuse Prevention and Consumer Protection Act of 2005.

4   As a consequence of the existence of a credible safety net for insured deposits for over 75 years, there were no major retail bank runs in the US during the crisis (but certainly wholesale runs until the establishment of the Temporary Liquidity Guarantee Program and other measures to rebuild confidence in the wholesale and repo markets). By contrast, deposit insurance in the EU for all countries was only introduced in 1995 by Directive 94/19/EC and was untested. Moreover, even in 2013, a number of important EU countries (Austria, Italy and the UK among others) still lacked pre-funded deposit insurance.[3]

5   While European regulatory authorities in most countries lacked a macro-stability view during the crisis, chasing individual failing banks one after the other, the US authorities were more inclined to see the crisis in systemic terms, as a crisis of the banking industry.[4] Thus, while in Europe only needy banks were recapitalised (except in France), TARP was available to all viable banks (and probably to some non-viable banks), all the US megabanks being forced to participate. In this way, panic and runs were avoided since the public had no way of knowing which TARP recipients really were in need of the money and which were not; everybody was treated alike. In Europe the major state-aided and/or state-owned 'zombies' still stand out to be occasionally flogged in the press: RBS, Bankia, Commerzbank, Monte dei Paschi di Siena, ABN AMRO and Eurobank among other.[5]

6   With the rapid response to the crisis in the US came a rapid return of confidence, aided not least by the harsh and hence credible stress tests carried out by the Federal Reserve, forcing a number of banks to raise a substantial amount of new capital. The European stress tests, on the other hand, were treated as a joke in the press and had probably more of a negative effect on confidence in the Old Continent's banking system.[6]

7   The gradual return to growth in the US, in contrast with the disastrous effect on confidence and growth of the European debt crisis, led to quite different outcomes for their respective banks. While the US banking system had already returned to profitability by the beginning of 2010, their European colleagues were mostly in negative territory until well into 2013.[7]

8   The return to profitability by US banks led to the possibility of raising more equity capital (see the enormous difference between the US and Europe in Figure 9.1). From 2007 to mid-2013, European banks raised a total of €248 billion in new equity as against €190 billion for US banks, but recall that total assets in European banks were five times those of US banks, American

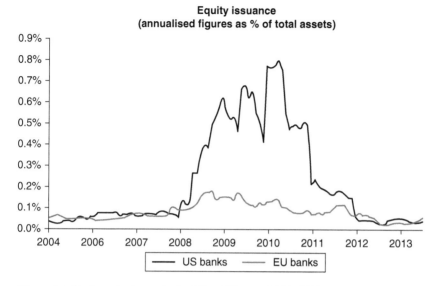

Figure 9.1 Bank equity issues in the US and Europe, 2004–2013, percentage of total assets.

Source: Dirk Schoenmaker and Toon Peek (2014) *The State of the Banking Sector in Europe.* OECD Economics Department Working Paper 1102, 27 January, p. 19 (for URL, see note 7).

corporates relying much more on direct access to the capital market than their European counterparts.

9 The profitability of US banks also gave them an advantage denied to European banks, namely to increase capital from retained earnings. The level of profitability allowed them to increase loan loss provisions at a much faster rate, putting the problems behind them.

10 Overall, the US handling of the financial crisis, while frequently improvised, turned out quite well. Instead of dismantling it, as Dodd-Frank largely does, it should be improved upon. Europe's leaders, however, have lots to learn from their US counterparts and this chapter looks at how/if they have learned their lesson.

Figures 9.2 (a)–(d) spell out the development between 2007 and 2012 of the 7,861 banks which existed in the EU (of 27 countries) in 2012. They focus on four aspects:

1 *Return on equity.* Having recovered from the financial crisis itself, profitability in the European banking sector suffered as a result of the sovereign debt crisis in the PIIGS countries (Portugal, Italy, Ireland, Greece and Spain), spilling over into Northern Europe, not least by the forced writedown of Greek debt. US banks had a return on equity of 8.8 per cent in 2012 as compared to −1.6 per cent in the EU.[8]

2   *Capital adequacy.* With government aid and by shrinking assets (and to some extent by issuing new capital), European banks improved their Tier 1 BIS ratio from 8 to 12 per cent. US banks had, however, a Tier 1 ratio of 13.1 per cent in 2012, despite assets having risen from US$13.4 trillion to US$14.4 trillion in the 5-year period.[9]

3   *Efficiency.* In terms of cost-to-income ratios, the US and Europe were surprisingly similar at around a 66 per cent.[10]

4   *Non-performing loans (NPL) ratio.* In a stagnating Europe, NPLs as a share of total loans doubled between 2008 and 2012 to 4.5 per cent and were still rising in 2013, whereas US banks had NPLs at 3.3 per cent (and falling from 5 per cent in 2009).[11,12]

Competition vs. stability aspects[13]

While there was some infighting between both American and European national regulatory authorities, the national European authorities (and their banks) also had to fight a supranational hydra in the form of the EU Commission. One of the major contentions of this chapter is that the Commission's focus on a 'level-field' competition and the single market to the disadvantage of stability was (and is) one of the major reasons why Europe has fared worse than the US in getting its banks back on their feet. I take a clear exception to the statement by Ferran (2012, 80–81) (in her otherwise excellent review) that:

> Pre-crisis, the primary aim of EU financial services policy was to "consolidate dynamically towards an integrated, open, inclusive, competitive and economically efficient EU financial market". The need to address at EU level the negative side-effects of removing internal barriers was not ignored, but nor was it the number one priority. Now, EU financial services regulation is all about improving safety and soundness.[14]

As the *dictata* of the European Commission concerning the legality of the national aid efforts made clear, the Commission was throughout the crisis and to this day almost exclusively focused on competition to the detriment of macroeconomic stability. Indeed, the EU Commission has acknowledged that, after the initial period of accepting state aid in the name of financial stability, it started to tighten conditions for state aid to the financial sector from the second half of 2010. The Commission writes:

> **All in all, in the second semester of 2010 the Commission considered that there was a sufficient level of stabilisation in the financial sector to embark on a gradual exit path, with a tightening of conditions to grant aid.** That process started with tighter conditions for government guarantees from 1 July 2010, and was then extended to the other temporary rules governing aid to both financial institutions and the real economy from 1 January 2011. In particular, from that date, every beneficiary of a

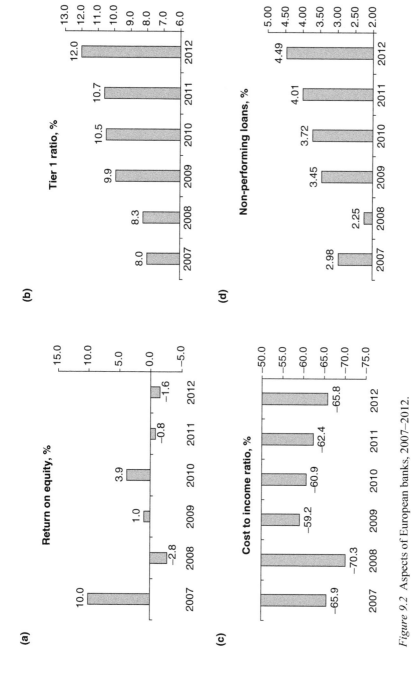

Figure 9.2 Aspects of European banks, 2007–2012.

Source: European Banking Federation, March 2014 (http://www.ebf-fbe.eu/publications/statistics/).

recapitalisation or impaired asset measure has been obliged to submit a restructuring plan to the Commission's approval, irrespective of the level of aid it received [. . .]

The tightening of the conditions for approving aid conveys the signal that banks have to prepare for a return to normal market mechanisms without State support when market conditions permit such a return. In particular, they should accelerate the still necessary restructuring. At the same time, the applicable rules afford sufficient flexibility to duly take account of the potentially diverse circumstances affecting the situation of different banks or national financial markets, and also cater for the possibility of an overall or country-specific deterioration of financial stability (emphasis in original).[15]

This period – mid-2010 – is precisely the time when the sovereign debt crisis entered into its most critical phase, putting pressure not only on the sovereigns and states in the so-called PIIGS countries but also on banks in Northern Europe, having invested in the sovereign debt from these countries and been severely hit by the writedown of Greek debt.[16]

What the EU wants to achieve in terms of bail-out vs. bail-in[17]

I am very pleased that finance ministers of the Member States have managed a few minutes ago to reach broad political agreement on the future rules for how to restructure and resolve failing banks. These rules are of utmost importance to protect taxpayers from having to bail out banks in the future. They will be instrumental to deal with the threat of banks which today are 'too-big-to-fail' and to help overcome links between states and banks which continue to weigh on economic growth.

[. . .]

The agreement represents a balanced compromise. I am pleased that the fundamental principles and provisions in the Commission's proposal have been accepted by Member States.

1. A comprehensive and credible framework

My first priority has been to ensure that the framework is robust and clear . . . Critically, a harmonised rulebook is established for how the costs of bank failure are allocated – starting with bank shareholders and creditors, and backed by financial support from resolution funds sourced from the banking sector and not taxpayers.

2. Integrity and unity of the Single Market

Banks in all Member States will be subject to harmonised provisions governing how resolution is carried out and how the costs are shared. No Member State will be able to subject banks to less onerous resolution arrangements, for example based on its fiscal strength.

3. A strong regime for financing resolution

Discussions today focused on the all-important details of how the costs of resolution are shared. From the start, I have insisted that the regime must convince markets and citizens that we are serious about ending public bailouts of banks. To the furthest extent possible, bank losses must be covered by private bank investors and the banking sector as a whole. (Remarks by EU internal-markets Commissioner, Michel Barnier, 27 June 2013.)[18]

Notice first that the emphasis of the Commission is still on the single market and the competitive aspects of the EU and only on stability concerns at one remove. Hence, parsimonious states with stable government finances are to be prevented from aiding their domestic banks in relation to prodigal states without sufficient domestic financial resources.

This Commission focus on competition and disregard for the need for a credible financial backstop has received a severe rebuke from the ECB, although framed in unobtrusive language so as to not insult a sister EU institution. Unfortunately, as I show below, its critique fell on deaf ears as the compromise result on the access to the common public purse is far too small to make an impact.

> The ECB is of the view that, while subject to the principle of fiscal neutrality, access to fiscal resources would be an essential element of the SRM's backstop arrangements. This is because private sources of funding may, especially at the start of the SRM, be scarce and temporarily dry up under acute financial market turmoil. The ECB understands that the Commission had not included an obligation on participating Member States to grant access to public funds as this could interfere with Member States' fiscal sovereignty which cannot be encroached upon under the legal basis of the proposed regulation. Against this background, the ECB considers it important that participating Member States cater for a joint and solid public backstop to be available upon the entry into force of the proposed regulation (p. 9).[19]

Also, (ibid., p. 10, the emphasis is mine)

> The ECB acknowledges that the State aid framework has proved essential in defining common parameters for national public support within the context of bank resolution across the Union. However, the ECB is of the view that the impact of the application of State aid control and its impact on resolutions undertaken by the SRM should be carefully assessed. Once the SRM is fully operational, resolution decisions will be taken at the Union level, thus preserving the level playing field and not distorting the single market. In view of this, the parallel assessment under the State aid procedure should not delay, duplicate or hinder the resolution process. The aim of preserving the internal market and not distorting competition between the participating Member States and non-participating Member States can be achieved within

the resolution process. Integration of State aid aspects into the resolution process may, in particular, be envisaged given that the Commission has the final decision-making power. *In any event, the application of the proposed regulation should ensure that state aid control neither results in any undue delays nor hinders the achievement of the resolution objectives, in particular given the need to protect financial stability.*

In a slightly earlier, leaked private letter to the Commission in July 2013, ECB President, Mario Draghi, sought, in vain, to modify the proposed rules limiting the possibility of taxpayer bailouts. Draghi said in the letter that mandatory burden-sharing with shareholders and junior bondholders was warranted when a bank was on the brink of collapse or its capital had fallen below the minimum regulatory threshold. There could be cases, however, when a bank had a viable business model and its capital was above the minimum threshold, but its supervisor still required it to raise additional funds. In such cases, if the bank could not raise the capital needed in the market quickly enough, the ECB President said state aid should be possible without junior bondholders getting hit first. The letter also said incentives should be in place to ensure that banks did their best to raise private capital before resorting to state aid.[20]

Second, I note the similarity with the US situation after Dodd-Frank. Should a bail-in of (unsecured) creditors prove insufficient, the banks under supervision will be subjected to an ex post levy to pay for the failures of other banks' risky adventures. This hardly creates the best incentives for careful and cautious bank management. Furthermore, it is hardly a credible policy in the midst of a systemic financial crisis. Since it is not credible, it invites speculation as to what would really happen in a (new) crisis.

Resolution as an integral part of a European banking union[21]

Broadly viewed, a true banking union needs five legs. They must also be consistently and simultaneously put in place and applied, otherwise it is like a stool with uneven length legs.[22]

A common currency and a common central bank acting as a reliable lender of last resort

In the US the Federal Reserve has existed since 1913; in Europe, the ECB started only in 1998. However, aggressive actions (quantitative easing in the US; long-term refinancing operations (LTRO) and, from September 2012, outright monetary transactions (OMT) in Europe) taken over the past crisis have given both central banks immense credibility, at the price of a dramatic growth of their balance sheets, rising three to four times. Neither of them may, after the adoption of the Dodd-Frank Act in the US, lend to individual non-banks. This may create a problem if the origin of the next crisis is located in the 'shadow banking sector', say a large hedge fund or an insurance company, or even a large non-financial corporate, facing liquidity problems.

Common minimum rules for solvency and liquidity

A worldwide standardised basis is provided through the adoption of the Basel III rules, introduced in the US by Dodd-Frank[23] and by the CRD IV package (Directive and Regulation) in the EU. The US has, however, chosen to demand more stringent leverage (capital-to-total assets) ratios of its TBTF banks (6 per cent as compared to Basel's 3 per cent). Some countries in the EU, such as Sweden, may fully utilise their right to charge its TBTF banks an extra capital charge in relation to risk-weighted assets of 5 per cent rather than the 1 to 2.5 per cent agreed upon by Basel's Financial Stability Board (FSB).[24]

An SSM [25]

There are clear similarities between the US and the EU in setting up a revised system of supervision. In Europe, the ECB is charged with the direct supervision of around 130 TBTF banks with assets corresponding to some 85 per cent of total euro area banking assets. It will also be the secondary supervisor to the 6,000 or so smaller banks supervised nationally in the euro area, but not to the residual 2,000 banks chartered by non-euro member states, unless these countries choose to join the SSM voluntarily.

In the US, in addition to the state banks that are members of the Federal Reserve System, the Federal Reserve will supervise just over 30 domestic bank holding companies, which have assets of over US$50 billion, the other banks and bank holding companies being supervised by the Office of the Comptroller of the Currency, the FDIC or by state supervisors, depending on their charter. Just as in Europe, these 30 banks have around 85 per cent of total banking assets. In contrast to the ECB, however, the Federal Reserve will also supervise such non-banking holding companies as are deemed systemically important by the Financial Stability Oversight Council. The ECB will have no such rights. In sharp contrast also to the US, for the foreseeable future, no common deposit insurance authority will exist in Europe to act as a secondary supervisor (and resolution authority, cf. below) to the central bank or to federal/state supervisors like the FDIC does in the US.

Common deposit insurance authority and common deposit guarantee fund

This is perhaps where the major difference between the US and the EU will be over the coming years. While there are rules for how much of deposits are guaranteed in both areas (US$250,000 vs. €100,000), the FDIC is the sole and unique deposit insurance authority in the US, whereas the deposit insurance system in Europe is, and will continue to be, nationally fragmented. Furthermore, in the US there is a common *ex ante* bank-financed deposit insurance fund (DIF), aiming at reaching 2 per cent of covered deposits in the years to come. In Europe many countries still lack pre-funded systems at all, and they will only be required to attain the desired 0.8 per cent of covered deposits by 2024. The critical difference is thus that banks in California may have paid their insurance fees to the DIF for saving depositors in a crashed Florida bank, whereas in Europe, the only cooperation among the national deposit insurance funds will be bilaterally-arranged loans on a voluntary basis.

A single resolution authority, a single bank resolution fund and a common backstop under the SRM

In the US, a decision on the resolution of a failing TBTF bank requires a vote with qualified majority by the FDIC and the Federal Reserve boards and the agreement of the Secretary of the Treasury. Once the decision is taken, however, the FDIC is in sole and total control of the process. In the EU, a resolution decision is a complex process involving the ECB as supervisor, the newly-created SRB, the EU Commission, the European Banking Authority (EBA), national regulators and ultimately the ECOFIN Council of (Finance) Ministers if the Board and the Commission have different opinions.

A common feature in Europe and the US is the insistence that not only shareholders but also unsecured creditors, junior as well as senior, be bailed in before any resolution fund or taxpayer money is used. In the US there is no fund strictly speaking despite the name Orderly Liquidation Fund – it is a drawing right on the US Treasury – and in Europe, the resolution funds, while pre-funded by bank fees on a risk-based basis, will be national for the time being and only gradually communalised and will attain only 1 per cent of covered deposits, or an estimated €70 billion (of which €55 billion will be in the euro area). A minimum of 8 per cent of banks' total liabilities and equity must be bailed in before the resolution fund is to be accessed (cf. below).

As a final backstop, the existing €500 billion European Stability Mechanism (ESM) may be used, but only partly (up to €60 billion), to recapitalise bridge banks directly and only once the SSM is in place and only provided that the ECB takes over the supervision of the bank in question, if it is not already the supervisor. The ESM would then become the (temporary) partial owner of the distressed bank, a role for which it has no prior experience.[26]

The €55 billion Single Resolution Fund (SRF) corresponds to approximatively 0.1 per cent of total banking assets in the EU, according to statistics from the European Banking Federation, and a slightly higher proportion of euro area bank assets, which comprise 72 per cent of the total. This corresponds to some 0.4 per cent of the area's GDP. Recall that costs of recapitalisation during the last crisis have been, on average, 3 to 4 per cent of GDP in the majority of countries, even after repayments, and an average of 7 per cent of GDP gross, i.e. during the crisis phase (and up to 40 per cent of GDP in some countries such as Ireland). The conclusion speaks for itself.

An additional complicating factor is that since member states could not agree, the SRF will not be guided entirely by EU rules, but its gradual mutualisation is decided upon by a separately-agreed mechanism among the participating countries outside of normal EU legislation.[27,28] The European Parliament objected to this feature, demanding that the fund be created through normal EU treaties, subject to the Parliament's decision.[29]

The five legs of the banking union are obviously interdependent and should ideally be introduced simultaneously. Without a resolution authority, the SRB and a sufficient financial backstop in place, markets may well panic, while pondering on where the necessary new capital infusion to banks that failed the test will come from. The SRB must be able to draw primarily on the resources of the ESM with the involved countries' taxpayers as ultimate back-up.[30]

The OECD has calculated that the 200 largest euro area banks need to raise an additional €300 billion to €400 billion in new equity to pass the stress test.[31] This may be compared with the €30 billion actually raised in the first half of 2014. It may also be compared with the actual results of the stress tests undertaken by the ECB and the EBA, which found a need for new capital in the banks studied of just €24 billion, reduced to €10 billion after taking into account amounts raised in 2014.[32] The huge difference speaks for itself.

Analysis of the legislation: SRM and BRRD

The new legislation consists of a regulation on the SRM and the BRRD partly overlapping. The regulation applies formally to all the members of the EU, but is applicable only to the euro area (and other participating) countries whose banks are supervised directly or indirectly by the ECB under the SSM, while the BRRD is applicable to all EU member states.

The regulation puts in place the path resolution authorities under the SRM must follow.[33] The procedure of how a resolution is to be conducted is spelled out in Article 16 of the SRM Regulation.

The ECB in its role as the overall supervisor, aided by national supervisors for smaller banks, would give the alarm when a bank supervised under the SSM mechanism finds itself in trouble and is likely to fail. The SRB with its five executive members and including representatives from the relevant national authorities (as well as representatives of the ECB and the European Commission as observers) would prepare for the resolution of the bank. Is the bank viable? What are its assets really worth? Can the bank be sold? Should a bridge bank be set up? Should good and bad assets be separated? Should the bank be continued after a bail-in of creditors, with unsecured bank debt being converted to equity or written off? Will resolution involve the SRF?

On the basis of the Board's recommendation, the EU Commission will decide whether and how to place a bank into resolution and it would also spell out a framework for the use of resolution tools (bridge bank, sale, asset separation and bail-in). The Commission's role would normally be limited to the formal decision to trigger the resolution of a bank and the decision on the resolution framework, thereby ensuring its consistency with the single market and with EU rules on state aid.[34]

This is because under existing EU treaties, neither the SRB nor any other agency such as the EBA may take such a decision at the EU level, which is reserved for an EU institution such as the Commission, the ECB or the Council. This limit on the delegation of powers follows the so-called 'Meroni doctrine', named after a case where the European Court of Justice (ECJ) in 1958 challenged a decision by the High Authority of the European Coal and Steel Community (the predecessor of the Commission)[35].

If the Commission objects to the proposal by the SRB, the matter is referred to the Council of Ministers, which takes a decision by simple majority. The Board is obliged to set out a revised resolution plan following the decision by the Council. After the first 24 hours the Board has a further 8 hours to formulate an alternative, i.e. a total of 32 hours, concluding it in the early hours of Sunday if the process is started, as it is hoped, on a Friday evening.[36]

In my view, given the lack of financial and economic competence of the Commission on banking issues, as well as its almost exclusive focus on the single market and competition aspects, it would be preferable to create the SRB within the ECB, thereby creating a parallel institution to the ECB in its role as the operator of the SSM. This would echo the Bank of England's (BoE) establishment of a special resolution unit within the bank in parallel with its Prudential Regulatory Authority (PRA), the country's main financial supervisor together with the Financial Policy Committee.[37] This would leave the Commission to focus on competition matters, a power the Financial Conduct Authority holds in the UK.

It would have been preferable to house the SRB within a common deposit insurance authority as in the US (and other countries such as Sweden), but given the absence of a common deposit insurance authority for the foreseeable future, the ECB solution seems to be the only feasible alternative.

Let me turn now to the issue of bail-in and bail-out. The conditions for state aid are spelled out already in the preamble to the BRRD:

(73) Where those exclusions are applied, the level of writedown or conversion of other eligible liabilities may be increased to take account of such exclusions subject to the 'no creditor worse off than under normal insolvency proceedings' principle being respected. Where the losses cannot be passed to other creditors, the resolution financing arrangement may make a contribution to the institution under resolution subject to a number of strict conditions including the requirement that losses totalling not less than 8% of total liabilities including own funds have already been absorbed, and the funding provided by the resolution fund is limited to the lower of 5% of total liabilities including own funds or the means available to the resolution fund and the amount that can be raised through ex post contributions within three years.

My view is that despite the words of Commissioner Barnier, quoted above, only the banking industry itself and bank owners and creditors should bear the costs of bank failures; a taxpayer bail-out is not outlawed, but made more difficult. Bail-in of shareholders and other creditors must amount to 8 per cent of total assets of the institution before a bail-out is allowed. Furthermore, the injection of capital must in the first place come from the built-up resolution (stabilisation) funds and may only amount to 5 per cent of the total balance sheet of the saved institution.

Given that the ratio of risk-weighted assets to total assets in European banks is, on average, around one-third, the demand for an 8 per cent bail-in would mean that only banks with Basel III CET1/RWA ratios higher than 24 per cent will be able to avoid bailing in subordinated and senior creditors. It may be compared with an actual average core Tier 1 ratio to risk-weighted assets of 11.7 per cent in December 2013.[38] Even the largest SIFI banks will not be required to have more than 12 per cent equity in relation to risk-weighted assets by 2018.[39,40]

For countries such as Sweden, which has already built up a resolution (stabilisation) fund in excess of 3 per cent of covered deposits, the requirement is lowered to 20 per cent of risk-weighted assets.[41,42] However, in no case must the resolution fund or taxpayers inject more than 5 per cent of total assets into a bank as new capital, and the money must be repaid within five years (the same timeframe as for the use of the US Orderly Liquidation Fund). The possibility of bailing in senior unsecured creditors has also been brought forward to 2016 from the earlier 2018.[43] Should a bail-in prove insufficient, the possibility exists of ex post charges on the supervised financial institutions, just like under Dodd-Frank.

Despite the optimistic proposal of the Commission in 2010, the result in the form of a common financial backstop (single bank resolution fund) is much more limited.[44] Only after ten years will the resolution fund reach 1 per cent of covered deposits (around €55 billion in the euro area), and it will stay national and only be gradually communalised during these ten years. It will be financed by a risk-based fee on the liabilities of the participating institutions.

The fund may be used to:

- guarantee assets or liabilities of the bank under resolution, or a bridge bank or an asset-management vehicle ('bad bank');
- make loans to the above-mentioned institutions;
- purchase assets from the banks under resolution;
- contribute capital to a bridge bank or asset-management vehicle.

The fund may not, however, be used to recapitalise a going concern and any amount spent must, as noted above, be repaid within five years.

The other and more important reason why taxpayers are likely to be involved in the next crisis is that the proposed structure is not credible, as indicated by the comments below. The domestic resolution funds and the common fund will not be sufficient. Neither will the threat to bail in senior bondholders and uninsured depositors. As well stated by Oliver Burrows from Rabobank: 'If you bail in senior bondholders, capital markets will freeze . . . and the bank concerned will not be able to fund itself again. If you're a regulator, the answer is not to drop a nuclear bomb but to find a diplomatic solution'.[45,46]

In my view, as was well said by the US Secretary of the Treasury, Jack Lew, the proposed European resolution fund is 'too little, too late'.[47] Furthermore, it will not break the 'doom loop' between sovereign risk and bank risk.

National funds are natural elements in those countries that prefer to stay out of the common resolution mechanism. These funds also need a financial backstop. As indicated earlier, Sweden's stabilisation fund already corresponds to 1.3 per cent of GDP and will ultimately reach at least 3 per cent of GDP. For these countries, it must be possible to use the national fund to recapitalise banks much earlier than present restrictions allow. The national stabilisation fund must also, as in the Swedish one, have an unlimited borrowing right in the treasury (in the Swedish case, the National Debt Office, an authority under their treasury).

For banks participating in the SSM and SRM, in the absence of a common SRF, the SRB must be given the financial means to fulfil its mission. For the time being, this can only mean using the resources of the ESM of €500 billion. At the demand of the SRB, it must be made possible for the ESM to lend to individual banks in the euro area directly rather than to their sovereign. However, as noted above, the ESM does not constitute an ideal owner of failing banks (even though it will create a subsidiary for that purpose). Hence, as regards recapitalisations, the ESM should extend the necessary funds to the SRB, which will then inject fresh capital into the ailing banks, with a subsidiary of the SRB becoming the partial and temporary owner of the (bridge) bank.

In order, however, to avoid subsidising 'zombie banks', the present restriction that the ESM may only participate in recapitalisations of banks having a minimum of 4.5 per cent CET1/RWA is sensible. Normally, this minimum amount would be expected to be provided by bail-ins or by the member state in question. The member state will also share 20/80 with the ESM in a further recapitalisation, in order to attain the capital ratio decreed by the relevant supervisor.[48]

What others think

Major criticisms of the SSM/SRM/SRF structure have begun to appear, many of which are similar in content to much of the critique enunciated above. First, the resolution mechanism is unwieldy and too politicised. Second, without common deposit insurance and a DIF, bank runs will be an inevitable part of the next crisis, in particular since deposits above €100,000 may also be bailed in. Third, there is no requirement for banks to hold sufficient amounts of bailinable instruments such as subordinated debt and contingent convertible securities (CoCos) (see, however, the addendum). Fourth, particularly on account of the limited size of the resolution funds, there must be a backstop in the form of the ESM and ultimately, the taxpayers. Fifth, the link between sovereigns and banks through banks' holdings of sovereign bonds remains and is becoming a gradually larger threat. As well expressed by Avgouleas and Goodhart (2014):

> [The paper] explains why bail-in regimes will fail to eradicate the need for an injection of public funds where there is a threat of systemic collapse, because a number of banks have simultaneously entered into difficulties, or in the event of the failure of a large complex cross-border bank, except in those cases where failure was clearly idiosyncratic.[49]

Another critical voice is Bini-Smaghi (2013), a former member of the ECB Executive Board:

> The mechanism is unsatisfactory from several viewpoints. The decision-making process is cumbersome and involves too many bodies. The funds are insufficient to tackle a big banking problem. The ability of the mechanism to borrow in the markets is still unclear. The period of transition to the final system is too long, at least compared to the frequency of banking crises. Overall, the separation between banking and sovereign risk – which was the main goal of the union – has not been achieved.[50]

Among critical articles that still show a way forward is Gordon and Ringe (2014):

> The project of creating a Banking Union is designed to overcome the fatal link between sovereigns and their banks in the Eurozone. As part of this project, political agreement for a common supervision framework and a common resolution scheme has been reached with difficulty. However, the resolution framework is weak, underfunded and exhibits some serious flaws. Further, Member States' disagreements appear to rule out a federalised deposit insurance scheme, commonly regarded as the necessary third pillar of a successful Banking Union. (Abstract)
> [. . .]
> The Single Resolution Mechanism just enacted by the European Parliament will fail in its essential mission of managing the failure of a systemically important bank in a way that overcomes the fatal link between sovereigns and their banks. The SRM simply provides no strategy to avoid contagion from a bank failure because depositors and short-term creditors are not adequately protected, due to an insufficient resolution fund and the absence of a credible, centralised deposit insurance scheme. If bank resolution is not a credible threat, then the Single Supervisory Mechanism of the European Banking Union will be a paper tiger.[51]

Others have been seemingly more positive (Ferran, 2014):

> Yet it is important not to lose sight of how far the EU, or more especially the euro area, has come in financial regulation since 2008. The overhaul of prudential regulation and supervision has been far-reaching. There has been a remarkable shift of power from national to supranational (EU and euro area) authorities. The links between banks and sovereigns may not have been fully broken but they have certainly been considerably weakened. From being a topic that was not even on the regulatory policy radar prior to the crisis, a sophisticated EU regime for the resolution of failing banks has been agreed, and it includes an array of procedures and tools, including bail-in powers that, in time, should reduce considerably the likelihood of a need to call upon public funding. An apparatus for industry funding of resolution processes

is emerging. Innovative legal thinking is continuing to refine approaches to resolution planning, including a much richer understanding of the interrelationship between the structure of banking groups and the choice of resolution strategies. There is even already a common public sector backstop of sorts for the euro area in the form of the ESM . . . The ESM has the potential to play a role in resolution funding support as well, as least for an interim period.

The conclusion that this points to is that there has been put in place a legal framework that, on balance, is sufficiently robust to equip the institutional apparatus of EBU with sufficient authority and credibility to begin to rebuild confidence and, in that way, to contribute to the reversal of the trend towards EU financial market disintegration. That is progress.[52]

But a caveat is that she is mostly concerned with the stability of the legal foundations of the treaties (SSM and SRM), not their economic stability. Or, as she writes (abstract):

From this analysis the paper builds the case for the claim that the legal framework for the two mechanisms is sufficiently robust for the new arrangements to have the authority and credibility to rebuild confidence and, in that way, to contribute to the reversal of the trend towards EU financial market disintegration.

Gros (2013) concluded (p. 2): 'This compromise on the SRM is an inelegant step in the right direction. It leaves as many problems unresolved as it addresses. The riders on the European bicycle will have to continue to pedal for some time'.[53] While Thierry Philipponnat, secretary-general of the Brussels-based Finance Watch research group, is reported in the *Financial Times* (8 May 2014) as saying: 'It is clear that important flaws remain in the design of banking union, not least the presence of banking structures that are incompatible with a credible bail-in and resolution mechanism'.[54]

What he was referring to, in particular, was the continued preferential treatment of sovereign debt in the banking book, which means that the 'doom loop' between sovereign and bank risk is far from broken, saying:

The current regulatory preference for sovereign debt gives rise to "moral suasion", a situation in which large banks hold undue influence over their governments through the purchase of their governments' debt. When this is combined with doubts about the behaviour of the SRM in a systemic crisis, it is clear that important flaws remain in the design of banking union'.[55]

The consulting and accountancy firm, PwC, labelled their analysis *EU Bank Recovery and Resolution Directive: Triumph or Tragedy*.[56] The last word has not been said on the European banking union.

Conclusion

While stressing the importance of common rules for capital ratios, supervision and resolution, it appears that important countries have, in fact, lost faith in the process and prefer to go it alone, being as independent as possible of others' mistakes. In the US, major international banks must in the future operate as local separately capitalised subsidiaries under the supervision of the Federal Reserve, whereas up till now, the Federal Reserve only looked at the banks' total (global) level of capital irrespective of where it was held. Sometimes, giant Deutsche Bank even had negative capital in the US; now it has to find US$20 billion in additional capital or shrink assets by some US$100 billion. Other banks hard hit by the new rules are major investment banks, such as Barclays and Société Générale.[57]

It appears that a number of European countries are drawing similar conclusions, in particular the UK.[58] In the future, the PRA will take a hard look at whether the supervisor in the bank's home country is a sufficiently tough regulator, otherwise the bank will have to enter the UK as a subsidiary, regulated and supervised by the PRA, rather than as a home country supervised branch office.[59] Some banks, such as Spanish Santander, already operate on this business model. Indeed, between 1997 and 2011, the share of cross-border assets in Europe held by subsidiaries rather than branches rose from 40 to almost 70 per cent.[60]

Would it not be a lovely compliment to the EU's financial integration if the PRA were to decide that the ECB is not a sufficiently strong supervisor and hence, all major euro area banks have to enter the UK as subsidiaries? Others have drawn even more drastic conclusions concerning the (failed) trajectory towards a European banking union.[61] Perhaps host country control is the answer if the European banking union were to fail? It would provide for an increase in average capital levels worldwide as well as facilitate the resolution of cross-border banks.

Addendum

The FSB has recently complemented the earlier work by the Basel Committee on Banking Supervision by a proposal for minimum levels of bailinable debt, total loss-absorbing capital (TLAC) as they put it, in the banks regarded as TBTF, or in Basel-speak, G-SIFIs.[62]

An additional 8 to 12 per cent of loss-absorbing capital (subordinated debt, CoCos, etc.) will be added to the present capital requirements under Basel 3, which are:

- 4.5 per cent minimum CET1[63]/RWA; plus
- 2.5 per cent capital conservation buffer in the form of CET1; plus
- 1 per cent other Tier 1 capital, totalling 8 per cent minimum Tier 1 capital.

Since the large banks are also subject to a 1 to 2.5 per cent SIFI charge[64] and may be subject to a 0 to 2.5 per cent countercyclical buffer,[65] this implies that the G-SIFIs will have to hold, at the discretion of the supervisory authority, 17 to 25 per cent capital in relation to risk-weighted assets. They must also hold a minimum of 6 per cent TLAC in relation to total (unweighted) assets, of which at least 3 per cent must be CET1. It has been calculated that the requirements will necessitate the issuing of US$480 billion to US$1,600 billion in CoCos and other Basel 3-approved bailinable debt to satisfy the new requirements.[66]

However, it is difficult to see that the proposal, while a step in the right direction, solves the problems highlighted in this chapter. Foremost, the threat to bail in even senior debtholders in a systemic crisis is not credible. As a bank reaches a position where a bail-in becomes possible, a run on its debt will ensue, which will increase funding costs for all (large) institutions. Some evidence of the nervousness of investors in bailinable debt has already begun to appear.[67] The solution, as put forward by Admati, Hellwig, Haldane and many others is to demand a much higher proportion of equity in the capital requirements.[68]

Notes

1 Among many useful references, see Viral V. Acharya and Sascha Steffen *The Greatest Carry Trade Ever? Understanding Euro Zone Bank Risks*. NYU Stern School working paper, 18 November 2012; Thorstein Beck, ed., *Banking Union for Europe, Risks and Challenges* (London: CEPR and VoxEU.org, 2012); Claudia M. Buch, Tobias Körner and Benjamin Weigert *Towards Deeper Financial Integration In Europe: What The Banking Union Can Contribute*, Sachverständigenrat (German Council of Economic Experts), Working Paper 2/2013, August 2013; Jacopo Carmassi, Carmine de Noia and Stefano Micossi *Banking Union: A Federal Model for the EU With Prompt Corrective Action*, CEPS Policy Brief no. 282, 18 September 2012; James R. Barth, Apanard (Penny) Prabha and Greg Yun (2012) The Eurozone financial crisis: Role of interdependencies between bank and sovereign risk, *Journal of Financial Economic Policy* 4(1): 76–97; Douglas J. Elliot *Key Issues on European Banking Union: Trade-Offs and Some Recommendations*, Working Paper 52, November 2012, Brookings Institution; Rishi Goyal, Petya Koeva Brooks, Mahmood Pradhan, Thierry Tressel, Giovanni Dell'Ariccia, Ross Leckow, Ceyla Pazarbasioglu and an IMF Staff Team *A Banking Union for the Euro Area*, IMF Staff Discussion Note, SDN 13/01,13 February 2013; Niamh Moloney 'The legacy effects of the financial crisis on regulatory design in the EU', chapter 2 in Eilís Ferran, Niamh Moloney, Jennifer G. Hill and John C. Coffee, Jr. *The Regulatory Aftermath of the Global Financial Crisis* (Cambridge: Cambridge University Press, 2012); Nicolas Verón *A Realistic Bridge towards European Banking Union*, Petersen Institute for International Economics Policy Brief 13–17, June 2013.
2 *The Banker* July 2008.
3 International Monetary Fund *EU: Publication of Financial Sector Assessment Program Documentation – Technical Note on Deposit Insurance*, IMF Country Report No. 13/66, March 2013.
4 See, e.g. Randall S. Kroszner 'Making markets more robust', chapter 2 in Randall S. Kroszner and Robert J. Shiller *Reforming U.S. Financial Markets, Reflections Before and Beyond Dodd-Frank* (Cambridge, MA: MIT Press, 2011).
5 For instance, 'Five years on and the RBS pain is still far from over', *Financial Times*, 28 February 2014; *German Competition Body Urges Govt to Sell Commerzbank*,

available at http://uk.reuters.com/article/2014/07/09/uk-commerzbank-sale-idUKKBN 0FE1AJ20140709; *Pireaus Bank Escapes State Control, Eurobank Does Not*, available at http://www.reuters.com/article/2013/04/22/us-piraeusbank-millennium-idUS-BRE93L0XF20130422; *Dutch Bank ABN AMRO's Top Salaries Hike Plan Sends Wrong Signal*, available at http://www.forbes.com/sites/marcelmichelson/2014/06/18/dutch-bank-abn-amros-top-salaries-hike-plan-sends-wrong-signal/.

6 Among many similar articles, see e.g. *The Guardian* 'Faith in European banks shaken by stress test results', 23 November 2010; *The Daily Telegraph* 'European stress tests weren't worth the paper they were written on', 23 November 2010; *New York Times* 'Doubts persist as most Europe banks pass stress tests', 23 July 2010.

7 See for instance the Deutsche Bank research *Bank Performance in the US and Europe, an Ocean Apart*, 27 September 2013, available at http://www.dbresearch.com/PROD/DBR_INTERNET_EN-PROD/PROD0000000000320825/Bank+performance+in+the+US+and+Europe%3A+An+ocean+apart.pdf; Dirk Schoenmaker and Toon Peek *The State of the Banking Sector in Europe*, OECD Economics Department Working Paper 1102, 27 January 2014, available at http://www.oecd-ilibrary.org/docserver/download/5k3ttg7n4r32.pdf?expires=1394983777&id=id&accname=guest&checksum=65C45A9C4A143FE59D71C61312F70424.

8 Source for the US: Federal Reserve Bank of St Louis, http://research.stlouisfed.org/fred2/series/USROE.

9 Source for the US data: http://www.bankregdata.com/allHMmet.asp?met=ONE).

10 Mc Kinsey data for the US from 'The triple transformation', *McKinsey Annual Review of the Banking Industry*, October 2012.

11 World Bank http://data.worldbank.org/indicator/FB.AST.NPER.ZS (last accessed 27 July 2015).

12 The data bank of the Federal Reserve Bank of St Louis shows US NPL falling from a peak of 5.6 per cent in 2009 to 2.7 per cent in the final quarter of 2013. http://research.stlouisfed.org/fred2/series/NPTLTL.

13 See also Stefano Micossi, Ginevra Bruzzone and Miriam Cassella *Bail-In Provisions in State Aid and Resolution Procedures: Are They Consistent With Systemic Stability?* CEPS Policy Briefs no. 318, 21 May 2014, available at http://papers.ssrn.com/sol3/papers.cfm?abstract_id=2445900.

14 Eilís Ferran, 'Crisis-driven regulatory reform: Where in the world is the EU going? chapter 1 in Eilís Ferran, Niamh Moloney, Jennifer G. Hill and John C. Coffee, Jr. *The Regulatory Aftermath of the Global Financial Crisis* (Cambridge: Cambridge University Press, 2012).

15 European Commission Competition *The Effects of Temporary State Aid Rules Adopted in the Context of the Financial and Economic Crisis*, Working paper, 5 October 2011, p. 17, available at http://ec.europa.eu/competition/publications/reports/working_paper_en.pdf. See also European Commission *On the Application, From 1 August 2013, of State Aid Rules to Support Measures in Favour of Banks in the Context of the Financial Crisis*, Communication C(2013) 4119, 10 July 2013, available at http://eur-lex.europa.eu/LexUriServ/LexUriServ.do?uri=OJ:C:2013:216:0001:0015:EN:PDF.

16 For an insightful and critical assessment of the reaction of the various EU authorities to the debt crisis, see Philippe Legrain, *European Spring: Why Our Economies and Politics are in a Mess – and How to Put Them Right* (New York: CB Books, 2014).

17 See also Eilís Ferran, op. cit.

18 http://europa.eu/rapid/press-release_MEMO-13–601_el.htm; see also remarks by Herman van Rompuy, President of the European Council *Towards a Genuine Economic*

and Monetary Union, 26 June 2012, EUCO 120/12, available at http://ec.europa.eu/economy_finance/crisis/documents/131201_en.pdf; and Rishi Goyal, Petya Koeva Brooks, Mahmood Pradhan, Thierry Tressel, Giovanni Dell'Ariccia, Ross Leckow, Ceyla Pazarbasioglu and IMF Staff Team *A Banking Union for the Euro Area*, IMF Staff Discussion Note, SDN 13/01, 13 February 2013.

19 European Central Bank *Opinion of the European Central Bank of 6 November 2013 on a Proposal for a Regulation of the European Parliament and of the Council* (CON/2013/76).

20 See http://m.ft.com/cms/s/0/13cc9614–397f-11e3-a3a4–00144feab7de.html and http://uk.reuters.com/article/2013/10/19/uk-banks-bondholders-draghi-idUK-BRE99I03220131019.

21 European Commission, Communication from the Commission to the European Parliament and the Council, *A Roadmap towards a Banking Union*, COM (2012) 510, 12 September 2012; European Commission *A Blueprint for a Deep and Genuine Economic and Monetary Union, Launching a European Debate*, COM(2012) 777 final/2, 30 November 2012; European Council *Towards a Genuine Economic and Monetary Union*, Herman Van Rompuy, 26 June 2012, EUCO 120/12, available at http://ec.europa.eu/economy_finance/crisis/documents/131201_en.pdf.

22 See e.g. Nicolas Véron *A Realistic Bridge towards European Banking Union*, Petersen Institute for International Economics, Policy Brief 13–17, June 2013; Elliot, op cit.

23 But modified by the Collins Amendment to Dodd-Frank.

24 However, only 3 per cent may be charged under Pillar 1 and hence anything above will have to be charged under Pillar 2.

25 See also Eilís Ferran and Valia S. G. Babis *The European Single Supervisory Mechanism*, University of Cambridge, Faculty of Law Research Paper no 10/2013, available at http://papers.ssrn.com/sol3/papers.cfm?abstract_id=2224538.

26 In the meantime, a country could request aid from the ESM. Yet policy makers say they purposefully made that option very hard to take. The chances of the ESM stepping in are 'very, very small', Dutch Finance Minister, Jeroen Dijsselbloem, told lawmakers in The Hague on 2 July 2014, available at http://www.bloomberg.com/news/2014-08-06/espirito-santo-shows-eu-s-need-for-speed-under-new-banking-rules.html.

27 The Inter-Governmental Agreement (IGA) on mutualising the SRF was signed by 26 of the 28 members, Britain and Sweden abstaining. See http://europa.eu/rapid/press-release_STATEMENT-14-165_en.htm.

28 In the Council agreement of December 2013, the Irish Finance Minister, Michael Noonan, pleaded the case for a backstop to underpin the bank failure fund given its limited capacity, saying markets need a sign that a plan is in place. 'When you think of European banks having multi-trillions of assets on their balance sheets, the fund itself is quite small', Noonan said. 'Maybe if we could bring forward the date of consideration of the backstop, or if we had an agreement that a backstop would be in place by a certain date, that might help the credibility of the system', available at http://www.irishtimes.com/business/economy/proposals-to-break-deadlock-on-bank-fund-put-forward-at-ecofin-1.1696134.

29 http://www.ft.com/intl/cms/s/0/7c1d0dda-7ec0–11e3–8642–00144feabdc0.html; http://www.bloomberg.com/news/2014-03–10/eu-bank-crisis-talks-resume-as-draghi-watches-attentively.html.

30 Stefano Micosse, Ginevra Bruzzone and Jacopo Carmassi *The New European Framework for Managing Bank Crises*, CEPS Policy Brief 304, 21 November 2013; Thorsten Beck,

Daniel Gros and Dirk Schoenmaker 'On the design of a single resolution mechanism', in European Parliament *Banking Union: The Single Resolution Mechanism*, Monetary Dialogue, 18 February 2013 (Nicolas Véron, Guntram B. Wolff, Thorsten Beck, Daniel Gros, Dirk Schoenmaker and Sylvester C. W. Eiffinger); Charles Wyplosz, 'Banking union as crisis management tool', in Thorstein Beck, ed. *Banking Union for Europe, Risks and Challenges* (London: CEPR and VoxEU.org, 2012); Dirk Schoenmaker *Governance of International Banking: The Financial Trilemma* (Oxford and New York: Oxford University Press, 2013); 'From bail-out to bail-in', *The Economist* 14 December 2013, available at http://www.economist.com/blogs/freeexchange/2013/12/european-banks.

31 http://www.bloomberg.com/news/2013-07-23/european-banks-face-capital-gap-with-focus-on-leverage.html.

32 EBA *Result of EU Wide Stress Test*, 26 October 2014, available at http://www.eba.europa.eu/documents/10180/669262/2014+EU-wide+ST-aggregate+results.pdf.

33 *Regulation (EU) no. 86/2014 of the European Parliament and of the Council of 15 July 2014 Establishing Uniform Rules and a Uniform Procedure for the Resolution of Credit Institutions and Certain Investment Firms in the Framework of a Single Resolution Mechanism and a Single Bank Resolution Fund and Amending Regulation (EU) no 1093/2010*, available at http://eur-lex.europa.eu/legal-content/EN/TXT/HTML/?uri=OJ:L:2014:225:FULL&from=EN. See also http://www.europarl.europa.eu/news/en/news-room/content/20140411IPR43458/html/Parliament-lifts-bank-bailout-burden-fromtaxpayers%E2%80%99-shoulders and http://www.consilium.europa.eu/uedocs/cms_data/docs/pressdata/en/ecofin/143925.pdf.

34 If within 24 hours the Commission has failed to react, the Board's proposal is put into action.

35 In 2005 the ECJ gave a clear signal that the distinctions outlined in the doctrine still apply. Referring directly to Meroni, the Court upheld the conferral of power to one of the organs of the European Central Bank, stating that:

> [w]ith regard to the conditions to be complied with in the context of such delegations of powers, it should be recalled that, as the Court held in *Meroni*, first, a delegating authority cannot confer upon the authority to which the powers are delegated powers different from those which it has itself received. Secondly, the exercise of the powers entrusted to the body to which the powers are delegated must be subject to the same conditions as those to which it would be subject if the delegating authority exercised them directly, particularly as regards the requirements to state reasons and to publish. Finally, even when entitled to delegate its powers, the delegating authority must take an express decision transferring them and the delegation can relate only to clearly defined executive power', available at http://www.publications.parliament.uk/pa/cm200809/cmselect/cmeuleg/19xxx/1905.htm.

36 If the bank were to enter resolution earlier in the week, then clearly this timetable will not work as the bank would fail to honour its obligations on the next working day since it would still be in limbo. Everything would have to be sped up [eds].

37 http://www.bankofengland.co.uk/FINANCIALSTABILITY/Pages/role/risk_reduction/srr/default.aspx.

38 Source: http://www.ft.com/cms/s/0/e4d05a72-0141-11e4-9750-00144feab7de.html#axzz39L5Hspwf.

39 Basel 3 establishes a 4.5 per cent minimum capital charge of Common Equity Tier 1 (CET1) to risk-weighted assets (RWA) on top of which comes a capital-conservation

buffer of 2.5 per cent, a cyclical buffer of a maximum of 2.5 per cent and a SIFI charge of 1 to 2.5 per cent for the largest institutions. See also the Addendum at the end of the chapter.

40 http://www.bloomberg.com/news/2013–12–16/eu-banks-shrink-assets-by-1–1-trillion-as-capital-ratios-rise.html.

41 The exception requires that the fund is entirely prepaid, which is not yet the case in Sweden, the government's start-up injection of SEK15 billion not having been paid up.

42 As of the end of 2013 the Swedish stabilisation fund contained SEK49 billion, which divided by some SEK1,300 billion in covered deposits yields a ratio of 3.7 per cent. This corresponds to 1.3 per cent of GDP and will, in the absence of payouts, increase with the annual charge of 0.036 per cent on bank liabilities, the earlier ceiling for the fund of 2.5 per cent of GDP having been scrapped.

43 http://www.ft.com/intl/cms/s/0/555f3ade-6303–11e3-a87d-144feabdc0.html?siteediti on=uk#axzz2vvM638At.

44 European Commission *Bank Resolution Funds*, COM (2010) 254 Final, 26 May 2010.

45 *Financial Times* 8 August 2014, 'Bank bond investors sleepwalk into bail-ins'.

46 It is remarkable that the Commission document on which the proposal is based makes no mention of possible runs by creditors as a bail-in becomes anticipated. See DG Internal Market *Discussion Paper on the Debt Write-Down Tool – Bail-In*, undated, available at http://ec.europa.eu/internal_market/bank/docs/crisis-management/discussion_ paper_bail_in_en.pdf.

47 http://www.reuters.com/article/2014/01/07/us-france-lew-idUSBREA060M120 140107.

48 European Stability Mechanism *ESM Direct Bank Recapitalisation Instrument*, Luxembourg, 20 June 2013, available at http://www.consilium.europa.eu/uedocs/cms_ data/docs/pressdata/en/ecofin/137569.pdf.

49 Emilios Avgouleas and Charles Goodhart *A Critical Evaluation of Bail-in as a Bank Recapitalization Tool*, paper prepared for the conference on 'Bearing the losses from bank and sovereign default in the Eurozone', organised by Franklin Allen, Elena Carletti and Joanna Gray at the European University Institute, Florence, 24 April 2014.

50 http://blogs.ft.com/the-a-list/2013/12/19/the-european-banking-union-is-a-disappointment/.

51 Jeffrey N. Gordon and Wolf-Georg Ringe *Bank Resolution in the European Banking Union: A Transatlantic Perspective*, Columbia Law and Economics Working Paper no. 465, 22 July 2014, p. 28, available at http://papers.ssrn.com/sol3/papers.cfm?abstract_ id=2361347.

52 Eilís Ferran *European Banking Union: Imperfect But Can It Work?* University of Cambridge Faculty of Law Research Paper, no 30, 2014, p. 28, available at http:// papers.ssrn.com/sol3/papers.cfm?abstract_id=2426247.

53 Daniel Gros *The Bank Resolution Compromise: Incomplete But Workable?* CEPS Commentary, 18 December 2013, available at http://www.ceps.eu/book/bank-resolution-compromise-incomplete-workable. See also his http://www.project-syndicate.org/ commentary/daniel-gros-examines-the-inelegant-but-fundamental-innovation-that-is-the-single-resolution-mechanism.

54 http://www.ft.com/intl/cms/s/0/7c3c8cd8-cee2–11e3–8e62–00144feabdc0. html#axzz38vvhivHT.

55 http://www.finance-watch.org/press/press-releases/858.

56 http://www.pwc.com/et_EE/EE/publications/assets/pub/pwc-eu-bank-recovery-and-resolution-directive-triumph-or-tragedy.pdf.

57 http://www.ft.com/cms/s/0/1a1110d4–9d7c-11e3-a599–00144feab7de.html.

58 'The Balkanisation of banking, the island defence', *The Economist* 1 March 2014; 'Regulators may disagree but should say who calls the shots', Gillian Tett, *Financial Times* 27 February 2014.

59 BoE *Supervising International Banks, The Prudential Regulation Authority's Approach to Branch Supervision*, Consultation Paper CP4/14, February 2014.

60 Dirk Schoenmaker *Governance of International Banking: The Financial Trilemma* (Oxford and New York: Oxford University Press, 2013), p. 44.

61 Wolfgang Münchau, 'Europe should say no to a flawed banking union', *Financial Times* 17 March 2014.

62 FSB *Adequacy of Loss-Absorbing Capacity of Global Systemically Important Banks in Resolution*, Consultative Document, 10 November 2014, available at http://www.financialstabilityboard.org/wp-content/uploads/TLAC-Condoc-6-Nov-2014-FINAL.pdf ; http://www.bloomberg.com/news/2014–11–10/banks-face-25-loss-buffer-as-fsb-fights-too-big-to-fail.html.

63 Core Equity Tier 1.

64 Sweden plans to introduce a 5 per cent SIFI charge for its four major banking groups; however only 2.5 per cent may be included under Pillar 1, the rest being added under Pillar 2.

65 Sweden proposed in the autumn of 2014 to demand a 1 per cent countercyclical buffer from its banks.

66 http://www.reuters.com/article/2014/11/20/banks-capital-idUSL6N0TA2V720141120.

67 'S&P warns of higher risk in bank bail-in bonds', *Financial Times* 6 February 2014, available at http://www.ft.com/intl/cms/s/0/4d6efa3c-8f57–11e3-be85–00144feab7de.html#axzz3L759BfTY; *Fannie Mae Debt Too Risky? Only When Investors Share Pain*, available at http://www.bloomberg.com/news/2014–12–04/fannie-mae-debt-too-risky-only-when-investors-share-pain.html; *Bank Holding Company Bonds Fray as Traders Fret Over Risk*, available at http://www.bloomberg.com/news/2014–11–27/bank-holding-company-bonds-fray-as-traders-fret-over-risk.html.

68 Anat R. Admati, Peter M. DeMarzo, Martin F. Hellwig and Paul Pfleiderer *Fallacies, Irrelevant Facts, and Myths in Capital Regulation: Why Bank Equity is* Not *Expensive*, Stanford University Working Paper no. 186, 2010, available at https://gsbapps.stanford.edu/researchpapers/library/RP2065R1&86.pdf; Anat Admati and Martin Hellwig *The Bankers' New Clothes: What's Wrong with Banking and What to Do about it* (Princeton: Princeton University Press, 2013); Anat Admati and Martin Hellwig *Does Debt Discipline Bankers? An Academic Myth about Bank Indebtedness*, Working Paper, Stanford University, 18 February 2013, available at http://www.gsb.stanford.edu/sites/default/files/research/documents/Academic%20myth-rev2%202-19–13.pdf; Anat Admati and Martin Hellwig *The Parade of the Bankers' New Clothes Continues: 23 Flawed Claims Debunked*, 3 June 2013, available at http://bankersnewclothes.com/wp-content/uploads/2013/06/parade-continues-June-3.pdf; Andrew G. Haldane *Capital Discipline*, speech before the American Economic Association, Denver, January 2011, available at http://www.bankofengland.co.uk/publications/Documents/speeches/2011/speech484.pdf.

10 Monetary policy and long-term trends

Charles A. E. Goodhart and Philipp Erfurth

The developing economies of the world are still drowning in debt, see Geneva Report by Buttiglione, *et al.* (2014). This is especially so in the case of housing finance (Mian and Sufi, 2014). In this chapter we aim to explain why this has happened and to suggest how the process of financial intermediation might be reformed to shift such financing more towards equity and away from debt finance, especially in housing. In the course of this exercise we focus first on the weakness of labour as a factor of production, as being a fundamental cause of both recent trends in the economy, i.e. the deficiency of demand and the arrival of deflationary pressures, and also of the, sometimes unavailing, policy effort to counter this by ever more accommodating monetary policy. This has led, since the onset of the great financial crisis (GFC), to a mutually inconsistent set of policies, with ever tighter regulations on banks, causing massive deleveraging (especially in cross-border lending), offsetting unprecedented and unconventional expansionary measures by central banks. The result has been a huge expansion of commercial bank deposits at the central bank, a blow-out of the bank reserve (R) to deposit ratio (D), R/D, with the banks caught in a liquidity trap whereby holding such reserves at the central bank is currently as attractive as any other usage of such funds. We end by suggesting how this trap might be sprung.

But first, we go back to the beginning of our story, which concerns the effects and implications of the weakness of labour, relative to capital, as a factor of production. There has been a long-term downwards trend in the share and strength of labour in national income, which is depressing both demand and inflation. This has prompted ever more expansionary monetary policies. While understandable, indeed appropriate, within a short-term business cycle context, this has exacerbated longer-term trends, increasing inequality and financial distortions. Perhaps the most fundamental problem has been over-reliance on debt finance (leverage).

The recent Bank of International Settlements (BIS) (2014) Annual Report, claimed that: 'Understanding the current global economic challenges requires a long-term perspective' (BIS, 2014 : 7) if we hope to find a 'new compass' for setting macroeconomic policies. This chapter aims to provide such a perspective by focusing initially upon one particular trend in developed countries, which is the trend decline in the adjusted wage share as a percentage of GDP in most developed countries since the end of the 1970s. This is shown for four main economies in Figure 10.1 and for a wider set of countries in Table 10.1.

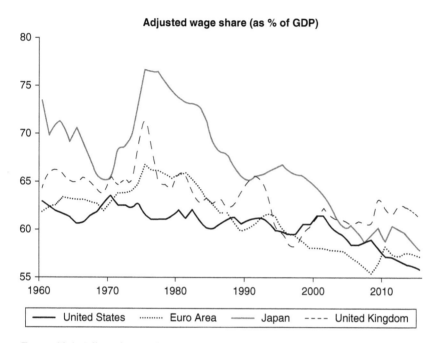

Figure 10.1 Adjusted wage share declining across developed markets.

Table 10.1 Developed markets adjusted wage shares (as percentage of GDP)

	1970	*1980*	*1990*	*2000*	*2010*	*2015F*
Germany	61.1	63.7	58.8	60.6	57.1	57.9
France	63	66.5	59.3	57.2	58.7	58.2
Italy	65.4	66.6	61.9	53.2	55.4	55.1
Spain	64.2	66.8	61.7	58.9	56.8	52.3
Canada	61	59.3	59.7	56.4	57.4	56.7
Australia	59.8	63.6	59.1	57.1	53.7	56.3
Denmark	60.2	62.3	59.3	56.4	59.5	57.7
Ireland	67.3	70	59.4	48.3	53.2	50.1
Greece	64.8	60.3	62.4	55.6	55	47.1
Norway	58.3	55.2	54	46.6	48.1	49.6
Netherlands	65.2	68.1	61.7	59.6	59.4	60.2

Source: European Commission AMECO database, Morgan Stanley Research.

While the rate of decline varies from country to country, it nevertheless appears to be broadly common. This has reflected an initial fall and flattening in the rate of growth of real compensation per employee since the early 1980s, which has been continuing through the ups and downs of the economic cycle, and is again common to most developed countries; it cannot easily be attributed to short-term

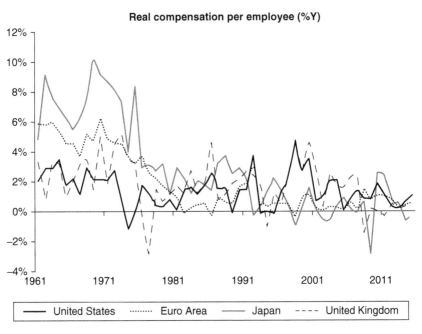

Figure 10.2 Real compensation growth weak across developed markets.

Table 10.2 Real compensation per employee (average annual percentage)

	1970–80	*1980–90*	*1990–00*	*2000–10*	*2010–15*
Germany	3.4%	0.5%	1.8%	0.6%	0.2%
France	4.2%	0.8%	1.2%	0.9%	0.5%
Italy	3.6%	1.2%	0.2%	0.7%	−0.1%
Spain	5.7%	1.3%	0.5%	0.6%	0.2%
Canada	0.8%	1.1%	1.2%	0.6%	0.7%
Australia	2.2%	0.4%	1.8%	0.1%	2.8%
Denmark	2.2%	0.4%	1.8%	0.1%	2.8%
Ireland	5.0%	2.3%	1.6%	2.6%	−0.8%
Greece	3.6%	0.0%	0.6%	0.9%	−2.8%
Norway	2.6%	1.9%	1.0%	0.7%	1.1%
Netherlands	3.2%	0.5%	1.2%	1.3%	0.7%

Source: European Commission AMECO database, Morgan Stanley Research.

political or macroeconomic policies. This is shown for a variety of countries in Figure 10.2 and for a wider set of countries in Table 10.2.

It is not our purpose here to try to explain why this has been happening; it is far too complex for us to tackle. Nevertheless, our preferred explanation is globalisation and, in particular, the entry of the Asian, especially Chinese, (and also those Eastern European countries that were formerly part of the communist system) labour force into the world's trading economy. This has allowed businessmen to apply a credible threat of relocating the production of any good, and of most services, to anywhere else in the world where labour costs are considerably cheaper. This has gone hand in hand with a decline in private sector unionisation almost everywhere, with causation going in both directions, and with a simultaneous decline in inequality between countries at a time when inequality within countries has been rising.

It is certainly possible that technical progress in the shape, for example, of IT and robotics has further weakened the share in output of labour, relative to capital and land (including natural resources, such as oil), but the measurement of this effect is fraught with difficulties. What we tend not to believe is that there is some immutable law whereby the return to capital must outstrip the overall growth rate of the country ($r > g$), as proposed by T. Piketty (2014) in *Capital in the Twenty-First Century.*

The macroeconomic consequences of a fall in the wage share

Be that as it may, what we do want to focus upon are the macroeconomic consequences of a trend decline in the wage share of GDP and relatively low real wage growth, relative to returns to capital and land. Workers tend to be poorer, more liquidity-constrained and less likely to aim (or be able) to pass on wealth in inheritance to subsequent generations than the owners of capital and land. Hence they will, as a generality, have a higher (marginal) propensity to consume. So, the trend weakness in returns to labour will simultaneously tend to hold down consumption, output and inflation (see, for example, the paper by Kumhof *et al.* (2013).

This weakness in consumption and output is likely to lead to some fiscal expansion and rebalancing, whereby welfare and benefits rise, financed by higher taxes on the rich. Whether there is scope for further fiscal expansion, in view of heightened public sector debt ratios and prospective future claims on the public purse from an ageing population, and for a more aggressive rebalancing and fiscal redistribution, is yet another major topic that is too large and complex to be tackled here.

What we do, instead, note is that circumstances in which both real output and inflation are held down compared to target by the relative weakness of labour would seem, superficially, tailor-made to be rectified by expansionary monetary policy. Just as the share of labour has been declining since the 1980s, so has the level of real interest rates to the point that they have become negative (Figure 10.3). This coincidence of a declining wage share and declining real interest rates is not, we believe, accidental.

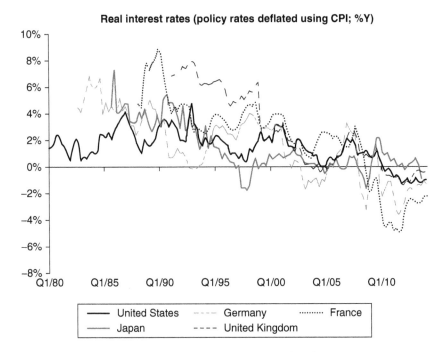

Figure 10.3 Real interest rates negative across developed markets.

From a short-term, business cycle viewpoint, a conjuncture of sluggish output growth and low inflation, surprising on the downside, should be met with and rectified by more expansionary monetary policy. But if one accepts the hypothesis that a (perhaps, the) longer-term driver of such a conjuncture is the relative weakness of labour as a factor of production, then this short-term response is unhelpful, indeed somewhat counterproductive, in a longer-term context. Its main effect is to raise asset prices and the relative value of land and capital, and thus benefit their owners who are rich, rather than workers who are poor. Hence, the trickle-down effect via the added consumption of the beneficiaries will be muted. More private sector capital expenditure would most likely benefit workers, e.g. by raising productivity and shifting the capital/labour ratio, but, alas, the empirical evidence shows capex to be notably interest-insensitive. Meanwhile, public sector investment is constrained by a variety of other factors, much to the dismay of Keynesians. What we are left with is the impact of monetary policy, whether conventional or unconventional, on housing and exchange rates. Movements in the latter are a zero-sum game globally: my depreciation is your appreciation.

This leaves housing. The financing of residential and commercial property has become central to our banking systems in recent decades, whether directly via mortgages, or indirectly via loans to construction companies, loans collateralised on property, etc. Furthermore, almost all such financing is done in debt form. The failure to reform housing financing modalities in the aftermath of the GFC has been a missed opportunity, indeed a tragedy.

The decline in (long-term) real interest rates has been a major factor leading to a rise in housing and property prices, relative to labour incomes. It has, of course, benefitted those already on the housing ladder, the old and the rich. So, affordability has been on a trend decline, though less in the US than elsewhere (Figure 10.4).

Against this background, the bipartisan political incentive prior to 2008 in the US to encourage more mortgage lending to the poorer, disadvantaged classes was entirely understandable. But it ended in the sub-prime crisis. Insofar as the main domestic transmission route of monetary policy to the real economy lies in the housing market, the authorities would appear to be caught in a dilemma. Either they encourage the young, the workers and the poor to take on an unstable and excessive burden of debt, or they pump up all other asset prices further and further for less and less effect on the real economy, with a potentially growing risk of some future (disorderly?) reversal.

The current mantra is to constrain any incipient overheating and excess indebtedness in the housing market by macro-prudential measures (e.g. the UK and Sweden), while pressing on with expansionary monetary policies to regain output inflation targets. This raises several queries. First, will the macro-prudential measures be pressed aggressively enough to work? But if they do, and the housing transmission channel is blocked, may not the resulting effects on other asset prices, including the exchange rate, have to be even more extreme (relative to labour incomes) and hence more distortionary and cause yet greater inequality?

There is, therefore, a longer-term, structural problem with monetary policy: As the BIS (2014) Annual Report noted:

> Policy does not lean against the booms but eases aggressively and persistently during busts. This induces a downward bias in interest rates and an upward bias in debt levels, which in turn makes it hard to raise rates without damaging the economy – a debt trap. Systemic financial crises do not become less frequent or intense, private and public debts continue to grow, the economy fails to climb onto a stronger sustainable path, and monetary and fiscal policies run out of ammunition. Over time, policies lose their effectiveness and may end up fostering the very conditions they seek to prevent. In this context, economists speak of "time inconsistency": taken in isolation, policy steps may look compelling but, as a sequence, they lead policymakers astray (BIS, 2014: 18).

Whether this is true for fiscal policy as well is a contentious issue, which we shall duck. Let us just state that policies of consciously allowing public sector debt ratios to rise further now are unlikely to prove acceptable in most countries. Having thus argued that expansionary monetary and fiscal policies have both largely 'shot their bolt', the BIS argues instead for: 'balance sheet repair and structural reforms'. Alas, we believe that its positive proposals are much less compelling than its criticisms of existing policies.

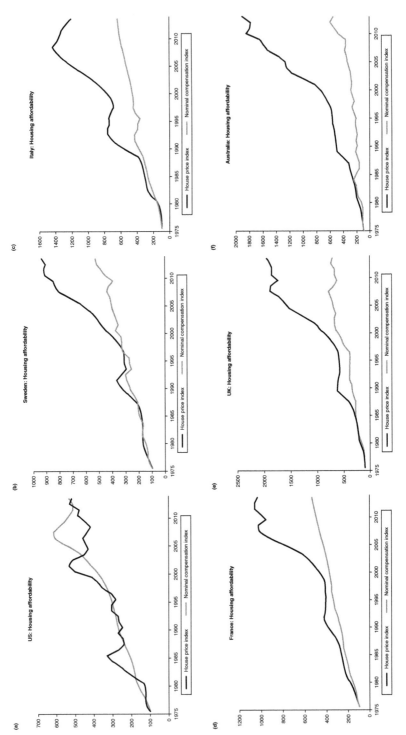

Figure 10.4 Housing (un)affordability driven by post-2000 surge in house prices.

Whereas structural reforms and deleveraging are beneficial in the longer term, almost by definition, they are much easier to achieve during periods of fast growth, rather than the current sluggish expansion. Moreover, structural reform commonly involves removing the monopolistic rents of protected sectors, and thus initially is deflationary, prior to the subsequent expansion of output and productivity. The longer the stagnation, the more difficult it may be politically to introduce supply-side reforms, such as cutting subsidies. In the absence of specifics, and there are virtually none in the BIS (2014) Annual Report, a call for more structural reform and deleveraging is akin to an appeal to a *deus ex machina*.

Improving the form of housing finance

A better proposal is to be found in the book by Mian and Sufi (2014), *House of Debt*, especially chapter 12. The GFC primarily impacted the poor, especially those subject to foreclosure, whereas the countervailing expansionary monetary policy mainly benefitted the rich, thereby worsening the longer-term trends already reported earlier in this chapter.

Their solution is for financial intermediaries to offer: '[A] shared-responsibility mortgage (SRM) [which] has two important differences: (1) the lender offers downside protection to the borrower, and (2) the borrower gives up [a part of his/her] capital gain to the lender on the upside . . . ' (Mian and Sufi, 2014: 192).

If housing price movements were independently and identically distributed, this would be a perfect solution. Unfortunately, they are not; they are strongly auto-correlated, with long periods of rising prices, sometimes culminating in a frenzy of sharp increases, interspersed with shorter periods of collapses in such prices.

The way that this would work is shown in the box below, which is mainly taken from Mian and Sufi (2014: 171–173).

How the SRM works

The key difference between the SRM and typical mortgage is that the SRM provides downside protection to the owner if house prices fall. The owner's mortgage payment schedule is linked to some form of local house-price index:

> For example, if her local house-price index is 100 when she buys the home, and falls by 30 per cent by the end of her first year of ownership, [the owner's] mortgage payment in her second year would decline 30 per cent (. . .) Her amortization schedule would remain the same. As a result, even though she will make a lower payment, her mortgage balance goes down according to the original formula. This in effect means

that [the owner] is given an automatic principal reduction when house prices in her area fall below her purchasing level. In our specific example, if [the owner's] house-price index remains at 70 for the remaining twenty-nine years of her mortgage, she will have received a 30 per cent forgiveness in principal by the end of her thirty years (Mian and Sufi, 2014: 172–173).

However, on average, house prices are expected to grow. At some point house prices are again likely to exceed the original purchase price. Increasing gradually, once the house-price index reaches that original level, the owner will be making full payments again.

The downside protection comes at the expense of the lender, who would therefore charge a fee. To eliminate that, Mian and Sufi suggest:

[g]iving the lender a small share in the upside as well. In particular, an SRM should also provide the lender with a 5 per cent share of the capital gain whenever [the owner] sells or refinances her house. The 5 per cent capital-gain rule is a small charge for [the owner], especially considering that capital gains on owner-occupied housing are otherwise tax-free (Mian and Sufi, 2014: 173–174).

During the upswing, and even perhaps especially in the final frenzy, home buyers may not be keen to share prospective capital gains with lenders, despite the self-insurance advantage. Some tentative attempts to introduce shared-equity mortgages in the UK apparently ran into consumer resistance during the long periods of rising house prices. Some complained that they had not understood the terms of the contract and had been missold.

Perhaps more seriously, would a lender be prepared to offer downside price protection, once the market had begun to crack? At what rate would lenders have offered such protection in, say, Las Vegas in 2008? Given the pattern of auto-correlation on housing prices, we fear that too few mortgage buyers would seek such SRMs in upswings, and that no sellers would offer it, or not at feasible rates, during downswings.

Nevertheless we think that the idea of greater (self-)insurance via a larger equity element in the housing market is good. This was a key feature of the UK government's Help to Buy equity loan, which has now been extended to 2020. It should be possible to build on this. For example, the government could decree that all house purchases had to have at least, say, a 30 per cent equity share, of which a minimum of 5 per cent would have to belong to the purchasers, though both such numbers are, at this point, somewhat arbitrary and would need much more careful analysis in any practical application. Insofar as purchasers were unable to reach the 30 per cent level themselves, they could either purchase an SRM in the market, or go to the government for equity funding. Of course, during downturns, the authorities would then be landed with almost all such housing finance, but this would be strongly counter-cyclical; it would be politically (more) popular (than bank bail-out); and, given all that we know about the housing market, it should be long-term profitable for taxpayers. The media has, in general, been critical of the Help to Buy equity loan scheme, but supportive of aggressively expansionary monetary policy. We reverse the argument: Help to Buy is part of the solution to a long-term structural problem, which has been, in part, exacerbated by aggressively expansionary monetary policies.

However, the more fundamental problem is not those policies, but the financing context in which they operate, which gives advantages to debt over equity financing. The most egregious is the relative tax advantage of debt finance, and the 'Holy Grail' would be to equalise, or even shift, such advantages to the benefit of equity finance. Moreover, in a world with massive existing debt overhang, the transition to a much higher equity ratio can be very painful to existing shareholders, usually including top management, who are in a position to block any such move.

Among such changes to a more equity-financed world could be a change in the pattern of government finance. Thus, a move towards nominal income bonds should help to make government finance less pro-cyclical, with less austerity during deflation and less temptation for ministers of finance to raid surpluses during booms. Of course, there are problems of revisions, and even falsification, to data, but these could be handled.

Reforming the structure of financial intermediation

It is not only the form of housing finance that needs reform but also the structure of financial intermediation through which such finance is provided. As Jordà *et al.* (2015) have demonstrated, it is the rapid growth of lending on real estate, both on housing and on commercial property, which has led bank loans to expand much faster than bank deposits in recent decades, since the 1970s. That funding gap was filled, until 2009, by increasing reliance on wholesale funding, mostly short-term, uninsured and provided by informed and flighty investors (Schularick and Taylor, 2009). As Turner (2013) has noted, banks changed from providing (short-term) finance for business to making much longer-term (mortgage) loans to households. This led to enhanced maturity mismatch and excessive leverage and took banking away from its traditional role and functions.

So long as housing prices remained strong, the system was stable, since the property was by itself good collateral for the original loan. Similarly, all financial markets that were derivative of the housing market, such as collateralised mortgage obligations, remained liquid and accessible. But once the housing market began to weaken, the system became fragile, though the extent of fragility depended on a variety of other factors, such as whether the mortgage loans were made on a recourse, or non-recourse, basis, the initial loan to value (LTV) or loan to income (LTI) ratio, the ease of foreclosure by the lender, etc. That fragility was evidenced by the frequency whereby financial crises were triggered by collapses in property markets in recent decades. In the UK all three recent crises, 1973–1975, 1990–1992 and 2007–2009, were triggered in this manner. Moreover, the demise of Lehman Brothers was caused by unwise investment in a portfolio of housing and property related securities, not by its derivative book.

For reasons that remain unclear, the main subsequent attack on the banking industry has been focused on the role and functions of investment banking, which, though undoubtedly culpable in several respects, was not primarily responsible for the GFC. The role of banking in the provision of property finance, which was at the centre of the crisis, was ignored. Indeed, the separation of universal banks, as proposed by Vickers, into separate investment and retail banking subsidiaries is likely to aggravate the tendency for the latter to concentrate on mortgage and property finance.

The need, instead, is to reverse the collapse of the housing finance specialist intermediaries – S&Ls in the US and building societies in the UK – into the arms of the banks. All housing, commercial real estate and property related lending (with a residual life to maturity greater than, say, one year) should be done by special-ist property finance companies, who should not be allowed to offer transactions accounts, or short-term deposit liabilities. There should be a much greater equity element in such mortgage loans (the Mian and Sufi (2014) SRMs), balanced by an equally large, or larger, equity ratio in the property finance houses. Such houses would be encouraged to securitise their fixed interest book, preferably in the form of Danish-style covered bonds, but banks would be forbidden to hold such secu-rities unless they had a remaining life of under one year. The aim would be to take banking back to its traditional verities and to revise a refashioned 'real bills' doctrine, whereby banks deploy their short-term deposit funding to lend on a short-term, self-liquidating basis, or to hold assets that would remain liquid in a crisis.

The shortage of equity prior to 2008 was, perhaps, most egregious in those banks taking a punt on the property market, e.g. Anglo-Irish, Northern Rock, RBS, etc., but leverage was excessive throughout the banking sector. The calls for much higher equity ratios, e.g. Admati and Hellwig (2013) and Miles *et al.* (2013), are correct in principle. But the problem is how to get there. With bank CEOs committed to trying to reach some desired level for their banks' return on equity (RoE), a weak market for bank equity and a massive existing debt over-hang, the incentive for bank management is to meet tougher capital adequacy requirements by deleveraging. With governments all imploring 'their own banks' to maintain domestic lending, such deleveraging has had an especially severe effect on cross-border lending.

The results have not been pretty, with the macroeconomic effects of tougher regulation counteracting the expansionary force of unconventional expansionary monetary policy and leading to the enormous pile-up of commercial bank deposits at the central bank. There are several possible routes to ease this conflict of objec-tives. One such route would be to try to adjust the incentive structure of manage-ment, perhaps along the lines suggested in Goodhart (2014). Another would be to force banks with insufficient equity capital to accept injections of public sector equity, but on terms expected to be highly profitable for the taxpayer and costly for the existing private sector shareholders. Whereas this was successfully done in the US with the Troubled Asset Recovery Program and the 2009 (Comprehensive Capital Analysis and Review Program) stress tests, it was, mistakenly, ruled out elsewhere by the wildly exaggerated hue and cry about the evils of bail-out.

So within Europe little has been done to mitigate the restrictive effect of much tougher bank regulation. This has played a role in Europe's continuing stagnation, though the scale of such effect is almost impossible to measure and highly contentious. Opinions vary widely.

Conclusions

There has been a long-term downwards trend in the share and strength of labour in national income, depressing both demand and inflation. This has prompted ever more expansionary monetary policies. While understandable, indeed appropriate, within a short-term business cycle context, this has exacerbated longer-term trends, increasing inequality and financial distortions. Perhaps the most fundamental problem has been over-reliance on debt finance (leverage). We propose measures, involving government intervention, to raise the share of equity finance in housing markets. Such reforms could be extended to other sectors of the economy. Similarly, we propose shifting the provision of housing finance from banks back to specialist property finance companies. These, like banks and other financial intermediaries, should hold a much higher equity ratio than heretofore. The problem is how to reach that goal without instigating massive deleveraging, a problem which has not so far been solved in Europe.

References

Admati, A. and Hellwig, M. (2013) *The Bankers New Clothes: What's Wrong with Banking and What to Do about It*. Princeton, NJ: Princeton University Press.

BIS (2014) *84th Annual Report*, released 29 June 2014. Available at http://www.bis.org/publ/arpdf/ar2014_ec.pdf (last accessed 19 July 2015).

Buttiglione, L., Lane, P. R., Reichlin, L. and Reinhart, V. (2014) *Deleveraging? What Deleveraging?* Geneva Reports on the World Economy 16, International Center for Monetary and Banking Studies, and Centre for Economic Policy Research. Available at http://www.voxeu.org/article/geneva-report-global-deleveraging (last accessed 19 July 2015).

Goodhart, C. A. E. (2014) Risk, reward and bank resilience. In Shigehara, K. (ed.) *The Limits of Surveillance and Financial Market Failure: Lessons from the Euro-Area Crisis*. London, UK: Palgrave Macmillan, chapter 10.

Jordà, O., Schularick, M. and Taylor, A. M. (2015) *Leveraged Bubbles*. Presented at the JME Conference, Swiss National Bank, Gerzensee, 7–8 November 2014. Available at http://conference.nber.org/confer/2015/EASE15/Jorda_Schularick_Taylor.pdf (last accessed 19 July).

Kumhof, M., Ranciere, R., and Winant, P. (2013) *Inequality, Leverage and Crises: The Case of Endogenous Default*. IMF Working Papers 13/249. Available at http://www.imf.org/external/pubs/ft/wp/2013/wp13249.pdf (last accessed 19 July 2015).

Mian, K. and Sufi, A. (2014) *House of Debt*. Chicago, IL: University of Chicago Press.

Miles, D., Yang, J. and Marcheggiano, G. (2013) Optimal bank capital. *Economic Journal* 123(567): 1–37.

Piketty, T. (2014) *Capital in the Twenty-First Century*. Cambridge, MA: Harvard University Press.

Schularick, M. and Taylor, A. M. (2009) *Credit Booms Gone Bust: Monetary Policy, Leverage Cycles and Financial Crises, 1870–2008*. National Bureau of Economic Research Working Paper 15512, November. Available at http://www.nber.org/papers/ w15512 (last accessed 19 July 2015).

Turner, A. (2013) *Credit, Money and Leverage: What Wicksell, Hayek and Fisher Knew and Modern Macroeconomics Forgot*. Stockholm School of Economics Conference, 12 September. Available at http://www.princeton.edu/jrc/events_archive/repository/ credit_money_turner/Credit_Money_Leverage.pdf (last accessed 19 July 2015).

Index

For Product Safety Concerns and Information please contact our EU
representative GPSR@taylorandfrancis.com
Taylor & Francis Verlag GmbH, Kaufingerstraße 24, 80331 München, Germany

www.ingramcontent.com/pod-product-compliance
Ingram Content Group UK Ltd.
Pitfield, Milton Keynes, MK11 3LW, UK
UKHW021615240425
457818UK00018B/569